A Sheffielder's Song:

The Recollections of Charles F. Hatfield

A Sheffielder's Song

The Recollections of
Charles F. Hatfield

The **Hallamshire** Press
1993

'Tha tells a good tale, can tha sing?'

Published by The Hallamshire Press
The Hallamshire Press is an imprint of
Interleaf Productions Limited
Exchange Works
Sidney Street
Sheffield S1 3QF
England

Typeset by Interleaf Productions Limited
and
Printed in Great Britain
by
The Cromwell Press
Wiltshire

British Library Cataloguing in Publication Data

Hatfield, Charles F.
  Sheffielder's Song
  I. Title
  942.821082092

  ISBN 1-874718-15-6

Contents

Chapter 1
'Grandparents and Parents'

M Y SURNAME is Hat*field*. I live in Shef*field*. For thirty years I lived in Abbey*field* Road. I now live at *Meadow*head. At one time I lived in Crab*tree* Lane. My middle name is *Farmer*.

One might think that with all these pastoral associations I would be an outstanding authority on agriculture. Not so.

My fingers might be described as greasy rather than green, as I have always been handier with a spanner than a spade. I have to confess that our garden owes much more to my wife than to me, as my activities there consist of very little beyond trimming the hedges, mowing the lawn and organising bonfires. My ignorance of almost all else horticultural or agricultural is abysmal.

In my schooldays I had mixed feelings about my Christian name, which I inherited from my father, Charles Evelyn, who also had an uncle called Charles. To carry on the family tradition, my son received the name of Roger Charles, and I have a grandson John Charles. Fortunately in these enlightened days, nicknames seem to be dying out. John is seldom called Jack, Richard is seldom called Dick, William is seldom called Bill, Robert is seldom Bob. But I was never Charles, almost always Charlie. That wasn't so bad—it saved me from being confused with my father, whose family always called him Charles— but at school I was often addressed as Chas, or Wag from the rhyme:

Charlie Wag
Ate the pudding and swallowed the bag.

Or Chuck:

Charlie, Charlie, Chuck Chuck Chuck,
Went to bed with three young ducks;
One died, Charlie cried,
Charlie, Charlie, Chuck Chuck Chuck.

My maternal grandfather, James Farmer

Had I been of an aggressive or pugilistic nature, I might have have attempted to do something about these indignities, but in the circumstances, it seemed politic to suffer in silence. So much for my name.

Autobiographies often begin with a chapter on the subject of the author's antecedents: some can boast a family tree going back to the days of William the Conqueror. I once read of a man who paid a researcher to trace the history of his family, only to discover that the earliest relation of whom any trace could be found had been hanged for sheep stealing. Such family skeletons are best left in the seclusion of their cupboards.

On the paternal side, I have no knowledge of any ancestor more remote than my grandfather, Jabez Hatfield, a steelworker, whose accomplishments consisted of playing the trombone and riding a penny-farthing bike, though not, I understand, simultaneously. Before I was born he and my grandmother (Sarah Ann) had separated, and he spent the rest of his life in Leeds, where he conducted a brass band. He was one of six brothers, of whom five played instruments, the sixth being a singer. I understand their father had also been a bandsman, and had in fact composed some band music in a manuscript book which was subsequently stolen from my grandfather, who claimed that the well-known tune 'Deep Harmony' was really of his father's composition. Music was my grandfather's whole life, and he had participated in the brass band contests at the Crystal Palace. When I was fourteen, my father took me to Leeds to see him for the first time. Except for a corner where he took his meals, the whole table was piled with copies of music.

My mother, Norah, was the daughter of James Farmer, a native of the Lincolnshire village of Hougham, which lies to the east of the Great North Road between Newark and Grantham. For 600 years his family had owned the farmed land there, but they had gradually lost it through payment of tithes. As a small boy he was sent into the fields at dawn to spend the day scaring birds off the land, with sandwiches of fat boiled bacon to sustain him. Having no means of knowing the time, he often ate his meal much too early in the day, with the result that he was very hungry by the time he was able to eat again. He never went to school, but taught himself to read by studying posters. He also learnt to write, and I still have his Bible with 'James Farmer, 1872' inscribed on the flyleaf in a beautiful copperplate hand. Eventually he left the farm and came to Sheffield, where he drove a horse van, delivering goods for Cole Brothers, then the town's leading drapers, now a vast multiple store. He married Ellen Eliza Cutts, a dressmaker, one of a large family of girls, and whose father was a highly skilled iron founder. It was he who cast the gates of the Sheffield Botanical Gardens, and for many years we had at home two examples of his art in the form of cast-iron plaques. One of these represented Jesus with the woman of Samaria at the well, whilst the other depicted 'Our Patriotic King, William IIII'. Throughout my boyhood this stood beside the Yorkshire range and was blackleaded and polished every week, giving 'our patriotic King' the appearance of a Nigerian chief in fancy dress.

My maternal grandmother, Ellen Eliza Farmer

My maternal grandmother's sisters had received some education at an 'establishment for young ladies', with not very impressive results, as one of them had never learnt to read, although she could copy handwriting beautifully and could work samplers. By the time my grandmother—the youngest—came on the scene her parents were unable to afford the fees, so she went to the Board School where each child paid twopence per week, and she received the best education of them all.

My mother's parents' life was tragic, though they were happy with each other. In the late nineteenth century, Sheffield was rife with disease, cholera and diphtheria claiming thousands, and none of the Farmers' first eight children lived to be teenagers. They started one year with five children and finished it with none, losing three in a fortnight, and I have heard that my grandfather's hair turned from black to white in a week. Mother was born years later when they did not expect to have any more children, and it was touch and go whether they would raise her. Once she had diphtheria, and on another occasion a bad fall resulted in concussion, and she was unconscious for several days. Owing to these circumstances, in later life her only relatives were cousins about twenty years older than herself.

A further misfortune fell when my grandfather contracted a spinal disease as a result of a soaking whilst driving his horse van in wet weather. Following this he was unable to work for the last sixteen years of his life. Of course there was no social security in those days, and Grandma had to turn her front room into a little drapery shop.

I cannot help reflecting how close together the generations really are. As I write I am in my late seventies. My grandparents would have been able to read the works of Charles Dickens as they were being published, railways were almost in their infancy, and motor cars were yet to be invented. I have already mentioned my great grandfather who lived in the reign of William IV, and I have heard that my great grandmother, travelling from Darlington to Sheffield, was robbed by highwaymen and her wedding dress taken.

In the year 1890 a group of Presbyterians, many of them Scottish steelworks managers and their families, living in the north-east Sheffield district of Pitsmoor, decided to found a congregation in that area. At that time, there was only one Presbyterian church in Sheffield, St Andrew's in Hanover Street. Grandma Farmer was a member, and when the new congregation was formed in premises only about a hundred yards from her home, she transferred her membership to it, becoming a founder member. Within a few months Grandma Hatfield also joined, and sent her six children to the Sunday School. And that was where my parents met.

My father had two brothers, George and John William, and three sisters, Edith, Elsie and Phyllis. John William and Phyllis, the two youngest, died of diphtheria at an early age. When they were old enough, the survivors all sang in the church choir, as also did Mother. She and Auntie Elsie sang soprano, Auntie Edie and her mother sang contralto, Uncle George sang tenor, and Dad sang bass.

After the Sunday evening service, the minister and some of his flock conducted a mission open-air service in the slum area. One carried a lantern on a pole, whilst Dad and another stalwart staggered along with a harmonium. Apparently only one person could master the playing of this instrument, a female by the name of Winnie Paul, as the pedals operating the bellows had to be treadled at a far faster tempo than the hands played the keys, the performance demanding a degree of co-ordination which was no mean feat.

Dad's education had been somewhat spasmodic, because he had attended several schools before he left at the age of twelve, owing to the family's rather frequent change of residence, occasioned by Grandad's habit of practising on his trombone *fortissimo* in the middle of the night, which did not endear him to his neighbours.

Immediately on leaving school, Dad was found a very menial job, scrubbing floors and doing domestic work, which he hated. His ambition was to become an engineer, and after a time he managed to get a job in a nut and bolt factory. What he did there was not engineering, but he regarded it as a step in the right direction, and eventually at the age of sixteen, after constantly pestering, he managed to start training as an engineering apprentice at the works of Samuel Osborne & Co. Ltd. On completing his apprenticeship he gained further valuable experience at David Brown's of Huddersfield, machining bevel gears to a very high degree of precision. Unfortunately, owing to the fact that his apprenticeship had started at the age of sixteen, and not fourteen, he was not allowed to join the Amalgamated Society of Engineers, but had to join the toolmakers' union, where the rate of pay was lower. His discontent with this, coupled with unhappiness at home when his parents separated, led him to decide to try his luck abroad, and in the year 1911, having saved forty pounds, he embarked on a liner for Canada.

In the shipping company's literature he had read of a place called Nelson in British Columbia, described as a rising township with engineering works, so he had decided to make that his goal. However, his mother's brother, Charles Palmer, had a farm on the prairie, so he decided to break his journey and spend a while with Uncle Charlie. He arrived in time to help to get the harvest in, but although he worked very hard from dawn till dusk, his uncle paid him no wages, only providing board and lodging, so he decided to leave and resume his journey to his first objective in British Columbia.

Imagine his disappointment on arriving there, having made a journey of 6,000 miles, to find that Nelson consisted of a small undeveloped township beside a lake, and that there was no prospect of employment for him. Soon his meagre supply of money was exhausted, and hearing of a job a hundred miles away, he rode there on a train buffer. It was an uncomfortable ride, and ash blown out of the huge chimney of the locomotive covered his head and shoulders. As the train slowed down to enter the station, he heard someone shout, so he jumped off the buffer and ran into a wood. He was unsure as to whether he was being pursued, but not wishing to take the chance of being arrested as a hobo, he ran through the wood in a big circle, and eventually arrived safely in the small town. He got a job, which involved cleaning out locomotive fireboxes, and it was fortunate that he was at that time very slim, as he had to get in through a ten-inch hole. In the succeeding months, he took whatever casual employment he could get, working at a lumber camp, and as a cook's assistant at a gold mine, all the time travelling back eastward, partly in Canada and partly in the United States, until he arrived in Montreal. There he took a job on a building site as one of a gang of men wheeling barrowloads of concrete and tipping it into the foundations.

Meanwhile, back in England, the girl he had left behind, Norah Farmer, was beginning to receive attention from a young man who was a student at the University, so she wrote to my father informing him of the fact as she wished to know where she stood. His reply was to catch the next boat home, where he arrived exactly as he had started, with forty pounds, after an absence of nine months. He applied for a job in one of the big Sheffield engineering works, and when asked where he had last worked, he gave the name of his last employer in Montreal, not mentioning the nature of the business, and describing himself as an engineer. His story was never checked, and at last he was able to join the Amalgamated Society of Engineers (now the AEU) and to earn the appropriate wage. About a year later he and my mother married, but owing to the fact that by now both her parents were invalids, they made their home with them in the little house in Petre Street. Grandma's little drapery shop was closed, and the newly-weds furnished that room and the front bedroom.

The next year I was born.

Chapter 2
'Unto Us a Child is Born'

I ENTERED this world on the 6th of March 1914—a momentous year for other reasons. After the midwife, the first visitor to arrive was, I believe, the minister, to hear my father singing in his fine bass voice:

> For unto us a child is born,
> Unto us a son is given.

The author as a baby

Little could he have known that in years to come that same child grown to manhood would have the privilege of singing—with the finest choirs in the locality—Handel's great oratorio from which he had heard that brief excerpt on the day of his birth.

The house in which I was born, 50 Petre Street, was a product of the Industrial Revolution. Petre Street, Grimesthorpe Road, Earsham Street, Carlisle Street and Savile Street were all long straight roads leafing from the vicinity of the Wicker, spanned by its impressive railway arch, to the industrial east end.

Our house was in the middle of a long terrace in a yard of six houses, and at the back was a breathtaking view of an equal number of lavatories and dustbins. Behind these was a row of similar properties in Writtle Street, and the only bit of greenery to be seen was a short untended length of grimy privet which rose above the wall. The houses at the two ends of the yard boasted the enviable addition of 'offshot slop kitchens'. Our house was next to the top house in the yard, and like the others had two ground-floor rooms, divided by a staircase which led to two bedrooms, over which was an attic. There was also a coal cellar. One side of the living room was taken up by a stone sink with a cold water tap over it, a coal-fired copper for washing the clothes, a Yorkshire range, and a built-in cupboard. The wall facing the entrance door and window had a door at each end, one giving access to the cellar, the other to the stairs and front room. Between these doors stood an old dresser, above which hung a large framed watercolour of a man-of-war sailing ship of about the time of Nelson. A mahogany-framed sofa, whose horse-hair upholstery prickled my legs as a boy, occupied most of the space along the wall facing the fireplace, and over it hung an ancient pendulum clock flanked by pictures of a religious nature. The space between the outer door and the window was occupied by the wringing machine. A deal table stood in the middle of the floor, surrounded by chairs that matched the sofa. On the pegged hearth-rug Grandad's Windsor armchair and Grandma's rocking chair faced each other.

I only dimly remember my little brother Clifford. When I was three and a half and he was a year and eight months we both had bronchial pneumonia. The treatment for this in those days consisted of applying hot poultices to the chest. Unfortunately Clifford was a chubby child, and the heat of the poultice was unable to penetrate to his lungs and he died.

An event I do remember with remarkable clarity, considering how young I was at the time, was the German Zeppelin raid on Sheffield in September 1916, when I was only two and a half years old. Dad had strengthened the ceiling of our cellar by placing under it heavy baulks of timber, supported by uprights resembling pit props, and I was snatched out of bed and carried down there. Some of our neighbours also came in to shelter. It was impossible to get Grandad down the cellar steps, so he was seated in a chair at the top, the narrow space between the walls in the middle of the house being considered the safest place for him.

No sooner had we taken refuge than there were two terrific explosions in quick succession. One bomb had fallen in Writtle Street, at the back of our house, and the other in Petre Street, a little higher up on the opposite side of the road, killing a man. All our windows were blown in, and the roof was badly damaged. Someone in the cellar started repeating the Lord's Prayer. It was pretty cold down there, and Dad dragged a slow combustion stove to a position where he could get the chimney pipe up the cellar grate, but when he lit a fire in it, a down-draught filled the cellar with smoke, causing us all to cough and our eyes to stream, so he had to put it out.

Presently I heard a sound, and said, 'Listen!' 'What can you hear, Charlie?', anxiously asked our next-door neighbour, Mrs Grayson, who was nursing her baby Leonard. 'I think they're putting the windows back in', was my reply.

For a long time we sat there in the candlelight, cold and miserable, until it was considered safe to return upstairs. We still had only candlelight, and Mother sat down on what she thought was a hassock, only to find it was a pile of soot that had fallen down the chimney. Our house was so badly damaged that we had to leave it and live with relatives until it was repaired.

Not long after the air raid, Grandad died of cancer. I remember him as a short, stout, kindly old gentleman with a shock of snow-white hair. He had never had toothache or been to a dentist in his life, and he went to his grave with a full set of his own teeth. He was keenly interested in politics, holding Liberal views, and had many heated arguments with cronies who visited him, whether Tory or Labour. On one occasion a political argument was at its height, both participants sweating profusely with the heat of their contention, when the Tory visitor suddenly broke off and turning to Grandma said, 'Excuse me, madam, what do you polish your oven knob with?'

In spite of their political differences the old gentlemen were the best of friends.

Incidentally, the steel knob which gleamed brightly on the glossy blackleaded oven door was polished with a damp rag which had been dipped in the ashes. All the doors had brass knobs, and when I was older it was one of my Saturday morning jobs to polish them and the brass fender and fire irons with Brasso or Komo metal polish. Although their homes were very humble, all the women in the yard were very clean and house-proud, and they used to whiten the doorstep and the edges of the stone window sills with what was known as donkey stone, or pipe clay. Any suggestion that Petre Street was a slum would have been met with a very indignant response.

One day in November 1918, Dad, having been on the night shift, was walking in Whiteley Woods when he heard the bells of Fulwood Church playing 'Peace, Perfect Peace', and he realised that the war was over. No more shells were required, and soon he became redundant. Always of an independent nature, he decided to go into business on his own account, and started by renting an old stable and forge in Jamaica Street, which was a steep cobbled side road off Petre Street. His small savings were invested in lathes and other machine tools, and he began to undertake general engineering and motor repair work. Around that time, many ex-servicemen were using their gratuities to start small businesses, and Dad began to buy and sell to them second-hand machinery, which he also installed.

Another of my memories is of a week's holiday in Blackpool when I was very small indeed. It was after Grandad had died, and Grandma went with us, wearing her customary black dress trimmed with Whitby jet, and her black bonnet and veil. Dad sported a straw boater, which had a string attached to a clip on his lapel so that he could haul it back whenever it blew off his head, and he carried a silver-mounted yellow walking stick. We went by train, changing at Manchester and Preston. In Blackpool we stayed in a boarding house kept by a Mrs Bearder, and I can still recollect the aroma of coffee and cooking that seemed to pervade the house.

On seeing the ocean for the first time I asked, 'Is *that* a sea?', then, noticing the miles of sand, I exclaimed in ecstasy, 'What a lot of muck!' One very windy day I was somewhat awe-stricken to see the huge Atlantic waves breaking over the promenade, and Dad's hat lanyard was in constant use. No doubt the memory of that holiday has remained with me so many years because it was to be the last holiday we were to have for a very long time.

In February 1919 my brother Douglas was born. It was soon noticed that one of his eyes wasn't straight, and he didn't start to walk as early as children usually do. Soon it became apparent that he was afflicted with a weakness of all his left side, a disability which handicapped him all his life. For some reason, Grandma had difficulty in remembering Douglas's name, and one day when she was nursing him, she turned to Mother and said, 'See, what do you call this child? Oh, Judas, that's it.'

Chapter 3
'Ellesmere Road Council School'

AFTER EASTER 1919 I started to attend Ellesmere Road Council School, conveniently situated at the bottom of our street. My first teacher was a young lady named Miss Hughes, and at the end of the first morning I went home and told Mother that I didn't think she knew very much, as I had drawn a motorbike and she didn't know what it was. To this day I am not sure whether that drawing was very bad, or avant garde, as it seems that in these modern times the less recognisable a work of art is, the more likely

Ellesmere Road Infant School, about 1920

it is to be acclaimed by the pundits. At any rate, the choice of subject showed in which direction my interest lay, even at that tender age.

Dad had already had one or two second-hand motorbikes, primitive contraptions with flat petrol tanks, sit-up-and-beg handlebars, and vee-belt pulleys that could be made to expand or contract in diameter to alter the gear ratio. Every journey was a precarious adventure, and was almost invariably attended by some form of breakdown. One of these vehicles was a Rudge Multi, with sidecar, the Achilles heel of which was the belt drive. There were two forms of belt: the Whittle, which consisted of leather links connected to each other with steel links, and the rubber belt. The former used to slip badly in wet weather, and the latter used to come apart when the fastener that held the two ends together pulled out of the rubber. Actually, both forms of belt suffered to some degree from both faults, and also in those days of poor tyres and bad roads punctures were very common. The current Rudge slogan was: 'Don't trudge it, Rudge it!', but Mother was inclined to think the rhyming words should have been reversed.

Our headmistress at the infant school was Miss Oakley, a strict and severe lady who wore Victorian dress and had a long enough neck to support not only a high stiff lace collar, but also a black band round her throat. She remembered having taught my mother, and always addressed me as Farmer. One day, for no reason that I was aware of, the teacher called me out and told me to go and stand outside the classroom door. Presently, along came Miss Oakley, and demanded to know what I was doing there, to which I replied, quite truthfully, that I didn't know, so she told me to go back to the teacher and ask. 'For wriggling about like a little worm' was the reply. Miss Oakley caned me.

I had not been long at school when the Peace Treaty was signed, and to celebrate this event we had a tea party at school. We had to take our own mugs and any large flags we might have to decorate the classrooms. Patriotic songs were learnt for the occasion, and each child was presented with a lead medal whereon was depicted an Angel of Peace precariously balanced on a very small globe, suspended on a red, white and blue ribbon. Dad brought some fireworks home and I got a clout for setting a banger off in the house, frightening the wits out of my poor old Granny. Peace Day!

I learned to read and write very quickly, but found sums harder to grasp. Like most children I had measles and chickenpox, but

My parents

worst of all on Christmas Day I was delirious, and everything in the bedroom seemed to be at a great distance. I was very ill for weeks.

I have often thought deeply about an incident that occurred just then. An old bearded Irishman named O'Neil came to our house every week selling tea, and Grandma told him of my illness. He said to me, 'Do you believe in Jesus Christ?' I wondered at this question, as ours was a Christian home and it had never occurred to me that anyone might exist who did not believe in Jesus Christ. However, I simply answered 'Yes', whereupon he anointed my head with oil and prayed.

I began to get better, but I was very weak for a long time and was away from school for three months. When I was well enough to go out Dad decided I needed some fresh air, so I was taken to Whiteley Woods. We went on a tramcar, which had an open bay at each end

of the upper deck, and we sat in the front one. I was taken in a
rowing boat on the dam, and for a long time I treasured the memory of this unusual treat.

My long absence from school had a further disastrous effect on
my arithmetic, as when I returned I found myself in a higher class,
among children who had learned most of the multiplication tables,
whereas the only tables I had ever heard of were dinner tables.
Then, as soon as I was eight, I went into the senior school, and
because I was 'good at composition' I was put into Standard 3 instead
of Standard 2. The rest of my schooldays were spent struggling to
catch up with arithmetic, although I was above average in all other
subjects.

Grandma died when I was eight. For years she had suffered from
bronchitis and ulcerated legs, and had never been happy since her
husband had died. She was a very kind, gentle old lady who had
seen much sorrow. Having been a dressmaker, she spent a good
deal of her time making clothes for Douglas and me when we were
small.

Throughout history, wars seem to have been followed first by a
short period of prosperity, then a depression. All too soon the depression came in the twenties and thirties, and it became common to

*Ellesmere Road Council School, Class 3, May 1925. The headmaster,
Mr Green, is on the left. The other teacher is Mr Simon.*

see groups of unemployed men standing aimlessly at street corners. There was no money about, and every trade suffered. Dad's little business was soon affected, as the bottom had fallen out of the second-hand machinery market, and in desperation he turned to making and repairing wringing machines, which were to be found in almost every home in the days before washing machines and launderettes had been thought of. Once again our front room was converted into a shop where the wringing machines could be sold. The piano was brought into the back room, replacing the old sofa, and the rest of the front-room furniture was somehow accommodated in the bedrooms.

By any standards, Dad was a good engineer, and he was versatile in other directions, such as blacksmith's work and joinery, but he was not really a good businessman, although Mother helped with the clerical work, which was not very extensive. Before her marriage she had worked in the secretary's office of Carter & Sons Ltd, manufacturers of gravy salt and druggists' supplies.

Dad's mistakes lay in starting a business with insufficient capital, having premises in a little-known back street, undercharging for his work, and in working alone; although it must be said that he had little option in the last respect, as he couldn't afford to pay wages. The trouble with the lone worker is that he has to waste his valuable time doing every menial job himself, even sweeping the floor, and at times he has to lock up his workshop and go out: either to buy supplies, to deliver finished work or to carry out work on customers' premises. A potential customer, finding the door locked, often will not bother to return and will take his custom elsewhere. Occasionally he would find it possible to employ a lad for a time, and sometimes he had the help of an unemployed steelworker, Tom Hunt, who was a very loyal friend, and who did a great deal of work for little or nothing. The only trouble with Tom was that he didn't realise his own strength. If a brick had to be knocked out of a wall for a pipe to pass through, Tom would demolish half the wall. If he tightened a bolt, either the bolt or the spanner was likely to snap under the strain, bringing from Tom the comment, 'Must have been a bit of poor steel.' Faced with any difficult job, he would mutter, 'It's got to go', and go it would if brute strength would achieve it. Once, sawing up an old wickerwork sidecar with an ordinary wood saw, he sawed right through a steel bar without noticing. He and Dad remained friends to the end, and now they lie side by side in adjacent graves.

Ellesmere Road Council School adjoined Ellesmere Road Wesleyan Chapel. The block nearest the chapel was the oldest part, and was built of stone. This was the infant school. Separate from it was a red-brick building which had been built between the times when Mother left school and I started. On the ground floor was the Boys' School, with the Girls' School above it, and each department had its own spacious asphalted playground. At that time the boys' head-master was Mr Egbert Green, and the girls' headmistress was Miss Wells. With hindsight, I am convinced that Ellesmere Road was a school ahead of its time in teaching methods.

In Standard 3 I was taught by a rather stout lady named Miss Chapman, whose only pretension to beauty was a fine head of deep auburn hair. She was a good all-round teacher and a firm discipli-narian, could play the piano, and taught art as a special subject. All but one of our teachers were musical: three were pianists, one was an organist, one was a choirmaster, and the headmaster played the violin, so we had a good grounding in music, and were taught to read both staff notation and tonic solfa. During his year of office as Lord Mayor, Alderman J.G. Graves, the head of a thriving mail order business, presented each of the city's schools with a supply of records and a gramophone which had a big fluted horn made of oak. This instrument occupied a prominent position in the assembly hall, and was played almost every day, thus improving our musical educa-tion. Also, at morning assembly after the usual hymn and prayer, the headmaster would refer to some current topic of news, or even to some film then being shown at one of the city's fifty or so cine-mas, from which he thought some lesson might be learnt. Books were also discussed, and I soon had the reputation of having read more books than any other boy of my age. Throughout my school life my teachers would frequently ask, 'What book are you reading now, Hatfield?' A great advantage I had was that one of Mother's cousins was a headmaster who received publishers' samples of school books which he gave to his nephews, the Wolstenholmes, who even-tually passed them on to me. Whenever time permitted, reading was one of my greatest pleasures, as indeed it still is.

Although I was encouraged at home to read good books, reading often had to give place to other things I had to do, such as sawing and chopping for firewood the old worn-out wringing machine rollers. As I grew older I helped more and more in the workshop, as it was expected that I would eventually become an engineer, and I often accompanied Dad to foundries, engineering works and small workshops where many diverse trades were practised. I also ran a lot of errands for both my parents, shopping for Mother and fetching such things as iron castings and paint for Dad. At that time, buying was a much more interesting experience than now, when we just select a tin from a shelf in a department store or supermarket. Then, we went to a paint shop, where a tin was placed on the scales, and into it went white lead, boiled linseed oil, turpentine, and some coloured power from the tiers of drawers that lined the back of the shop. This was real paint that would protect wood and metal for years, not like the synthetic colouring that now masquerades as paint and peels off after a year or two. Admittedly, the lead content was probably harmful.

Chapter 4
'Christmas 1922'

THE YEAR 1922, when I was eight years old, was ending badly. Work had been steadily declining, and the outlook for Christmas looked bleak, but in December one big job presented itself. A woodworker in Coal Aston bought from Dad a gas engine to drive his machinery, and this meant laying a concrete foundation, with rag bolts inserted, fixing the engine on it, installing a cooling water tank and fitting water pipes, gas pipe, and exhaust system. Then an overhead line shaft had to be supported on bearings known as 'Plummer blocks', all of which had to be correctly aligned, and belt pulleys of carefully calculated diameters fitted so that every machine ran at its correct speed. This was the job that would pay for our Christmas festivities.

On the Saturday before Christmas I went with Dad to Coal Aston. We went on the tram to Woodseats Terminus, which was near the old Chantrey Cinema, before reaching the 'Big Tree' Inn. I even remember the name of the film being shown at the cinema—'The Lost City'. From there we had to walk, trudging through the snow up Meadowhead, I carrying my little bag of tools with the neck tied round a hammer shaft. At last we reached our destination, which was a very cold workshop, and while Dad was working I tried to warm my feet in a pile of wood shavings.

The job took several days to complete, and was finished on Christmas Eve. The gas was turned on, the engine was cranked causing it to burst into life with a steady beat, pulleys spun, belts sang, and machines whirred. A good job had been done. Dad presented his bill.

The customer said he couldn't pay till after Christmas.

With a heavy heart and an empty pocket Dad tramped wearily homeward through the snow. When he reached the city he saw crowds of happy people carrying home their turkeys, geese, Christmas trees and parcels. For our family there was little likelihood of any of these things, and my little brother and I would be hanging up our stockings without much hope of Father Christmas filling them.

Utterly dejected he reached home, to be greeted by Mother with a bright smile, and at least a warm fire. How could he tell her? Wretchedly he imparted his tale of woe.

Mother heard him to the end and then said, 'Would a hundred pounds be any good?' He started in stunned amazement at the bundle of notes she held out.

Then she told him. A week or two previously he had advertised for sale a big screw-cutting lathe, but there had been no response until that day. A man had come along expressing interest, so Mother had taken him to the workshop, shown him the lathe, and succeeded in selling it to him for a hundred pounds cash.

In those days shops remained open until ten o'clock on Christmas Eve. As soon as our meal was over, my parents sallied forth with some of their opportune windfall to buy Christmas goodies.

When Douglas and I awoke on Christmas morning, we found our stockings filled with presents, and our eyes fell on a brightly trimmed Christmas tree. Then came dinner, a plump goose cooked to perfection, with the usual accompaniments of apple sauce and sage and onion stuffing, followed by Christmas pudding.

In later years I have often faced difficulties, and taken fresh heart from the memory of that Christmas so long ago, when with a near miracle God provided for us in our need.

Chapter 5
'The Happiest Time of our Lives'

MY BROTHER Douglas's disability gave great concern, and at the suggestion of the family doctor, he was taken to the Children's Hospital, where both his legs were encased in plaster, thus completely immobilising him. This treatment proved to be an unmitigated disaster, and could only have been prescribed by someone with no knowledge of the problem. For a start, as only the left leg was defective, it is difficult to imagine why the right leg was also put in plaster. As time went on, it became obvious that the child was in pain, and one day Dad took the matter into his own hands, and with a saw removed the plaster to reveal some bad sores.

When Douglas started school, the school doctor became concerned, and decided that he should attend what afterwards became known as the Edgar Allen Physical Treatment Centre. The doctors there were aghast on hearing of the former treatment, as they recognised that exercise and not immobilisation was needed. Mother had to take him there every morning. First of all he went into a bath through which an electric current flowed, then the muscles of his arm and leg were exercised on machines, and finally he was massaged by a Swedish lady, Miss Olga Landa. This treatment was undoubtedly beneficial, but of course it resulted in his missing morning lessons over a very long period of time, and when he eventually left school he was ill-equipped for either manual or clerical work.

When I was ten and Douglas five, we had another addition to our family, a little brother who was christened John Geoffrey, but who was always called Jack. He was a bright intelligent little boy, and I was always very fond of him. Here again tragedy struck. One morning, just before his fourth birthday, Mother had to go to the shops, and left him playing with another little boy, having asked a very good neighbour to keep an eye on him. Unfortunately, at a moment when her attention was diverted, the two children ran down the passage onto the road, and Jack was knocked down by a coal lorry. By the time Mother arrived home, he had been taken to the Children's Hospital, where it was discovered that he had a broken pelvis and a ruptured bladder. The pelvis mended but the bladder never did, and he spent the rest of his life in and out of hospital, and had many operations. In spite of all he suffered he was very cheerful and had a keen sense of humour. He was very clever with his hands.

Our teachers used to tell us that our schooldays were the happiest time of our lives, but this was not so in my case, partly because I dreaded the arithmetic period, and partly because of the conditions at home. My father was very strict, and kept a piece of leather belting about eighteen inches long by about an inch wide hanging on a nail beside the fireplace, a constant reminder of his authority. Many times I was thrashed unmercifully for quite trivial offences, and so nervous did I become that I went through a period of stammering, which I eventually overcame by reciting poetry. We were always short of money, often quite desperately so, and my parents found it difficult to afford the basic necessities of life, let alone any luxuries. To make things worse, my father had turned in his desperation to backing horses, with the usual disastrous results. On one occasion there were only three horses in a race, and he backed them all to be sure of getting a winner. I don't understand anything about gambling, as I have never backed a horse in my life, but I believe he had backed these horses at different prices, so that no matter which one won he would have something to draw, but the one he really wanted to win was called Cargo. The race started, and one horse fell at the first fence. Then another fell, leaving Cargo with nothing to do but finish the course to win. Cargo jumped into the canal, and it was declared 'no race'.

Of course, school was not all gloom by any means. One popular diversion was the headmaster's slide show. His projector, or magic lantern as we called it, was a bulky contraption with incandescent illumination, which required a gas supply and an oxygen cylinder. The slides shown were all of a geographical nature, and included some of Mr Green's own holidays in Devon and elsewhere. We also used to enjoy his science lessons, with bunsen burners, retorts and test tubes. During the week before we broke up for our annual four weeks' holiday, he used to organise cricket matches in the playground, a team from each class playing a team from the next higher class. The rule was 'tip and run', that is, once a batsman hit the ball he had to run. For the sake of the windows, a tennis ball was used. Remarkably, I cannot remember the weather ever being anything but fine during our cricket week.

Many of the school playground games of my boyhood are no longer played. What has happened to spinning tops? Every boy had a peg top, and probably also a whip top or a monkey top. Buttons were laid in a chalked circle, and the boys attempted to win them by knocking them of of the circle with the spinning peg top. Marbles were also popular, and I had a bag full of the ones that came out of broken lemonade bottles dumped by a mineral water factory near Dad's workshop. We also played games with cigarette cards, and swapping these to make up our sets went on every playtime.

It amazes me that in these days of supposedly advanced education, so many boys and girls leave school after having been there for about a dozen years unable to read. No one, however backward, ever left Ellesmere Road School (where every class had over fifty children) unable to read. The really backward ones were not promoted into higher classes until they reached something like an acceptable standard, and they would be individually taught by Mr Green himself.

One day in an English lesson, we were learning prefixes and suffixes, and we were asked to give words beginning with 'un-', meaning 'not'. To everyone's astonishment, a boy named Sidney Jones, who had seldom if ever been known to answer any question, put up his hand and rose eagerly to his feet calling 'Sir, sir!' 'Yes, Jones?', asked the teacher. 'Onion, sir' came the answer.

There was a boy named Wilkins who was a poor reader and who seemed to have difficulty with most of his lessons, until it came to the singing lesson, when his voice rang out, pure and clear. He seemed to have no difficulty reading tonic solfa, he watched the conductor, and his attack was instant and precise. Most people have ability in some direction, if only it can be discovered. It is said that no one is entirely useless—even the worst of us can serve as a horrible example. Even Jones the Onion distinguished himself by succeeding in climbing the greasy pole at Grimesthorpe Fair.

One year, when we returned to school after the summer holiday we found a transformation had taken place. The gas lighting had been replaced with electric, and the classrooms had been redecorated. A year or two later, all the houses in our yard were converted from gas to electricity, with penny-in-the-slot meters. At that time Sheffield probably had the cheapest electricity in the country. Once the first eight hundred units had been consumed at a price of fivepence per unit, the installation was deemed to have been paid for, and we then paid a small standing charge, based on the rateable value, and one-fifth of a penny a unit.

My first male teacher was a Manxman named Mr Corkill, for whom I had a great deal of admiration. We were now in Standard 5, in the crucial year of the dreadful eleven-plus examinations, the results of which would probably determine the whole course of our future lives. There was not one, but two examinations that had to be passed for entrance to a secondary school. I passed the first exam in all subjects. In the second, more difficult exam I received high marks in every subject except arithmetic, in which I failed by a narrow margin, and had therefore failed the whole examination, it being obligatory to pass in reading, English and arithmetic. Had I passed, it had been decided, on the headmaster's recommendation, that I should have gone to the Pupil Teachers' Centre. No doubt I would have become in due course an adequate teacher; whether I would have always been happy in that profession is open to question.

During those years we were never able to afford any holidays. The Rudge Multi motorcycle had long since gone to the scrapyard, and our only means of transport was the tramcar. Sometimes we would have a ride on one of these to one of the termini—the adult fare was three ha'pence, and the children's fare a ha'penny—and then walk in some of the beautiful countryside that surrounds Sheffield. When we visited Auntie Edie at Ecclesfield, we usually rode on a tram to the terminus at Firth Park, and then walked the rest of the way, pushing Douglas's pram. There was a short cut across fields to Auntie Edie's cottage, and to the left of the path were some old cottages, the basements of which had windows which were only a little above ground level, and through these windows it was possible to watch the file cutters at work. The file blanks were laid on a block of lead, and then with amazing skill and speed the teeth were cut with a hammer and chisel. So skilled were these file cutters that they could cut a hundred, or indeed almost any specified number, of teeth to the inch. This must have been one of the last surviving cottage industries.

Auntie Edie lived in the first of a row of very old stone cottages known as Oliver Cottages. The walls were about a yard thick, and there was no gas or electricity, lighting being by oil lamp and candles. There was still a communal pump in the yard, but this was disused as water had been piped into the kitchens. A Yorkshire range in the living room had obviously been fitted into the original open-hearth fireplace, and a relic of a roasting jack was still fixed to the low ceiling. An old copper kettle gleamed in the hearth. The sanitary arrangements were primitive in the extreme, consisting of a communal privy midden up the yard, with a box-like seat with two apertures cut in the top, enabling two persons to enjoy the amenities of the place companionably together if they were so minded.

Auntie Edie was small and hump-backed, a disability caused by some childhood accident that no one would talk about. Owing to her unfortunate lack of physical attraction, it would not have been surprising if she had never married, yet she outlived three husbands, all of whom shared the name Edward. She met the first one, James Edward Charlesworth, hereinafter referred to as Uncle Jim, when she somehow managed to stop his runaway horse and milk float. How she managed to do this with her small stature and disability I have never been able to understand, but she must have been very courageous. Uncle Jim was a very likeable man, countrified and friendly. Like so many at that time he found himself unemployed, and was pleased when at last he managed to get a job with a gang of men who were laying an electric cable. One dark night he was attending to the red warning oil lamps around some road works, when he was run down by a lorry and killed. Auntie Edie had one little boy, Eric, and was then expecting her second, Eddie. In order to subsist, she had to start taking in lodgers, men who worked at the Brightside Foundry and Engineering Works, which was about the first industrial works to be sited in the area, across the fields from her cottage, near the railway.

A few years later she married one of her lodgers, Edward Townsend, known as Ned. He was a widower with a grown-up family, quite a kind generous man, but being a lot older than Auntie Edie, in a few years he left her a widow again. History repeated itself once more, when some years later she married another old widower lodger, Edward Rodgers, nicknamed Ted, who was also nearing the end of his days, and she outlived him by quite a number of years.

Sometimes in the summer holidays I spent a few days with Auntie Edie, enjoying playing in the fields and spending the evenings in the lamp-lit cottage listening to her old phonograph with its cylindrical records. The titles of the records were recorded on them. One I remember started with the announcement: 'Edison Bell Record, "All Aboard for Margate", sung by Miss Florrie Ford.' Then began a churning indeterminate noise that was the orchestral introduction, followed by the strident tones of Miss Florrie Ford. It was a far cry from today's hi-fi stereo recording, but then we thought it very entertaining.

One year, Mother decided we ought to have a day out, by way of a holiday, so she produced a collecting tin, and for several weeks I pushed this under the noses of the family, collecting their pennies. My spending money was supposed to be twopence per week, but there were many weeks when I got nothing. My chief source of income was our next-door neighbour, Mrs Loukes, who was a dressmaker. When she had completed a dress, I used to deliver it for her, in return for which she gave me twopence.

At last the eagerly awaited day of our holiday arrived, a bright sunny August Saturday, and the few shillings we had saved were extracted from the tin. Mother packed some food, and full of excitement we set off for the station. We were actually going on a train!

Standing on the platform, we could watch trains coming and going, and see all the bustle of passengers and porters. Presently, in came our train, a great green shiny monster emitting clouds of smoke and steam, with its fascinating movement of piston rods, connecting rods and valve gear. We scrambled into a carriage, and soon the wheels were clattering over the points and crossings as we left the Midland Station. For the first mile or so there was little to see but factories, then the train gathered speed as it ran alongside the pleasant green expanse of Millhouses Park. Next came the upper-middle-class houses of Beauchief and Dore, and then we roared into the blackness of Totley Tunnel, where the windows had to be closed to keep out the smoke. What an adventure!

Almost as soon as the train had emerged from the tunnel, it stopped at Grindleford station, where we got off, having reached our destination. The fact that we had only travelled about ten miles from home never occurred to me—I had been on a train; I had just come through the second longest tunnel in England, as was proved by the evidence of a notice over the tunnel entrance; I was now in another county—Derbyshire—and all those hills I could see were the mountains of the Peak District! As a traveller, I considered myself to be practically on a par with Marco Polo or Columbus. Leaving the station we walked down to the River Derwent, and spent the rest of the day in the woods along its bank in that lovely stretch between Grindleford and Hathersage. When we returned home on the train that evening, I don't think many people can have enjoyed a fortnight in the Costa Brava more than we enjoyed that day's outing to Grindleford.

The following year, the collecting box came out a little earlier, and we were able to have a day's outing a little further afield, at Torksey in Lincolnshire, where Dad and I fished for gudgeon and bream. This was another enjoyable day. The year after that, we achieved the ultimate—a day at the seaside, at Cleethorpes.

Chapter 6
'All Saints' School'

IN 1926 Douglas caught mumps, which of course he passed on to me, to my great disgust. Although I was not really very ill, I was not allowed to go to school in order not to spread the infection. Someone had given me an old melodeon (a kind of accordion) and I sat with that on my knee most of the day playing such tunes as 'Drink to Me Only with Thine Eyes' and 'Swanee River', until the neighbours probably wished I was in the Swanee River.

Later that year the Sheffield Chrysanthemum Society held their annual show in Edmund Road Drill Hall, and sent a number of free tickets to the schools to admit scholars on the Saturday morning. Prizes were to be awarded to those writing the best essays describing the show.

Three of us went from Ellesmere Road school: John Russell, Harold Hooper, and myself. We found parties of children going round with their teachers, making notes. Some of them were from secondary schools, and were therefore up to sixteen years old. We were only twelve, took no notes, and of course larked about. None of us had the slightest idea of anything to do with the exhibits. Nevertheless, John and I decided to have a go at the essay competition, and we wrote our effusions during the weekend. The rules stated that only the best one should be sent from each school, but having read our offerings, Mr Green decided to submit both.

Several weeks passed, until one afternoon the entire school was summoned into the assembly hall. Mr Green began by reading out a letter he had received from the city's Tramways Department complaining of boys having committed the dangerous practice of riding on the backs of trams. Having delivered an ultimatum regarding

the dire punishment that would be meted out to any such offend-
ers, he cleared his throat and continued, 'Now we come to something more pleasant', and proceeded to read another letter, this
time from the Sheffield Chrysanthemum Society, stating that I had
won the first prize in the recent essay competition. The prize, repos-
ing on Mr Green's desk, proved to be a wooden crate containing
twenty pounds of Grimes Golden apples, produce of British Columbia.
With the aid of a poker from the teachers' room, the lid was prised
open, and I made a donation of apples to John Russell as a conso-
lation prize, and also presented an apple to each of the teachers.
An account of my achievement was inscribed in the school record
book, and I was the hero of the hour.

As soon as the rest of the scholars had returned to their classes,
the lid of the crate was hammered back on with the ubiquitous
poker, and Mr Green sent me home with my prize, as he knew
there was a likelihood of there being few apples left in the box if I
left school with it at the same time as the others.

I still have a copy of that essay, now yellow and cracking at the
folds. Here it is:

Charles Hatfield   Std VII   Ellesmere Road Cl. School

The Sheffield Chrysanthemum and Fruit Show.

On Saturday last I had the pleasure of visiting the Drill Hall where
the above show was being held. The committee very kindly invited
scholars on Saturday morning at a greatly reduced entrance charge,
and I was exceedingly pleased to take advantage of their generous
offer.

I was delighted with everything I saw, particularly the gorgeous
flowers. At first sight the exhibition appeared like long lines of
varied colour, then as I looked at each individual table, my pleasure and appreciation increased, until after I had repeatedly surveyed each table, I thought that there could not be a more delight-
fully interesting occupation than that of a gardener.

When I thought of the time and money spent on the exhibits,
both in cultivating them and arranging them, I thought it a pity
that more scholars had not been sufficiently interested to avail
themselves of the opportunity offered of viewing so charming a
display.

The central figure was a tall pyramid of apples and oranges.
Though I had heard all the names, I had never before realized
that there were so many species of apples. The pyramid was sur-
mounted by a pineapple, the lofty and conspicuous position of
which made it the cynosure of all eyes.

To advertise the fact that if you wish to prosper in business you must have a good window display, two models of shop windows were placed side by side. In Mr. B. Hind's shop, fish, rubbing-stone, firewood, nuts, mouldy fruit, and shrivelled vegetables were mixed in haphazard fashion, while mis-spelt notices such as "Logins," "Back in a minnit," and "Errand Boy wanted to find customers" adorned the establishment. In the centre of the window, in a large basket lined with pink paper, reposed a solitary tomato, in the final stage of decay. This bore an antiquated tin label, "English." A set-out of disreputable-looking and evil-smelling kippers found a resting-place on a pile of unhealthy looking onions. From a dilapidated gas-bracket, suspended by a piece of string hung some skins which, it is to be supposed, may at some remote period have clothed rabbits. A copy of the "Early Bird," presumably for wrapping purposes, occupied a prominent position. The brickwork outside the shop was adorned by a shadowy sketch which may have been meant to represent a girl, since the name "Rosey" was scrawled beside it. Evidently the children of the district found this a suitable spot for exercising their educational accomplishments, as in addition to the drawing was a sum, and an exhibition of noughts and crosses. The whole effect was one of entire neglect.

The next shop, the proprietor of which was Mr. C. Progress, bore an entirely different aspect. Everything was of the very best quality, temptingly displayed with utmost good taste. Clean, bright-looking advertisements were set out to the best advantage, those representing the banana trade being specially attractive. The contrast presented by these two shops could not fail to convince anyone that business, to be successful, must be run on modern lines and given careful attention.

In various parts of the exhibition were beautiful vegetables: cabbages, leeks, beetroot, savoys, cauliflowers, tomatoes, onions, potatoes, carrots, parsnips, celery, etc.

The finest sights of all were the innumerable flowers. Single blooms and wreaths were in profusion in all colours. Although their stems were not in water, they did not wither as they were sprayed by means of pumps. There were large and small varieties, and I liked the smaller ones just as much as the larger species.

The pretty leaves and ferns took my attention, as beautiful leaves are seldom seen by town dwellers.

On one stall flowers and vegetables were exposed for sale, the proceeds to be devoted to the hospitals.

A number of prizes to be awarded to the most successful exhibitors were on show.

My visit to the exhibition afforded me much enjoyment, being so full of interest, and I should like to thank those whose kindly thought provided this opportunity for the schoolchildren of Sheffield

Despite the sentiments expressed at that early age, gardening has never been one of my hobbies, as I have always been involved in other interests, although a well-kept garden is always a pleasure to the eye. Around the time when the above essay was being written, the seeds were being sown of an interest that has remained with me to the present day, namely music. Periodically we were marched from school to the city to attend a concert in the Victoria Hall, which was the principal concert hall in Sheffield before the City Hall was built. There we were introduced to some excellent vocal, instrumental and orchestral music performed by the best local musicians of that period. On the day following these excursions, we had to write the inevitable composition describing our impressions of the concert, and the two that were considered to be the best were sent to the Education Committee offices. Mine always went, and the other was usually that of my friend John Russell. He was a clever boy, and I often wondered what became of him, but I never heard anything of him after we left school.

One day, a few weeks before my thirteenth birthday, Mother was doing her weekly wash when something went wrong with one of her eyes, and she could only see flashes of light. She went immediately to the doctor, who diagnosed a detached retina, and sent her straight to the Royal Infirmary. There she had to lie flat on her back, motionless, and her eye was irrigated by pouring liquid into it from a glass vessel with a long spout.

The management of the house now fell squarely on my shoulders. Whilst Douglas and I were at school, our good neighbour Mrs Loukes looked after little Jack, who fortunately had not yet suffered his accident. At mid-day, I had to dash home, peel potatoes and put them on to boil, and get the dinner ready for when Dad came in. After school, I opened the shop, dealt with any customers who might come in, prepared the tea, looked after the kids, washed up the day's accumulation of dirty pots, chopped the sticks for the next day's fire, did my homework and got the children to bed. Dad was pretty useless in the house, and in any case he visited the hospital, and almost always went back to the workshop and worked till about ten o'clock, sometimes even later. On Saturdays I did the housework, scrubbed the floor, dusted, blackleaded the Yorkshire range, polished the brasses, and did the shopping. One evening I also made sixteen pounds of marmalade. I admit to having been puzzled to know how to pass my spare time.

One evening, Dad had been to the hospital to visit Mother, and he came home looking more upset than I had ever seen him. Mother was so ill and so disfigured that he had walked past her bed without recognising her. It appeared that she had been prescribed a dose of calomel each morning, and a dose of salts each evening to clear the calomel out of her system. A nurse had confused two prescriptions, and instead of the salts she was giving Mother heart tablets which should have gone to another patient who was getting the salts. The result was mercury poisoning, and Mother almost lost her life. The inside of her throat swelled so that she almost choked, and her lower lip turned yellow and curled outwards until it almost touched her chin. Panic ensued in the ward, with doctors and matron called in, and a tragedy was only narrowly averted.

As a result of that carelessness, Mother suffered misery for the next thirty years, in fact some effect remained until the end of her life. Previously, her skin had been clear and flawless, but now ulcers began to appear all over her body, and once she had no less than sixteen at the same time. The following Christmas she had a hole about an inch in diameter in the back of one of her hands, and it was possible to see the bone. She was unable to cook, and following her directions I made the bread and stuffed and cooked the goose.

Mother had been in hospital for three months, and during that time I had my thirteenth birthday, at which point I had to move to another school. For the final year our class went to Grimesthorpe School, which was too far away to give me time to get home, prepare the dinner and return, so Dad arranged for me to go to All Saints' School, which was hardly any further away than Ellesmere Road. I started there on All Fools' Day 1927, and some joker had put the church tower clock back a quarter of an hour, so half the school arrived late. However, we were finally mustered in the hall, and proceeded to sing 'O Happy Band of Pilgrims'.

I did not enjoy my year at All Saints' very much, although my education did benefit in just one direction, as will presently be seen. All Saints' Church (which boasted the highest spire in Sheffield) and the adjoining school had been built out of the generosity of the steel magnate Sir John Brown—some detractors saying from the profit he had made from supplying munitions for the Crimean War. The buildings were therefore old, and the stonework blackened with the smoke that came from the valley of the River Don, where the works of Thomas Firth and John Brown still lay. From the school, the sound of the great steam hammers could be clearly heard, and at times it was possible to smell the whale oil in which the hot steel was being tempered. The playgrounds were small compared with those of my previous school, and the classrooms were overshadowed by the height of the church. Our classroom was upstairs, half of it built out like a shelf over a playground, and when the teacher stood in front of the class, his trousers flapped in the draught that came up between the floorboards. There was also a two-inch gap under the door, which again contributed to the Spartan conditions that prevailed in winter.

That the teacher did not care for me soon became apparent. All Saints' was run on completely different lines from Ellesmere Road, where much the same importance was attached to each subject, and a great deal of general knowledge taught. At All Saints' all the emphasis was laid on passing examinations. The walls of the hall were hung with honours boards recording the names of boys who had gained scholarships over the years. Unfortunately for me, on one of the first days I was there, the headmaster, Mr W.H. Simon, decided to give our class a general knowledge test, and with what I had learnt at Ellesmere Road, I was able to outshine the rest of the class. Mr Simon was pleased with me, and jokingly christened me 'The Professor', but the class teacher, whom generations of boys had dubbed 'Pongo', resented me as a newcomer, and soon made the fact obvious. Of course, he immediately discovered my weakness, as arithmetic was knocked in at all times of the day. This was the year of the Examination for Certificates of Merit, and we were constantly reminded of the dire consequences of failing to pass it. For the first time in my life I went to the bottom of the class, notwithstanding the fact that when it came to grammar I could analyse and parse the most complex sentences and answer every question that was set, scarcely ever losing a mark. At Ellesmere Road we had been taught a round style of handwriting, whereas at All Saints' a narrow upright style prevailed. Pongo insisted that I should change to this style, with the result that I fell between two stools and finished up with a very bad inconsistent style which I did not lose for years. Every afternoon began with a 'tot', an addition sum which had to be completed in one minute. Everyone with a wrong answer, or who had not finished, was caned. I was caned every day for about six months; then the light dawned. By this time Mother was out of hospital and once more able to do a certain amount of work, and so I was able to concentrate more on my school work, and spent the greater part of each evening doing homework.

Every week we had a test to determine our position in class, and by Christmas I had moved from the bottom to the top, and remained in that position until I left school three months later, passing the Merit Examination in all six subjects, gaining distinction in five subjects, including arithmetic, in a year when no one else in the school gained more than two distinctions. A burning sense of injustice had driven me to make this great effort in order to show my contempt for the way I had been treated.

We had been told repeatedly that there was no hope of any of us being able to get a job unless we had a Merit Certificate, but I had been working for two or three months before I heard the result of the exam. A special evening function was held at the school for the presentation, which was made by the Bishop and the Schools Inspector, who said that mine was the finest certificate to be presented that year. From the school I received as a prize a copy of the complete works of William Shakespeare.

Before describing what happened after I left school, there are a few other anecdotes of my childhood to relate.

Chapter 7
'Jamaica Street'

MENTION has already been made of my father's workshop in Jamaica Street, and as what went on there has had such an influence on my life, I will describe it.

It was part of a row of similar buildings in a yard behind terraced houses on a steep cobbled hill. The property belonged to an elderly man named Mr Lawrence, who occupied one of the houses with his wife who served in the sweet shop at the front. Two sons of theirs and their families lived in two of the other houses. Access to the yard was through an archway between the houses, and the double doors of our workshop faced this entry. The premises consisted of two parts, forming an 'L' shape. The first part, which we always called the top shop, was on the ground floor of a two-storey building and had once been a stable, and there were still two mangers at the far end. At right angles to this was the bottom shop, single-storey, with a leaky roof of wood and glass. Evidence that this had been a blacksmith's shop was there in the form of an old forge. A large opening had been made in the wall dividing the two shops to give access from one to the other, and also to give more daylight to the top shop.

To power the machinery, Dad installed a large gas engine in the top shop at the end near the mangers. A dynamo driven by a belt from one of the flywheels of the engine provided the electric light. Overhead, a steel shaft in bearings ran the length of the shop. This was driven by another belt from a pulley on the engine, and belts from pulleys on the shaft drove two lathes, a hacksaw machine, a pillar-type drilling machine, a milling machine, a slotting machine, a double-headed grinder and a circular saw. Near the door was a strong bench, bolted to which was a large engineer's parallel vice, and cupboards and shelves to hold drills, taps, dies, reamers, chasers, callipers, micrometer, spanners, files, hammers and engineering tools of every description.

In the bottom shop was the blacksmith's hearth, bellows, anvil and a great collection of hammers and tongs. Here was another heavy bench supporting a very strong leg vice and a pipe vice. There was also a joiner's bench, with a good supply of tools appertaining to that trade. Shelves along one wall contained various tins of paint, and new timber was stored overhead. A coke-burning slow combustion stove in the middle of the floor supplied a little warmth. The wringing machines were built in this part of the shop, and there were piles of cog wheels for these.

Brought up in the days of twin-tubs and automatic washing machines, my grandchildren may ask, 'What was a wringing machine?' Well, it performed two functions: wringing and mangling. When the clothes had been washed, before they were hung out to dry, they were passed between the wooden rollers of the wringing machine, and when the handle was turned causing the rollers to revolve, most of the water was squeezed out into the washboard, running out through the semi-circular hole cut in the front of this, back into the washtub. If the rollers were in good condition, such items as sheets when dry could be mangled, that is, folded and passed through the rollers again, which eliminated ironing.

Some of our machines were made from new castings, particularly the ones that could be folded to form a table, but most of the upright ones were reconditioned second-hand. I helped a great deal with this work from about the age of eleven, dismantling the machines, scouring the frames with a wire brush and painting them: green for the sides, red for the edges, black for the hand-wheel and gear wheels, chocolate for the top board, aluminium for the hand-screws that applied pressure to the rollers, and gold for the maker's emblem. I also made new washboards and mangling boards, thus getting valuable experience in joinery.

The rollers were turned on one of the lathes, usually from blocks of sycamore, which is a very white, close-grained wood, but the very best rollers were turned from lignum vitae, and these would last almost a lifetime, but few of our customers could afford the cost of them. Rollers measured from about twenty to twenty-four inches in length, and from five to six inches in diameter. When Dad had roughly turned a roller in the lathe, he used to bore a hole right through it, take it out of the lathe and drive the spindle right through. It then went back in the lathe, with the spindle now held in the chuck, and was turned to the correct diameter and length. A three-inch-diameter groove was turned in each end, into which iron rings were hammered to prevent splitting. The rollers were sand-papered, beeswaxed, and varnished, and the ends treated with bitumen. People often asked for old rollers to be replaced. This entailed going to the customer's house, dismantling the machine, bringing away the old rollers, removing the gear wheel, splitting the old rollers off the spindles, turning the new rollers, replacing the gear wheel, and returning to the house to reassemble the machine. For all this work he charged one pound two shillings and six pence per pair of rollers, having paid six shillings for the wood. Sometimes if the machine was situated close to a hot fire, the rollers would split, and the customer would demand a replacement. It was a poor living.

Besides making and repairing wringing machines, of course Dad would accept any job that came along, and he could repair almost anything.

If snow was on the ground, he made sledge runners. The forge was lit, and bars of steel cut to various standard lengths. Each end in turn was brought to red heat, bent at a right angle, and forged to form a spike which could be driven into the wooden framework of the sledge for which it was intended. An added attraction for the boys who came to buy the runners was that they were allowed to work the forge bellows, and on a good day they queued to do this. Dad also made complete sledges for sale in our shop.

One day after the shop was closed, we heard someone knocking on the back door. Mother opened it to find a small boy standing there. 'Yes?', she asked. Holding out a small brass cog-wheel he said, 'Can you put a clock on this wheel?' Like tempus he had to fugit.

In our shop we sold (or tried to sell) not only wringing machines but car spares, toys, fireworks, paperback books, wireless sets and parts, broomsticks and even Indian clubs. On Saturday mornings, children came in to spend their Saturday pennies, and long consideration preceded every purchase. Sometimes they would look at all we had, ask for two ha'pennies for a penny, and then leave for the sweet shop. A variety of sweets could be bought for the price of four ounces for fourpence, and there were penny, and even ha'penny bars of chocolate to be had.

Each year as the fifth of November approached, a poster on our window announced that 'LION FIREWORKS' were 'SOLD HERE'. To comply with the law, we had to buy a licence costing five shillings, keep the stock in a closed metal container, and ensure that any fireworks on display were covered with glass. Our metal container was an old-fashioned coal scuttle with a hinged lid. For the display cabinet we made a box exactly the size of the frame of a picture of the Good Samaritan which graced one of our walls. With the picture removed, the frame and glass served as a lid for our display box. The inspector surveyed these arrangements with a disapproving expression, but they came within the law—just!

To advertise the fireworks further, we made a Guy Fawkes and placed it in the shop for about a week before bonfire day. Dad's oldest working suit, very oily, was stuffed with wood shavings, a mask served for a face with a firework stuck in the mouth like a cigarette, and an old cap placed on his head. Many children came in to see the guy, and we sold quite a lot of fireworks.

On the fifth, the women who lived in the yard brought out their cast-iron oven shelves and laid them together on the asphalt opposite our house. As a further protection, an old galvanised bath was placed on them, and in this some bricks were laid to support the old bucket, punched with air holes, which would contain the fire. All the neighbours contributed some fuel from their precious store. Directly over the bucket a strong wire ran to the clothes post to support Guy Fawkes.

About six o'clock, our yard began to fill with all the boys of the neighbourhood, not to mention a few girls, and the fire was lit. Soon fireworks were banging in all directions: roman candles, golden rain, sparklers and catherine wheels giving their colourful displays, and rockets whooshing through the air. At the climax, the guy was brought our of the shop (which was still open) hung by his shoulders onto the wire, and slid along until he was over the fire. Soon he was well ablaze, and the fireworks in his clothing banging away. Those who had exhausted their supply of fireworks wheedled extra coppers out of their parents (who were enjoying themselves as much as the children) and before closing time at eight o'clock we had sold our last firework. Then potatoes were laid in the embers to roast, and our mothers brought out home-made 'bonfire toffee', and slabs of the treacly dark brown cake known as Yorkshire parkin. My little brother Jack once said, 'I think bonfire day's the happiest day of all the year!'

The next day, the Good Samaritan was returned to his frame and his place on the wall, where we could contemplate him for the next eleven months.

In our shop window, by way of advertisement, were two wringer rollers standing on end. One, bearing the legend 'Before' was the most badly worn and splintered old roller I ever saw. Beside it was a new varnished roller labelled, of course, 'After'.

One day when Mother had gone into the cellar, she overheard the conversation of two men who were standing on the cellar grate looking into the window. 'I don't believe it!' said one. 'No, neither do I', agreed his companion, 'He could never put all the wood back like that.'

An officious Inspector of Weights and Measures came in one day. 'Have you any scales?', he demanded suspiciously looking all round. 'No,' answered Mother in her mildest voice, 'We don't sell wringing machines by weight.'

In the mid-twenties, the wireless had become the greatest wonder of the age, and for many men constructing a set provided greater interest than listening to the programmes. Dad made the biggest crystal set I ever saw, and the reception was very clear. When we were listening with our headphones on, our dog, Nigger, would sit up and beg for a pair to be put on his head, and he would listen to music with rapt attention. I made up several simple crystal sets from kits of parts, and these were sold in the shop for five shillings each. Usually we also managed to sell a pair of headphones at twelve and sixpence, and probably a coil of aerial wire. Later, I made a two-valve set which was a little ahead of its time in that the receiver, speaker and batteries were all contained in a single cabinet, whereas most people then had all these components as separate units, connected to each other by a maze of wires festooned around the furniture. News items I recollect hearing on the wireless were the announcement of the death of Queen Alexandra, Amy Johnson's famous solo flight to Australia, and the burning down of Crystal Palace.

Lacking a vehicle for transporting the wringers, Dad had constructed a sort of very large barrow, about six feet long with cast-iron wheels (actually wringing machine hand-wheels) on a spring axle, and an iron bracket like those on sack barrows at the front to retain the load. The machines were laid on this, with the load balanced over the axle, and we pushed it all over Sheffield. Even the dog was sometimes harnessed to it to help pull up the hills, and he did his best

Nigger was probably the best loved and the most entertaining pet we ever had. A man once asked what breed he was, and Dad answered that he thought he was a Manchester terrier. 'Oh?' said the man, 'Mine's a Crookes hound!' His ancestry may have been doubtful, but his intelligence and loyalty were never in question. He was black with a white patch on his chest, smooth haired, and had long legs which gave him a great turn of speed. He was the friendliest of dogs, and everyone around seemed to know him. All the children loved him. One of his great assets was that his popularity made him almost self-supporting. Regularly he would come home carrying a large bone or a parcel of food that some unknown well-wisher had bestowed on him, and in the evening he had a round of fish and chip shops where he would sit up and beg with his paws crossed in such a comical manner that most of the customers would throw him a few chips or a bit of fish, which he caught expertly.

At the top of our street was a grocery shop kept by a man who rejoiced in the name of Democritus Davis (pronounced by one of our neighbours 'Demo-*cry*-tus', but generally known as 'Demmy') and who in the summer sold ice cream from a freezer near the door. Nigger was extremely partial to ice cream, and he would hang around until somebody bought some, when he would go through his chip shop routine, and the customer would say, 'Ah, look at him. I'll have to give him a bit.' He was a remarkable runner, and once chased a whippet round a field until he caught up with it and nipped its tail. On another occasion he was running at full speed down Jamaica Street, when to Dad's horror, some children appeared in his path. There was no chance of him being able to stop, and it seemed certain that they would be knocked down, but he jumped clean over their heads. Of course, he had occasional lapses from grace, as when he went into our shop and chewed the monkeys-up-sticks, rendering them unsaleable.

Before Nigger, we had had another dog, a little black Pomeranian, found by Dad lost and terrified of fireworks one fifth of November. Her owners were never traced, so we kept her and made a great pet of her until she died. She was very intelligent, and would carry messages tied to her collar between our house and the workshop. Dad used to grind scissors for twopence per pair, this being his cigarette money, and once when he had forgotten to take the scissors, he tied to her collar a note, on which he had written 'Please send scissors'. She went home and held up her head to Mother, who saw the note, read it, and sent her back with the scissors tied to her collar. One might think that a lot of scissors would have to be ground at the price of twopence per pair to buy many cigarettes, but it must be remembered that the cheaper brands, like Woodbines and Park Drive were only ten for fourpence, and the better brands, Players and Gold Flake, etc. were ten for sixpence.

Close to Demmy Davis's shop was another grocery shop kept by a Mr Moore, which today could well form part of a museum, although it was typical of many such shops of that period. Very few things were pre-packed. Sugar was weighed into strong paper bags which were invariably blue in colour, in fact 'sugar-bag blue' was a current term sometimes applied to clothing. Flour was contained in a large wooden bin, and weighed out as required into bags containing a stone, or half a stone. Salt was in the form of a block, from which a piece would be sawn. Treacle was dispensed into the customer's own jar from a tank with a large brass tap. Tea could be blended from the contents of a series of black and gold tins which were aligned on the top shelf. Various other commodities were sold from sacks or wooden boxes. Mr Moore scorned the use of a bacon slicer, and with a long razor-sharp knife could slice bacon or ham perfectly to whatever thickness the customer required.

Another local tradesman was the milkman, Mr Walker, who was assisted in his business by his wife, sons and daughters. He never took a holiday, and was to be seen every day of the year with his horse and two-wheeled milk cart, which carried two churns of milk. From these he replenished a large can which he carried round to his customers, and measured out pints or half pints into their jugs.

Often I had to fetch a hundredweight of coal from the coal yard in Canada Street, the next street to Jamaica Street. The coal was weighed into box-shaped barrows which we were allowed to borrow and return. If I remember rightly, it cost one and sixpence a hundredweight, and was a better quality than we ever saw after World War II, as then all the best was exported.

Most of the streets had gas lighting, and before the days of automatic lighting, the lamplighter used to go round at dusk, lighting the gas lamps with a torch on the end of a long pole. Postmen wore a uniform with a red stripe down the trouser seams, and a hat which had a peak at the back as well as the front to shed rain away from their necks.

Pushing 'the wagon', as we called it, with the heavy wringers was hard work, besides being time-consuming, and eventually Dad acquired a motorcycle combination, a 1912 Matchless with an eight-horse-power J.A.P. vee-twin engine, double belt drive and a wickerwork sidecar, and which was identical to the machine that had competed with distinction in the Isle of Man Tourist Trophy Race in the year of its manufacture. If it were still in existence it would be worth a great deal of money. The sidecar was soon replaced with a large box with a hinged tailboard which could be lowered to allow a wringer to be tipped on its side and slid in. Later, the rear end of the frame was modified to allow a gearbox, chain drive and a more efficient brake to be fitted.

The box could be converted to a sidecar by adding seats, wind-screens and a luggage grid. Dad's mother had a sister, Aunt Florrie, at Boston, Lincolnshire, and after Mother had written to her, she invited us to go there for a week. At the beginning of August, we set off on (or in, as the case may be) the unusual vehicle: Douglas on a seat in the front of the box, Mother and Jack on a seat in the back of the box and I on the pillion.

Driving a motorcycle of that era was much more of an art than is driving a modern machine. Three levers had to be constantly adjusted: the throttle lever, the air lever, and the ignition advance and retard lever. The engine was lubricated by means of a hand pump situated on the side of the tank, and the driver had to remember to keep operating this. The gear lever worked in a long quadrant, and selected bottom gear, second, and ten variations of top gear!

This was to be the first whole week's holiday we had ever enjoyed as a family. The eagerly awaited day arrived, and we embarked on our strange-looking equipage. It was a fine day, and we set off in good spirits, with a large box of home-made food and a fishing bas-ket on the luggage grid, and fishing rods sticking out of the rectan-gular sidecar, which I had repainted the previous day.

For a good many miles all went well, until one of the sidecar couplings broke where it was joined to the frame of the bike under the saddle. In the next village, we were lucky enough to find a blacksmith who fabricated a somewhat rough-and-ready part from a piece of wrought iron.

We went on our way rejoicing, until the front-wheel spindle broke. From somewhere we managed to obtain a bicycle spindle, which in spite of grave doubts somehow sustained the weight for the rest of the journey. Sleaford and Swineshead were behind us and Boston Stump could be seen across the flat landscape when yet another calamity occurred. The throttle cable broke. Undeterred, Dad removed it from the outer casing, tied it round a spanner, and controlled the speed by holding this in his hand until we reached our destination. This adventurous journey occupied a whole day; in any modern car it could be accomplished in about a couple of hours. In Boston we obtained a new throttle cable and front-wheel spindle, and enjoyed our holiday from then onwards without too much drama.

Boston became our holiday venue every year until 1937, when our financial position had improved to the extent that we were able to take a holiday in the West Country.

Boston was quite an interesting old town, with its ancient church and 'Stump', and its market on the green. Besides spending one or two days fishing in one or other of the many waterways, we always had a day at Skegness, which was twenty-two miles away by a twisting road, and occasionally a day at Mablethorpe. Our pleasures were very simple and inexpensive, but none the less enjoyable.

Chapter 8
'Pawson & Brailsford's'

IT HAD ALWAYS been assumed that when I left school I should follow in my father's footsteps as an engineer and go into his business. True, my old headmaster at Ellesmere Road thought I ought
to become a teacher, whilst another of my teachers was of the opinion that I should become a journalist. I had no notion of how a boy
of fourteen could set about becoming a journalist, and my failure
to pass the eleven-plus examination had precluded any possibility
of my becoming a teacher. Therefore it seemed that I was destined
for a trade, so in addition to the practical experience I was getting
in the workshop and the school woodwork class, I was reading
books on engineering and practising machine drawing.

Nevertheless, as the time when I should be leaving school drew
near, I began to entertain some serious doubts as to whether this
was really the way I was going to earn a livelihood, and one day I
dropped a bombshell by saying, 'Dad, I don't want to go into your
business.' He seemed to be utterly astonished, until I pointed out
that if he couldn't make a decent living, it was unlikely that my
prospects were very good. I was sick of our precarious existence,
and longed for security.

The problem was that I could not think of any alternative employment that appealed to me, and unemployment was so widespread
that there was keen competition for any kind of job. School-leavers
who in desperation became errand boys found themselves on the
scrapheap on reaching the age of sixteen, when their employers
would sack them and engage another fourteen-year-old boy to avoid
having to stamp their National Insurance cards.

One day Dad said to me, 'Have you ever thought about the printing trade?' I answered, 'No, but I think I could become interested

in it.' 'Well,' he said, 'Your Uncle Jack's connected with it, and he's never been out of work. I think we'd better ask his advice.' Uncle Jack was his sister Elsie's husband, and he was not actually a printer, but a process worker, that is, engaged in making the blocks from which photographs were printed by the letterpress method. His advice was that I should apply to the old-established form of Pawson & Brailsford Ltd, where he had served his own apprenticeship, and who had a reputation for teaching their apprentices well.

Three months before I was due to leave school, I wrote an application to this firm, quoting Uncle Jack as a reference. The reply I received was that they had no vacancies, but would retain my application. And that, I thought, was that. However, just over a fortnight before I was due to leave school, another letter arrived stating that a vacancy had arisen in the bookbinding department, and offering me an interview with their Mr Wilkinson, the manager of that department.

Mr Wilkinson proved to be a white-haired old gentleman, not very tall, wearing a high stiff old-fashioned collar encircled at its lower end by his tie, and grey spats over his boots. On hearing my name, he consulted a foolscap book, on two pages of which were recorded the names of boys who had applied for jobs. Probably assisted by my references, I was selected from this lot, and offered an apprenticeship, subject to my having proved satisfactory during a probationary period of six months.

During the week of my interview, a little crack at the corner of my mouth began to give me trouble, and to my consternation turned to a sore which quickly spread all over my face and neck, and being infectious caused me to have to miss my last two weeks at school, and prevented me from starting my new job for a further fortnight. It was, in fact, impetigo, and very miserable it made me. After various ineffective remedies had been tried, our doctor told Mother to take me home, boil some Robin starch, spread it on a cloth whilst it was still very hot, wrap it round my face and tie it in a knot on top of my head. It was to be left there until the starch cooled and dried, and then removed, when the sores would come away with it. After that I was to apply some ointment he had given me. Bizarre as this sounds, it actually worked, and the trouble was cured, but I shall never forget the horrible sensations I experienced, as first the stinging hot starch was applied, then as it went cold and clammy, and then as it dried and stiffened. Added to this, I must have presented a comical sight with the cloth wrapped round my face and head, and must have resembled nothing so much as a suet pudding.

Once rid of this embarrassing and painful complaint, albeit with a red and blotchy face, I presented myself for work. The hours of work were: Monday, 8.00 am to 5.00 pm; Tuesday to Friday, 8.00 am to 6.00 pm; Saturday, 8.00 am to 12 noon—a total of forty-eight hours per week. During my six months' probationary period I received five shillings a week, out of which a penny was deducted for the hospitals. After giving Mother three and elevenpence, I was left with one shilling, out of which I had to pay my tram fares. Every morning I walked to work, walked home for dinner, rode back on the tram (having walked past the nearest stop to our house to the fare stage, so it only cost me a penny to ride to the city) and walked home at the end of the afternoon. My actual spending money was therefore sevenpence, the rest of my wage being a necessary contribution to the upkeep of the home.

A journeyman's wage in the printing and bookbinding industry was then three pounds, fourteen shillings and sixpence, and ours was considered to be the highest-paid artisan trade. A bound apprentice in his first year received 15% of this, which was eleven shillings and threepence, and each year he received a rise of 5%, so that on reaching the age of 15 his wage became fourteen shillings and ninepence.

At the end of the first six months, my father and I had to go to the firm's solicitors to sign my indentures of apprenticeship. This document, which I still have, sets out the obligations of the firm, of the apprentice, and of his father, and with a seal against each of our signatures I thought it very impressive.

When I began my apprenticeship as a bookbinder and finisher in 1928, Pawson & Brailsford's, founded in 1855, was one of the most reputable and high-class firms in the Sheffield area. Although the loose-leaf system was beginning to make inroads into the account book making industry, there was still a demand for the books, and their manufacture comprised the greater part of our work. We also bound the University library books, and valuable books for private customers in fine leather with gold tooling.

Some years before my time, the firm had had a sales shop situated at No. 1 High Street, near the Cathedral, but this was now a bank, and the shop was behind it in East Parade and York Street. Certain work, such as die stamping stationery and process engraving, was also carried on in these premises, but the main works were at the corner of Mulberry Street and Norfolk Street, now the premises of the Central Health Clinic. The offices were on the ground floor facing Norfolk Street, and also on this floor were a warehouse and packing department. Under it was the biggest basement I have ever seen, containing rows and rows of high shelving full of paper of every description. Three large cylinder presses were housed in another part of the basement, whilst other parts contained a stereotype foundry and the central heating boiler.

Ascending the stone steps from the ground floor (for there was no lift, only a small goods hoist) one arrived first at the letterpress printing department, which was divided into the quiet composing room and the noisy machine room. Above this was the lithographic printing department, and on the top floor the bookbinding department, at which lofty height it was possible to count fourteen churches from one or other of the many windows.

Ours was a long rectangular room, with an area at one end where strawboards for the book covers were stored and cut, and equipped with a special bench for the gilding of book edges. The main part of the room had bookbinding benches running continuously along one wall, overlooked by Mr Wilkinson's desk which stood on a dais at right angles to the end of the benches. From this vantage point he could survey all his staff and scowl at any backsliders. The binders worked facing the windows, and behind them was a row of tables on which were bolted the iron nipping presses, and under which were shelves accommodating dozens of rolls of cloth of various shades and textures for covering books. The centre of the room was occupied by a huge wide table, where the girls worked, sewing books by hand on wooden frames, stripping down old books for re-binding, pasting, collating and numbering. On the Mulberry Street side of the room, which also had a row of windows, were a number of machines for ruling lines on account book paper. Also in the department were wire-stitching machines, paging machines, perforators, a book-sewing machine, a huge noisy folding machine, two big paper guillotines, several large presses, and two gold blocking presses. The staff of the department consisted of the manager, five men, two apprentices, a forewoman and twelve girls.

At first I was set to work with a man called Harry, who constantly took snuff, and who I subsequently discovered had earned, from his peculiar speech, the nickname of 'Clake-iddy-Wakes', which was his way of pronouncing 'Clerk of the Works'. On hearing that the Conservatives had won an election, he remarked gloomily, 'Vis country's sinking faver and faver into ve abcess.'

Although elocution may not have been his strongest point, he was an efficient bookbinder, and soon began to initiate me into the mysteries of account book binding. At first I was only allowed to bind quarter-bound books, which were cheap books such as delivery books and receipt books with a strip of cloth up the spine, marble paper covering the boards, and the edges then cut flush on the guillotine.

I had only been working there a short time when Harry left to work elsewhere, and I had to work with George. George was a small man who at home was domineered by a large wife, and he tried to compensate for this by being aggressive and overbearing at work. Unfortunately he was the least competent of all our staff, and made many mistakes. Every day, as part of the British Federation of Master Printers costing system, we had to record on a docket the time we had spent on each job, and the total number of hours recorded for that day was expected to match the number of hours we had been working. As fixed times were allowed for each operation, we had to work fast and lose no time. George would plod along at a leisurely pace until about four o'clock in the afternoon, when he would suddenly become aware of the time, start to rush about, chase me around and swear at me, and probably finish up by spoiling some work.

One of our jobs consisted of mounting showcards. Standing on a box, because I was not very tall, I would have to glue the printed sheets while George mounted them on strawboard. The adhesive was animal glue, melted in a large iron glue pot, standing on a gas ring. I had to work at such a pace that there were always three sheets glued, to give time for the glue to soak in and the sheet to finish stretching before it was applied to the board. According to George I was always: (a) too slow; (b) too fast; (c) the glue was too thick; (d) the glue was too thin; (e) I was putting too much on; (f) I wasn't putting enough on; (g) I wasn't picking the bits off—the 'bits' being the bits of bristle which the brush shed as it wore down. As we might spend several nine-hour days on one of these jobs, I was always glad when they were finished and I could get on with something less monotonous, away from George's constant stream of invective.

A condition of my apprenticeship was that I should attend the practical bookbinding class at the Sheffield College of Arts and Crafts, where we were taught fine art bookbinding under an elderly man who was acknowledged to be one of the finest binders in the country, Mr Walter Slinn. About that time, he left his employment with the old-established firm of William Townsend & Sons Ltd and started working for himself in the front room of his house in Ecclesall Road. He specialised in binding exquisite books in fine leathers, sometimes with inlaid designs and beautiful gold tooling, every book an individual work of art. He bound all Sir Osbert Sitwell's manuscripts, won a highly coveted national prize, and even had customers in America. Under his guidance we bound books of our own and learnt to enjoy the satisfaction of creative art.

The Monday class was for design, and I have to say that none of the bookbinding students learnt much of value. The instructor appeared to have little knowledge of the practical side of our craft, and was at the same time trying to teach other students such things as silverware design, and even heraldry.

One evening he told us to draw a design for a book about Africa, oblivious of the fact that the tools used by a bookbinder can only be used to form geometric and floral patters, unless very expensive brass blocks are engraved for long runs. At the end of the session he came round to inspect our designs, and saw that one of the apprentices from the Municipal Printing and Stationery Department had simply drawn a rectangle. 'Where's your design?' he demanded. 'That's it,' was the reply, 'The desert.'

To another who had drawn some triangles he said, 'These pyramids look like tents.'

'They are tents.'

'Oh, I thought they looked like pyramids.'

Occasionally a bit of humour crept into the practical class. A few day-school teachers started attending the class, as simple bookbinding was beginning to be taught as a craft subject in some schools. One of these was a pompous headmaster, who as soon as he had learnt a little, started trying to teach the apprentices things to which they were accustomed in their daily work, which as may be imagined didn't go down very well.

One evening, he was trying to letter a book with gold leaf. Real gold leaf is obtained in little books of rouged tissue paper in sheets about three and a quarter inches square, and has been beaten to a thickness of about three hundred thousandths of an inch, and is so thin that it cannot be handled. Each sheet has to be lifted out of the tissue paper book with a spotlessly clean knife onto a leather cushion,

*Bill Newsam, who taught me my trade. The ledger was bound in
white rough calf leather, with bands of dark red Russia leather,
laced with white vellum. The word 'Ledger' is gold-tooled on a
bright red leather label, and the lower lettered label in black.*

where by judicially blowing on it, the finisher can cause it to lie flat
and unwrinkled, a feat that demands a degree of skill that can only
be acquired by much practice. Our headmaster friend blew a little
off-centre, which caused the leaf of gold to leave the cushion and
float into the air. His efforts to retrieve it with a piece of cotton
wool only created a draught which blew it further away, until it was
finally lost. One of the apprentices said to him, 'Shall I tell you the
secret?' The harassed headmaster nodded assent.

'Just before you blow, suck up quickly.' Unsuspectingly, his victim did this, with the result that the leaf of gold instantly rose and
stuck to his mouth and moustache, the helpful apprentice having
smartly disappeared in the direction of the toilet.

I attended the college for the required three years, and certainly
gained a lot of valuable tuition and experience there, but was glad
when I was able to leave and have the time to pursue other interests.

The man who undoubtedly taught me most at work was Bill Newsam.
Resulting from the First World War, he had an artificial leg, but was
remarkably active. He used to descend all the steps down to ground
level by hopping down four steps at a time on his good leg with his

right hand on the rail, and steadying himself by pressing the palm of his left hand against the wall. No able-bodied person could go down as fast as he could. Besides being a good all-round book-binder, he was the finisher; that is, he executed the gold lettering and ornamentation of the books. I was apprenticed as a binder and finisher, and the other apprentice, Sidney Mee, was apprenticed as a binder and ruler. Actually, he spent most of his time on the ruling machine. He had already been there a year when I started. He became an excellent craftsman, and we were very good friends

During the years of my apprenticeship, Bill Newsam taught me to bind every type of account book and letterpress book, and to become an efficient finisher. Finishing demands a high degree of skill, and I spent many hours practising with tools on odd bits of scrap leather. I also worked with other men who were employed from time to time on a temporary basis, and learnt something from all of them.

The girls in the department were of a good type, and were all very friendly, although I never had any romantic associations with any of them. We were all kept too busy. For a few years we had an annual works trip, and on these of course we enjoyed each other's company. On one of these trips we went to New Brighton and Liver-pool, where we were conducted around the liner *Samaria*, which will receive further mention much later in my story.

Meanwhile, Dad was still struggling to make a living. When I was fifteen, Mother had another baby, whom she named James after her father. Unfortunately, the mercurial poisoning from which she still suffered affected the baby, who died after only ten days, and Dad had the sad task of making the little coffin himself. James was buried in a stranger's grave which had been opened for the interment of an adult.

The ramshackle premises adjoining our workshop in Jamaica Street had been taken over by an enterprising ex-army officer, Mr A.L. Simpkin, for the purpose of manufacturing sweets. He started in a small way, using second-hand equipment, and as his machines were constantly giving trouble, Dad had the job of repairing them. Even-tually, Mr Simpkin paid him a retainer of thirty shillings a week to give his work priority. Some weeks he earned a little more than the thirty shillings as he was spending so much time on Simpkin's work, so a new arrangement had to be made whereby he became their maintenance engineer.

Over the years, Simpkin's prospered, the breakthrough coming when they stopped making cheap sweets and concentrated solely on making medicated sweets to be supplied to chemists. As more sophisticated machinery was installed, efficiency improved and output increased until better premises were needed. When at last the firm moved into a modernised factory at Hillsborough, Dad was appointed Works Manager, and he played a big part in designing the layout of the new premises. His own business was closed down, and some of his engineering equipment sold to Simpkin's to equip a maintenance workshop, and he wisely invested the money in shares in the firm. It was the best thing he ever did.

Chapter 9
'Long Sammy, Fish Billy and the Duke of Darnall'

AT THIS STAGE of my narrative, I would like to regress and mention some of the characters who were well known to Sheffielders in the twenties and thirties.

One of the most famous was Long Sammy. He was very tall, and had the misfortune of being what used to be described as 'K-legged', that is, his legs were bent sideways. He was employed by Suggs the sports outfitters to advertise their goods, and could regularly be seen around the city carrying a sandwich board, wearing a ridiculous cricket cap and other sports gear. For many years he was a familiar figure, but was eventually found dead in a disused brick kiln, where he had been sleeping rough.

Another harmless eccentric was known as the Duke of Darnall. He was often to be seen around the city wearing shabby finery, carrying a pair of yellow gloves, and politely raising his bowler hat to all the ladies.

Quite a lot of bow-legged men were to be seen in the twenties, the condition caused by rickets in childhood. A lot of men who worked in the cutlery trade were self-employed, and were known as 'little mesters'; some forging blades, some grinding, some polishing and some making and fitting handles. For a while, one of these men, whom I facetiously nicknamed the Master Cutler, ground our firm's guillotine blades. Not far away in Sycamore Street (now demolished) was the firm of John Batt, where this man, along with many others, rented a grinding hull. He was the perfect caricature of the Yorkshire Tyke. His dress consisted of a cloth cap, an old jacket, a red muffler round his neck, corduroy trousers tied round with string below his knees, clogs, and he smoked a clay pipe upside down.

The grinding hull he rented was one of a long row on one of the upper floors of the building, and consisted of a trough containing water, in which a grindstone ran. This was driven by a belt from one of the pulleys which were mounted on a shaft running the length of the workshop at a height of about three feet. Power for the entire works was supplied by an old steam engine on the ground floor.

This was operated by another character. In a newspaper article at the time of his retirement he was reported to have said that he had been minding the engine for fifty years, and if he had been able to continue it could have run for another fifty. He said that at the beginning of his career he had to open and close the close the valves by hand, but he had himself adapted the mechanism to do this automatically. I don't blame him!

Also in Sycamore Street was a blacksmith's shop, probably the last in the city, where horses were shod. There had been a blacksmith's shop in Canada Street, just behind our Jamaica Street workshop, and next door to that was a wheelwright's workshop, As a boy, I often watched these craftsmen at work. Besides shoeing horses and doing general smith's work, Jack Mellor made the ironwork for the carts his neighbour was making, including the iron tyres for the wheels. Making the wooden wheels I thought was the most interesting part of the wheelwright's job.

During the economic depression, many men, usually wearing an ex-serviceman's badge, went from door to door trying to earn a meagre living by selling boot and shoe laces, matches, etc. from a tray supported by a band round their shoulders. Tramps occasionally came round begging, usually saying they were on their way to Barnsley, looking for work. As a rule they would be going to the casual ward at Firvale Workhouse.

Every Saturday morning a blind man came into all the yards playing an accordion and singing ballads. He had a good voice, and sang such songs as 'When Other Lips', 'Thora', and 'Home Sweet Home'. He was accompanied by one of his several children who guided him, and came to the doors collecting pennies in a little enamelled mug. As each child reached a certain age, he or she would be succeeded by the next younger one. One little girl coming round for the first time obviously felt her position deeply, and cried bitterly as she went from door to door.

Then there were the hawkers, of whom Fish Billy was the most noteworthy. He sold wares from a hand cart, which he had pushed from the other side of the city, and although small of stature he had a voice like a foghorn, and could be heard proclaiming the quality of his fish for half a mile in every direction. I believe he was of Welsh extraction.

A greengrocer named Mr Hays came round every week with a horse and dray, and a van bearing the legend 'Atora Beef Suet' was actually drawn by an ox, an incongruous sight in Petre Street. Another individual with a strange intonation sold lemons, and could be heard calling, 'Two a penny lamons!'

Chapter 10
'The Good Companions'

SUNDAY was a special day at our house. For six days a week, break-fast consisted of bread and dripping and a mug of cocoa, but on Sunday we rose to the dizzy heights of bacon and eggs and coffee—a great treat. Also I wore my best suit and white shirt to be ready for Sunday School, which I always attended. We kept the Sabbath, and I valued it if only because it gave me an opportunity for reading.

When I was very small I attended Ellesmere Road Wesleyan Sunday School because it was so near and there were no roads to cross, but as soon as I was eight I started going to St James' Presbyterian where, as I have already mentioned, my parents had become acquainted; although by this time the congregation worshipped in new premises in Scott Road, which was at some distance. I enjoyed going to this Sunday School, and for many years hardly ever missed, eventually becoming a teacher. As soon as he was old enough Douglas went with me, and later on Jack went too when he was well enough. Each year I entered for the scripture examination, and still have all my certificates, which in those days were attractively printed in colour. When I was about ten I made my first stage appearance in a Nativity play as a shepherd.

As I grew older I began to attend the church services as well, and became involved in all the young people's activities. At the age of sixteen I became a full member of the church.

Ever since I had been quite a small child I had entertained the family by singing humorous songs, of which I had quite a reper-toire, in a strong treble voice. My voice broke when I was thirteen, and I began to sing the bass part in the hymns. At first I sang by ear, but the old lady who had been Mother's Sunday School teacher presented me with a hymn book with tunes when I became a committed church member. I was able to read music because I had had some piano lessons given by the older sister of one of the boys in my class at All Saints', but never became a pianist, partly because I had little time to practise, partly because my fingers and brain did not co-ordinate, and partly owing to the decrepit state of our old French piano, which had a wooden frame that had shrunk and had not been tuned for about twenty years. Every now and then I used to take the action out, repair the hammers with wooden meat skewers, and rub down the lead balance weights at the ends of the keys with sandpaper; otherwise when I struck a key its neighbours would go down at the same time.

Once, when I had been practising a piece for about two months Mother suddenly said, 'Oh, I've just realised what it is he's supposed to be playing!' The composer was probably revolving rapidly in his grave.

I have forgotten to mention that about a year before I left school to add to my educational accomplishments I had some French lessons given by a Madame de Boé-Scott, the 'de Boé' part being her maiden name, and Scott that of her English husband. For those attending the children's class, she charged sixpence per lesson, and we all sat round a circular table in her front room and conversed to the best of our limited ability in French. One by one her pupils stopped going until I was the only one left, and as she couldn't afford to run a class for sixpence, and my father couldn't afford to pay for private lessons, I had to give it up. In later life, I have felt sorry about this, as I have always been interested in languages.

Being so fond of singing, it became my ambition to join the church choir, but was unable to do so as the choir practice was held on Wednesday evenings when I had to be at the College of Arts and Crafts. As soon as I was seventeen and could leave the college, I joined the choir, and within a year was singing the bass solos.

The years from 1930, when I was sixteen, to 1939 were some of the happiest of my life. The shadow of poverty was gradually lifting, I enjoyed my work and the company of my colleagues, and I had found an outlet for my interests in the church and its services and activities. There were a lot of young people of both sexes, and besides the choir we had an indoor games night in the winter and a tennis club in the summer. Sport never appealed to me a great deal, and none of the top players would have had much to fear from me, but I could play tennis just well enough to be able to enjoy a game.

When I was eighteen it was decided to form a concert party. The Girls' Club had staged a little operetta, and they thought the time had come to join forces with the boys. A meeting was held to discuss the matter, and our young organist, Bill Rathmell, along with our resident elocutionist, Miss Elsie Willoughby, were appointed to be joint producers. The party was given the not-very-original name of 'The Good Companions'. Rehearsals began and quite a wealth of talent emerged. Black and white costumes were made; volunteers erected the stage, made scenery and curtains, and organised the lighting; programmes were printed and sold; and the evening arrived when the curtains opened to reveal us all in The Opening Chorus.

Then followed a programme of solo and concerted items, sketches and what used to be known as comic turns. The kind of show we put on was popular with audiences of that era, and The Good Companions continued to give concerts in various parts of the city until the outbreak of war.

The very first song I ever sang in public was an old comic song of George Robey's called 'In Other Words', and the occasion was a church social event. Whilst the audience were amused by the song, some of them remarked on the depth and quality of my voice for a boy of eighteen. Soon afterwards, coached by the organist, I sang the solo part in an anthem sung by the choir on the Sunday School Anniversary. Next, I was asked to sing at a Sunday afternoon meeting at a Methodist chapel. The songs I sang were 'Friend o' Mine', 'The Lost Chord', and 'Love's Old Sweet Song'.

After I had sung in our own church one evening, the minister's son said to his mother, 'That lad's got a good voice, but he doesn't know how to use it. He should have lessons.'

It so happened that the daughter of our minister, the Rev. James Wallace, had recently married Dr Traugott Ernst Gumpert, who was to become eminent in his profession as a cardiac specialist, and who was the son of a former German consul and an English mother. Dr Gumpert's sister, Margarete, had studied singing first in England, and then for four years in Frankfurt, from where she had recently returned and started to teach. With characteristic kindness, Mrs Wallace offered to pay half the fee if I would go to Margarete Gumpert for lessons. Of course, I was only too delighted to take this advantage, and I always remember Mrs Wallace with deep gratitude. I had lessons for five years, but of course I didn't impose on Mrs Wallace's generosity for that length of time.

Part of every evening was now given up to practising vocal exercises, doing breathing exercises, learning songs, studying theory and transposing songs into lower keys to suit my voice. Apart from the popular bass ballads, I learnt quite a lot of *lieder*, particularly Schubert and Brahms, which I was taught to sing in German, and I also sang some songs in Italian and French. Over the years, I have often been congratulated on the excellence of my German pronunciation, but I could never pronounce French at all well, and have never considered it to be a good singing language, with its nasal inflections.

Our old piano still proved to be a handicap, and as soon as I could afford it, I started looking round for a good second-hand one. Several were seen and rejected, until one with an impressive specification was advertised in the local paper by a firm of furniture dealers. When Dad and I went to see it we were told it had been sold, but that there was a good selection of second-hand pianos in the basement; from which we suspected that the one so glowingly described in the advertisement was fictitious. However, we descended to the basement, which was indeed full of pianos. After a long examination, I decided that there were two pianos that were outstanding, both German in black cases, and finally decided on one made in Dresden. The price asked was thirty-seven guineas, but Dad, who was a hard bargain driver, managed to beat the salesman down to twenty-five pounds and the old piano. When tuned, it proved to be a first-class instrument which served me well for many years, and is now in my son's possession. I never became a pianist, but when learning a new song I was able to play the melody, and I had friends who would accompany me.

Soon I was being asked to sing in various parts of Sheffield, and though I have never gained much financially I have had a lot of enjoyment through my singing, and I like to think I have given other people pleasure.

Chapter 11
'Bookbinding'

MY APPRENTICESHIP had continued to pursue its rather uneventful course, and as the years progressed I became proficient in all branches of my trade, finding a great deal of interest in it. I bound the University books, and I would occasionally borrow one overnight to enrich my knowledge of some subject in which I had an interest.

At the time I started work, the firm was in great need of modernisation. Instead of an internal telephone system, there were speaking tubes linking the various departments. These had a whistle in each end, and if you wished to speak to someone in another department, you took out your whistle, blew down the tube to blow the whistle at the other end, then applied the end of the tube to your ear and listened, until it was your turn to speak into it. In our department, the speaking tubes were housed in a dark cupboard under the stairs leading to the attic, and the manager allowed no one but himself to answer the whistle. If he happened to be at the other end of the department when it blew he would take no notice for a few minutes, then say, 'Was that the whistle?'

On arriving at work, we did not clock on. On the wall just inside the works entrance was fixed a board with rows of numbered hooks, and on each hook was a brass disc stamped with a corresponding number—mine was eighty-four. Each worker took his or her disc off the hook and dropped it through a slot in the time office door into a box. Exactly at 8.00 am the timekeeper, Sam Hatfield (no relation of mine), removed the box and substituted another for the latecomers, whose names and time of arrival he entered in a book in red ink.

Besides being timekeeper Sam was warehouseman, packer, guillotine operator and custodian of the boiler. On very cold Monday mornings he would have to arrive extra early to light the boiler to get the building warm, and if he hadn't managed to attain the required temperature just before the managing director arrived, he would take the thermometer from his office and warm it on the boiler. A few minutes later, the managing director would arrive in his office, rub his hands, mutter, 'Cold this morning', then glance at the warmed-up thermometer and say in tones of surprise, 'Sixty-three, I wouldn't have believed it!'

Pay packets were as yet unknown at Pawson & Brailsford's. When we finished work on Friday afternoon, we went down to the warehouse and filed past the cashier, told him our number, and were each handed a little round tin, a semi-circular lid half covering the top, on which the number was stamped. We then tipped the money out into our palm, threw the tin into a box, and went on our way rejoicing.

Longevity was a characteristic of Pawson & Brailsford's staff. There was a little old clerk called Mr Llewellyn who claimed to have been the first man in Sheffield to have used a typewriter. By this time he was in his eighties, and he had been given progressively lighter duties, until finally he was put in charge of the postage stamps. The poor old lad was loath to retire because he was said to have a nagging wife. One day he collapsed at work. His son-in-law was sent for to take him home, and I believe he died the next day.

Another ancient retainer was Mr Watson, who served in the front shop. Although in his seventies, he was as straight as a die, tall and slim, walked briskly, and used to go for an outdoor swim every morning with the Water Rats, breaking the ice in winter time. One day he dropped dead.

All the department managers were old. Our Mr Wilkinson I have already described. In the letterpress department Mr Finnegan stayed until he was so old that the department was really run by his two foremen, the compositor Mr MacLaughlin, and the machine minder Mr MacDonaugh. One disgruntled printer who did not hail from the Emerald Isle was heard to say that his own name ought to have been MacHine (machine!). The manager of the lithographic department was Mr Woodcock, nicknamed for some obscure reason 'Timber-tool'. He had charge of the first-aid cabinet, and once when one of the bookbinders cut his finger rather badly with a leather paring knife, he went to Mr Woodcock to have it wrapped up. At the sight of the blood, Mr Woodcock fainted, whereupon the patient fainted too, and the artist had to fan them both. Our Mr Newsam was urgently sent for to deal with the pair of them, and having served in the Royal Army Medical Corps and had his own leg shot off, he was not very squeamish at the sight of a cut finger. Why he had not been appointed first-aid man was always a puzzle, as he usually had to be sent for if anyone had an accident; but of course it is a fact of life that the most obvious person for any post is seldom the one appointed. On one of the few occasions when Mr Woodcock was able to get a bandage round someone's finger, it fell off within two minutes.

Despite his shortcomings in this respect, in his own field he was supreme. He was a superb litho artist. Those were the days of direct litho, when the image to be printed had to be drawn in reverse on polished slabs of cream coloured stone. The stones were then laid in a flatbed machine, damped, and inked with a roller. The principle of lithography relies on the fact that grease and water will not mix, whilst the stone had an affinity for both. When water was applied, only the blank areas received it, the water being repelled by the slightly greasy image. Then when the ink was rolled on, it adhered only to the dry image, being repelled from the blank areas by the water. The paper was printed by being pressed against the stone when the operator pulled down a great lever. Many of the stones were so large and heavy that the litho department had much the appearance of a cemetery. Nowadays the stones have been superseded by thin aluminium plates which are easy to move and store, but the basic principle is much the same.

Sometimes a customer would order an illuminated address, and Mr Woodcock would do this by hand. The border and initial letter would be an artistic triumph in red, blue and gold, and the text would be hand-written in beautiful Old English script. When I became experienced, I often made covers for these, using fine morocco leather on padded boards, and tooling them to my own design in gold leaf.

Just before I was twenty, Mr Wilkinson retired and Bill Newsam became manager. To my delight, he gave me his former job as finisher, although I still had a year of my apprenticeship to complete. Nowadays, many lads would regard this as exploitation, being asked to do a man's work for an apprentice's wage, but I regarded it as a heaven-sent opportunity to gain experience and to become proficient in my craft before I was twenty-one, when I might have had to move to another firm. Most of my time was now spent in lettering and tooling the books, edge gilding, and marbling the edges of account books. Sometimes I left the finishing bench to bind such things as legal books in white calf with red leather panels for lettering; exquisite books of poetry, and large expensive account books, occasionally bound in cream, red or green vellum, sometimes bound in rough calf decorated and strengthened with wide bands of red Russia leather, laced with narrow strips of white vellum.

Some of the books we bound were of great interest. Once we bound original copies of the Journal of the House of Commons for the period of the Civil War. The oldest book I ever bound was a volume of Aristophanes in Greek, printed by Aldus Manutius of Venice (the inventor of italic type, and after whom the Aldine Press and Aldine Court are named), dated 1498.

Another of my regular jobs was stamping initials on leather goods. All the shops in Sheffield where suitcases, attaché cases, wallets, purses, dressing cases and handbags were sold sent them to us to have the customers' initials embossed in black, gold or silver. In the period before Christmas, when these articles were being bought for presents I lettered lots of them every day. Gold leaf and silver leaf were applied with heated brass tools exactly as if lettering books. Brown leather suitcases were often lettered in black, and to do this I held the tools in a gas flame until they were not only heated, but well blackened with soot, when they were pressed into the leather. It was possible by this means to achieve a deep shiny black impression, and the lettering was absolutely indelible.

Pocket diaries were another seasonal line, and we made many thousands each year. These had round corners, gilt edges and real leather covers, and if my memory serves me right, were sold for one and sixpence. The steel firm of Arthur Balfour ordered a huge quantity to be sent to their agents all over the world, and I had to letter the name of the recipient in gold on every one. This meant working a lot of overtime. The extra money was useful, but they were long days from 8.00 am to 8.00 pm, with an hour for dinner and a quarter of an hour for tea. There were no mid-morning and mid-afternoon tea breaks in those days.

Chapter 12
'The 1930s'

FEW PERIODS in modern history have been so maligned as the thirties, and whilst it is true that for much of that decade unemployment caused widespread misery, towards the end of it most people's living standards had actually improved. Wages had remained stable, and prices had actually fallen. Whole areas of slums had been demolished, and the former occupants housed on new estates. In the suburbs, new semi-detached houses cost between £350 and £500, and could be secured for as little as £20 deposit. Many of the houses which were then bought for about £400 are being sold around forty to fifty years later for over £60,000; in some cases a great deal more.

Prices of all commodities at that time seem incredibly low by today's standards. It was possible to furnish a house completely for £100. Our food, which came almost entirely from Britain and the Empire, was very cheap. On the other hand, of course, it must be remembered that wages were correspondingly low. Most men earned around £3 per week, and comparatively few married women worked.

In our family, although we were still far from affluent, our financial position had greatly improved since Dad had started to work for Simpkin's for a regular wage, and of course my own wage helped. We began to enjoy some of the small luxuries of life.

Our old Matchless motorcycle had finally gone to the scrapheap, and had been replaced with a home-built machine with a Zenith tank and frame with altered back end, a huge vee-twin J.A.P. engine, Sturmey-Archer gearbox, Indian front wheel, and Royal Enfield rear wheel. Alongside this fearsome contraption was bolted an improved box sidecar with rounded aluminium front. This enormously strong outfit had given good service for a number of years, but now it was replaced with our first car, a 1925 bull-nosed Morris Cowley saloon, which had cost the princely sum of £3.00. It was a remarkably good car, and gave little trouble before it was replaced with a slightly newer Morris Oxford which we nicknamed 'Sausage' because its previous owner had been a butcher, and it came to us still having a faint aroma of meat. Luggage boots had not yet been invented, and our luggage was carried in a tea chest on a grid at the rear.

I also had an eye for a bargain. For some years we had had an old gramophone, graced with a large metal horn garishly painted red, blue and green, from which blared the strains of the overtures to 'Tannhauser, Poet and Peasant', a strident cornet solo entitled 'Showers of Gold', 'Abide With Me', and Caruso singing 'M'Appari' from 'Marta'. One Saturday I staggered home bearing a heavy 'His Master's Voice' hornless gramophone in an oak cabinet. I had come across this treasure in the rag market, and had managed to beat the price down from seventeen and sixpence to fifteen shillings. The previous owner had spoilt its appearance by coating it with dark varnish, which I removed to reveal the original light oak. This instrument had an infinitely better sound than the ancient horn gramophone, and provided hundreds of hours of pleasure over the years. I made a matching oak cabinet for it to stand on and to contain my growing collection of records, and over fifty years later it survives to contain darkroom equipment.

Photography was another subject in which I became interested at that time, having bought from one of my workmates for £1 a Kodak Autographic No. 2 camera, with a negative size of 4¼" by 2¾", big enough not to need enlarging. I still have this museum piece, but films for it have not been available for many years.

With the end of the wringing machine business, I no longer had to make washboards, but I was very interested in woodwork, and working in the attic I made a number of very useful household items, and learned to French polish.

On Monday evenings at the church we had an organisation known as The Fellowship, where speakers expounded various topics of general interest, and where we sometimes had debates. I participated in these, holding forth upon such subjects as the life of Charles Dickens (almost all of whose books I had read), James Nasmyth (the Victorian engineer who invented the steam hammer), and the history of bookbinding. This early experience in public speaking stood me in good stead in future years.

One summer in the 1930s, our local evening paper, the *Yorkshire Telegraph and Star*, ran a 'Brighter Sheffield Competition', and Dad decided to enter it, although he knew nothing about gardening. He made a number of boxes, one for each window sill at the back of the house, a big one to stand on the ground under the window, one to stand on the dustbin enclosure, and a very big one to stand on the yard opposite the house. At that time he still had the motorbike and box, and he would get up very early and drive to a wood where he would fill the box with soil and leaf mould to fill his window boxes, etc. Soon the back of our house was covered in foliage and flowers, sweet peas climbing canes each side of the window to meet tendrils hanging from the box on the bedroom window sill. The big box across the yard sported a rhododendron among other things, and nasturtiums beautified the top of the wall. He won third prize. Spurred on by his example, some of the neighbours also made window boxes, and the yard was quite transformed.

King George V's Silver Jubilee took place in 1935, with nationwide celebrations. Only a year before, the King had suffered a critical illness, and daily bulletins were displayed in electric lights on Coles's Corner at the junction of Fargate and Church Street, which I could just see through a gap in the buildings from the window in front of my bench on the top floor of our firm. Apart from the Jubilee, 1935 marked a milestone in my own life, as I completed my apprenticeship at the age of twenty-one.

My parents decided that I should have a birthday party, and all my friends in The Good Companions concert party were invited, as well as a few others. Mercifully by this time the shop had been given up, and had reverted to being a front room, and had been decorated and furnished. Realising that our old kitchen table wasn't going to big enough for all our guests to get round, I added an extension made of tongued and grooved boards. It was unfortunate that my party was held at the end of the week in which the Good Companions had been performing the main concert of the year, and we were all too tired to enjoy the party quite as much as we might otherwise have done. My friend at work, Sidney Mee, brought his piano accordion to enliven the proceedings, and being quite a good-looking lad, he scored quite a hit with some of the girls.

During that year, there was a shortage of work in our department, and Sidney was put on short time. In September, the situation had worsened to such a degree that he and I were suspended for three weeks. During that time we drew seventeen shillings and sixpence a week unemployment pay, and a pound from the National Union of Printing, Bookbinding and Paper Workers. Each day we had to go to the Union office to sign the unemployment register. To pass the time, we went for bike rides into Derbyshire together, this being a cheap and pleasant activity. At the end of three weeks, the manager sent one of the girls to our house to say work had picked up, and I could return. That was the only time in my life when I was out of work.

Sidney was not quite so lucky. He married the following year, but soon found himself on short time again. For some while he looked around for another job, and eventually was fortunate in securing a post as foreman ruler at a firm in Newport, Gwent.

Once I was out of my apprenticeship, I was quite well paid by the standard of those times. Having paid my board, I had enough left to enable me to attend the excellent concerts that were held in the newly built City Hall, to buy clothes, including evening dress which was then *de rigueur* for singers, and to buy some National Savings Certificates. From being a child, I had made up my mind that I would never pay rent, and had always tried to save what little I could.

Chapter 13
'The Sheffield Philharmonic Chorus'

EARLY IN 1934, it had been given out that the second Sheffield Triennial Musical Festival was to be held in 1936, and as a special chorus was being formed I had gone for an audition. For this, one had to sing a short passage of music which we had been given an opportunity to practise, and then a sight-reading test. The people conducting the audition were out of sight behind a screen. I sang my set piece without any difficulty, and then came the dreaded sight-reading test. I was given the music, one chord was played, and I was on my own. How closely my interpretation approximated to what the composer had in mind I shall never know, but it couldn't have been too bad, because in due course a letter arrived telling me I had been accepted. I believe I was the youngest second bass in the choir.

The Musical Festivals of 1933 and 1936 were probably the greatest musical events to take place in the city, even though it has the reputation of being a musical city. The list of artistes who performed in 1936 contains many of the most famous names of that era: singers Isobel Baillie, Eva Turner, Muriel Brunskill, Parry Jones, Walter Widdop, Keith Faulkner, Roy Henderson, Alexander Kipnis and Harold Williams. Pianoforte soloists were Rachmaninoff and Solomon, violin soloist Adolf Busch, and cello soloist Suggia. The conductor was Sir Henry Wood, the orchestra was the London Philharmonic, and the chorus consisted of about four hundred voices, with the addition in one work of a hundred and fifty boys and girls from the elementary schools.

The concerts were performed on the evenings of Wednesday, Thursday and Friday, October the 21st to 23rd, and the works consisted of

Berlioz's 'Te Deum', Brahm's 'Violin Concerto in D', Rachmaninoff's 'The Bells', Bach's 'Magnificat', Rachmaninoff's 'Piano Concerto in C' (played by the composer), Richard Strauss's 'Death and Transfiguration', Vaughan Williams's 'Sea Symphony', Verdi's 'Requiem', Mozart's 'Haffner Symphony', Haydn's 'Cello Concerto in D', Walton's 'Belshazzar's Feast', Beethoven's 'Mass in D', Tchaikovsky's 'Piano Concerto in B flat', Delius's 'Brigg Fair', and Handel's 'The King Shall Rejoice'.

The choir rehearsed for a total of three hundred hours over a period of eighteen months under the chorus master Dr J. Frederic Staton, the organist and choirmaster of the crooked spire church at Chesterfield. He was a very popular and efficient conductor, and his keen sense of humour helped to make the rehearsals enjoyable. The experience I gained at that time in choral singing proved to be of enormous value.

At a fairly early stage in the preparations for the festival, an unfortunate row arose between Sir Henry Wood and Sir Thomas Beecham, who normally conducted the London Philharmonic Orchestra, of which the leader was Paul Beard. Whilst our rehearsals were in progress, Paul Beard left the LPO to joined the BBC Symphony Orchestra, and David McCallum was appointed in his place.

Sir Henry Wood contended that as he had been engaged to conduct the Sheffield Festival, he should have been consulted on the choice of the leader of the orchestra.

A deplorable and undignified slanging match ensued between the two great conductors which received great publicity in the press, and when at last the orchestra and Sir Henry came face to face at rehearsal, their lack of regard for each other was very apparent. The worst confrontation occurred at an afternoon rehearsal of Verdi's 'Requiem' and Walton's 'Belshazzar's Feast', which we were to perform the same evening. Sir Henry appeared to be in a thoroughly bad mood, and began by crossly reproving Eva Turner, the famous soprano, for arriving a little late. Sections of the orchestra were constantly being made to go over passages, and even the bass drummer had to give a solo performance. 'I want to hear a bass drum—not a tea tray!' roared Sir Henry in his high voice.

Then followed a moment of real comedy. Verdi's 'Requiem' contains a passage describing the Last Trumpet, and at the words 'Tuba mirum spargens sonem', a fanfare of trumpets in the orchestra is echoed by four trumpets off-stage. Local trumpeters had been recruited for this, and to everyone's horror, their performance was both off-beat and off-key!

The expected storm broke. Included in Sir Henry's caustic comments were the words, 'There'll be children coming tonight, and saying "Daddy, the trumpet's out of tune!" ' In fact, the performance that evening was stupendous, and all the daily papers carried enthusiastic reviews.

One of the highlights of the Festival was the performance of Berlioz's 'Te Deum', which raised the curtain on the opening night. This mighty work deployed the entire resources available: an outstanding quartet of international famous soloists, the orchestra, a brass band, the great City Hall organ, the Festival Choir of four hundred voices, and at the climax the choir of a hundred and fifty boys and girls. For sheer volume of sound, I have never heard anything to approach this masterwork.

Behind the scenes, we saw the famous at close quarters, and I secured some interesting autographs, including that of Leon Goossens, whose manner was as gracious as his superlative playing of that lovely instrument, the oboe. I hadn't quite enough courage to ask Sir Henry for his autograph. Someone told me that he charged half a crown for it, but I don't know if this was true.

Among the distinguished patrons in the audience were the Duke of Kent, the Duke and Dowager Duchess of Norfolk, and the composer Granville Bantock. In spite of the support the Festival received, the costs associated with it were so high that they were not covered, and the guarantors had to defray the deficit. The original intention had been for a Festival every three years, but no future one ever materialised.

After the Festival was over, all the members of the choir received an invitation bearing the City Coat of Arms embossed in gold to a Lord Mayor's reception and social evening in the Town Hall.

Out of the Musical Festival Chorus and the disbanded old Sheffield choral societies was born the Sheffield Philharmonic Chorus, of which I became a founder member. One of the old societies which was merged was the famous Musical Union which had toured the world in the year 1911 under its conductor, Sir Henry Coward. At an early stage in my singing career, I was singing in a programme of Schubert's songs when I noticed to my dismay Sir Henry Coward sitting in the front row. He was then a very old man. At the end of the concert he came and spoke to the young soloists very kindly and encouragingly, without any criticism at all.

The time I spent in the Sheffield Philharmonic Chorus before the war enlarged my experience of great choral music, and gave me the privilege of singing under Sir Thomas Beecham and Dr (later Sir) Malcolm Sargent.

My love of music was developing, and for some time I had attended the Saturday evening concerts in the Victoria Hall, where for an admission fee of only sixpence one could hear singers of the calibre of Peter Dawson (a great favourite of mine), Denis Noble and Harold Williams, as well as many excellent instrumentalists. Later I went to the International Celebrity Concerts at the City Hall, where I heard the Berlin Philharmonic Orchestra conducted by Fürtwangler, and great solo instrumentalists such as Kreisler, Cortot, Edwin Fischer, and such famous singers as Gigli, Paul Robeson, John McCormack and Richard Tauber.

Chapter 14
'Pexton Road and a London Talbot'

WHILST WRITING of my musical activities, I have bypassed what was for us a momentous event in 1935, being nothing less than our removal from 50 Petre Street to 9 Pexton Road. Mother had been born in the Petre Street house, and I was 21 when we moved. We had long been dissatisfied with the old house, which was too small for a family of five, inconvenient, and lacking any modern amenities. My grandparents had originally paid a rent of only five shillings a week for it, but of course this had risen over the years.

When we moved out, my Uncle George and his family moved in. They had been living in a wooden dwelling in Cyclops Street, which ran parallel with Petre Street at the Grimesthorpe end. Rows of these huts had been built during the First World War to house munition workers and Belgian refugees, and owing to the housing shortage they were still occupied for many years after the war. By reason of their construction, they had become bug-ridden, and our old house with all its shortcomings was hailed as a great improvement by our relations.

Uncle George was an iron moulder, and had been out of work for years during the depression. Having a gift for playing the piano by ear, he had supplemented his income by playing at a workingmen's club. Sometimes he accompanied a friend who played the cornet, and once when they were playing together in a pub, the cornet hit a high note and the ceiling fell down! Undeterred, they adjourned to the next pub.

Notwithstanding our long association with the old house, we all left it without regret. It had seen some happiness and much sorrow.

Our new house was in most ways a great improvement. It was in a somewhat better district, and I immediately gave it the name of

'The Cloisters', because in Sheffield parlance, it was 'cloise to t'church, cloise to t'cemetery, and cloise to t'chip shop'. It had good-sized rooms, a kitchen and a bathroom—these being two luxuries we had never previously enjoyed. At the back was a nice level garden. Some of our old furniture was not deemed fit to bring into this mansion, and our old dresser was replaced with a new sideboard, and the old deal table gave place to a big second-hand walnut dining table.

One day Dad drew up at our front door with a fresh car. He had swapped Sausage for a magnificent London Talbot saloon, which he had acquired for the princely sum of eighteen pounds five shillings. Its previous owner had been a director of a well-known local steel firm. It had a six-cylinder engine with polished aluminium rocker cover and sump, spring-spoked steering wheel, real leather upholstery which could be inflated with a bicycle pump to any degree of firmness, a sunshine roof, and a well-nigh rustless body of tinned steel with a thick coat of dark blue enamel. Nowadays it would be highly prized as a fine example of a vintage car.

I was immediately filled with a desire to drive this car, and persuaded Dad to start teaching me. Armed with 'L' plates and a provisional driving licence, I took the wheel for the first time and trundled along at a modest pace with growing enjoyment. This vehicle had both the gear lever and the handbrake on the right-hand side. The gear lever worked in a gate, and it was necessary to double-declutch for all gear changes. First gear was where fourth gear is situated on most cars. My experience with this car stood me in good stead a few years later, as will presently be seen. After three months' practice, I applied for a driving test. Driving tests had only been introduced during the previous year.

The driving test started from behind the City Hall, and was conducted by a morose individual in a bowler hat who had the demeanour of an undertaker. He asked me to read the number plate of a car which was parked some distance away, which was no problem, after which he asked me the usual series of questions, some of which are still asked by examiners over fifty years later. Having burned some midnight oil swotting up the contents of a sixpenny book entitled *Your Oral Driving Test: How to Pass It*, I managed to answer all the questions to the examiner's evident satisfaction, and the practical part of the test began.

Following instructions, I made a circuit of the City Hall, and drove in a westerly direction away from the city centre, giving somewhat exaggerated hand signals and peering ostentatiously in the mirror from time to time. Reversing into a narrow gateway and doing a three-point turn were accomplished successfully, and I drove back towards the starting point by a different route. However, I was still not out of the wood, as I had to stop and restart on a steep hill, and I was aware that the clutch was slipping. Somewhat desperately, I revved the engine hard and made sure the clutch was likely to be biting before I released the handbrake. The ensuing take-off was rather precipitate, and the examiner nearly lost his bowler hat, but at least the car hadn't rolled back, and that was what the exercise was all about. All the same, I completed the course with some misgiving, which some admonitory words from the examiner did not allay. However, the rest of my performance must have been satisfactory, as he passed me, to my great relief. I had never been to a driving school, and my father who taught me was himself self-taught, but I had been taught to double-declutch by his employer's chauffeur, who drove a Sunbeam which was very similar to our Talbot. Years later the two firms merged.

Chapter 15
'Crabtree Lane'

MUCH AS WE liked our house, it had one serious drawback. It was the end house of a terrace, and it was obvious that the builder had intended to build another house onto the end of it, but had never done so, with the result that the end wall was continually damp. Complaints to the landlady via the rent collector went unheeded, and when the roof also began to leak and she still refused to do anything about it, we decided to move again. This was in 1937, when we had lived there two years.

With regular employment, we were coming up in the world, and we moved to a bigger and better house. Its official address was Ecclesbourne, Crabtree Avenue, which was a short cul-de-sac, but the back entrance had the address 50 Crabtree Lane, and as this was easier for the postman, we usually used it. The front garden sloped down from the house, and on the other side of the avenue was a line of trees which improved the view from our windows by screening the main Barnsley Road which was separated from us by allotment gardens.

Crabtree was then a rather unique unspoilt little hamlet, containing some very old picturesque little cottages and a tiny Methodist chapel: an oasis in the northern suburbs. Batley Street, which connected it with Barnsley Road, was the only thoroughfare in the postal district of Sheffield 5 with the appellation 'Street', all the others being Road, Avenue, Crescent, etc., but in recent years it has been renamed Crabtree Close, in deference to the wishes of the residents of the new houses which have taken the place of the old cottages.

Soon after we had moved to this house, I decided to furnish my own bedroom. Having painted and papered it to my taste, I bought

Our family, 1938

a new oak suite, bedstead, carpet, chair, clock and bedside lamp. Mother supplied new curtains and matching bedspread, and with a wall mirror for a birthday present I was established in luxury. The whole lot only cost me around £30, and subsequently proved to have been an invaluable investment.

Dad was now becoming very interested in gardening, and soon had our sloping front garden looking very attractive with shrubs, roses, peonies and many other plants and flowers. Not content with this, he took on allotment in the rather distant Heeley Green area, with the idea of having somewhere to take Jack at the weekends. There had been little building around there at that time and the allotments were in fairly open countryside. It was a nice level green garden, with a small greenhouse and a well, and was fairly well stocked with vegetables and flowers.

He soon decided to extend the greenhouse, and we all spent many hours dressing second-hand bricks. I was much more useful at the building than the gardening, though I did once plant some irises, and no one was more surprised than I when they bloomed in due season. Dad's speciality was chrysanthemums, of which he had many exotic varieties. We made the greenhouse about four times as big as it had originally been, and equipped it with a firegrate and washbasin. At last it was finished and ready for painting. Then came a shock. All the allotment holders in that area received notice to quit, as the land was required for the building of flats.

One Saturday afternoon there had nearly been a tragedy. Dad was watering the plants, taking the water from a large rainwater barrel. Douglas was getting a bucket of water to refill the watering can, when his feet slipped on the wet ground, and the weight of water in the bucket caused him to fall head first into the barrel. Luckily Jack saw him and gave the alarm, and Dad rushed to pull him out before he drowned.

Faced with the notice to quit, Dad explored the neighbourhood and found another allotment to rent a short distance away. Although the soil was good, it was not so convenient to work as the other garden, being triangular and sloping, but it had the advantage of being surrounded by a thick hawthorn hedge which vandals and pilferers could not penetrate. The greenhouse which had taken so many hours to build was demolished, the materials conveyed to the new garden, all those bricks dressed again, and the greenhouse rebuilt. Then we dug a well. The Hatfields have always been gluttons for punishment.

The demolition and rebuilding of the greenhouse occupied several months, and it meant that the chrysanthemums had to stay out in the open throughout the winter, and of course many varieties were lost.

Some Saturdays, when we had spent the day at the garden and had our tea there, we rounded off the day by going to Heeley Green Theatre to see a variety show. Variety was by then nearing the end of its popularity, having been largely ousted by talking pictures, which had also meant the demise of cinema organs and orchestras. Whilst the Heeley Green shows were not of the highest calibre, we found them quite entertaining.

My singing teacher thought I ought to broaden my experience by entering the world of light opera, so I applied to the Sheffield Teachers' Operatic Society for an audition. The fact that I wasn't a teacher appeared to make no difference. For my audition I sang 'Even Bravest Heart May Swell' from Gounod's 'Faust' to demonstrate my vocal capabilities, and I was not only accepted, but given the part of Captain of the Scottish Archers in 'The Vagabond King'. This was performed in the Lyceum Theatre in 1938. I suspect that I was given the part, not because of any histrionic ability, but because I could sing a song that ended on a bottom D that could be heard throughout the Lyceum. The part wasn't a particularly rewarding one, but I learnt a lot about acting from the producer, Mr W. Jenkins Gibson, and performing in the old Lyceum was a memorable experience. The musical director was the learnèd Dr George Linstead, organist, composer, and later, music critic of the *Morning Telegraph*.

A press photo from 'The Vagabond King', performed by the Sheffield Teachers' Operatic Society

In 1939 we had our last holiday together as a family, touring Somerset, Devon and Cornwall in the Talbot. The highlight of this holiday was a day in Plymouth, where the Navy Week displays were in progress. We went on conducted tours of some of the great warships: HMS *Rodney* with its sixteen-inch guns, HMS *Newcastle*, the aircraft carrier *Furious*, and a submarine. Very soon all these vessels were to be on active service in the Second World War. From the deck of one of the great vessels we were able to watch naval displays in the basin; a reconstruction of a First-World-War engagement between a Q ship and a German U-boat, and an episode featuring a half-scale model of Drake's *Golden Hind*.

It was a glorious summer, just as I have heard the summer of 1914 was. On our way home, we passed a convoy of tanks heading towards the coast. Some people were preparing air raid shelters in their gardens.

Chapter 16
'Peace in our Time'

A MAD DOG was loose in Europe. Adolf Hitler could easily have been muzzled and rendered harmless a few short years before, but all the opportunities had been ignored, and now he was out of control and on the rampage. As everyone knows, an Austrian corporal of the First World War, a failed artist turned house painter, had in Germany formed the Nazi Party, consisting of a gang of ruthless thugs. In 1933, Britain and France were militarily immeasurably more powerful than Germany, and for some years after would have had no difficulty in suppressing Hitler's territorial aggression without firing a shot. Unfortunately, Britain was saddled with one of the most weak, inept and short-sighted governments of modern times, led alternately by Ramsay MacDonald and Stanley Baldwin, whilst the French political scene was constantly unstable, with ever-changing governments. So, whilst these two powerful nations followed a disarmament policy, and systematically weakened themselves, Germany was allowed to break all her treaty obligations and re-arm at will, until eventually the balance of power was reversed, and Hitler was in a position to invade and annexe the territory of neighbouring nations. For years Churchill had warned of the danger, but few of those in high office would listen until it was too late. His letters and speeches of that time show how strenuously he was trying to avert war, but yet his political opponents accused him of being a warmonger.

In 1938, Chamberlain met Hitler in Munich; Czechoslovakia was vainly sacrificed on the altar of appeasement, and he came back waving his scrap of paper and promising 'peace in our time'. Few people believed that we had gained more than a breathing space, and the country began desperately to prepare for war. Gas masks were issued to all civilians, air raid shelters were prepared, and the great engineering works were quickly adapted to the manufacture of armour plate, guns and all the munitions of war.

Our house had three cellars, and Dad and I converted the middle one into an air raid shelter. Sheets of corrugated iron were held up to the ceiling with rolled steel joists, the end of which were cemented into the walls, and further supported by a great wooden beam which ran the length of the cellar under the joists. The roof would have withstood anything but a direct hit. We equipped the shelter with all possible amenities such as seats, lights, ambulance box, fire extinguisher, radio, and tools to dig a way out if this should ever be necessary. It was also made possible to seal doors against the entry of poison gas. Out in the yard was a stirrup pump and a long-handled shovel for dealing with incendiary bombs. I also made wooden blackout shutters for all the windows.

My friends of military age considered their position, and several of them volunteered for what they thought might be the lesser of many evils, such as RAF ground staff. A few decided to be conscientious objectors. I thought long and deeply about the options. With my knowledge of engineering, and with the influence of various people I knew in that industry, it might have been possible for me to get a job in a reserved occupation, and so keep out of the armed forces, where I was quite sure I would be a square peg in a round hole. Everything I had ever heard about military life repelled me. All my life I had listened to stories told by men of my father's generation who had fought and suffered in the First World War. Even at school I had been a duffer at drill, physical training and all outdoor sports. I was a home bird, a lover of books and music, had never slept in a tent, never joined the Boys' Brigade or Scouts, and never spent an evening in a pub. In the event of my having to join any of the Forces, I was under no illusions as to the rough time that awaited me.

All the same, I rejected the idea of trying to get into a reserved occupation, because I felt that it would be a dishonest thing to do. Similarly, I gave little thought to the idea of becoming a conscientious objector, because I would have been ashamed to shelter behind the consciences of millions who thought it was their duty to go, even though they probably liked the prospect no better than I did. In the end, I decided that if war came I would volunteer for nothing, but leave the matter in the hands of God, and go wherever I was led, and try to make the best of whatever might befall me.

So convinced was I of the insanity of war, that until the very moment it was declared I found it incredible that so-called intelligent civilised nations should enter into it with the memory of 1914–1918 so recent. No one who heard the sad voice of Neville Chamberlain on that Sunday morning in 1939 will ever forget the chill that gripped our hearts as he told us the dreadful news that for the second time in a generation we were at war with Germany.

Just as in 1914, people were saying that it would be all over by Christmas. My own opinion was that it would last about three years. Had I known that the misery would go on for twice that period, I would have been even more horrified.

With the outbreak of war, our lives underwent an immediate change. Soon after the Prime Minister had made his doom-laden announcement, air raid sirens sounded in the south of England, as a raider was believed to be approaching. Scheduled radio programmes were cancelled, and only gramophone records interspersed with news bulletins were broadcast. After dark, the blackout was total, and wardens patrolled the streets on the lookout for any chink of light that might be showing. Car headlights were masked with tin covers which had narrow louvres to show a little light in a downward direction, and bumpers were painted white so that they might be more easily seen by the drivers of other vehicles. Torch batteries were in great demand, but with the exception of U2 cells they were unobtainable. Various items of food were very soon in short supply, notably bacon, and people tramped from shop to shop to queue for anything that might be available. Soon, of course, rationing was introduced. Sandbags were stacked around many public buildings, and windows were adorned with a latticework of adhesive tape to prevent shattered glass from flying in the event of a bomb blast. Everyone carried a gas mask, and at Pawson & Brailsford's we did a roaring trade covering the cardboard boxes in which they were supplied with blue Rexine and attaching a long loop of blind cord to enable them to be carried over the shoulder. Our apprentice, Jesse, had joined the Territorials, and he was called up a week before the declaration of war.

As I was now 25, it was some time before I was summoned to appear before the Medical Board. A succession of five doctors inspected and tested every part of my anatomy, and as none of them could find anything whatsoever wrong with me, I was passed A1. Then came the crucial moment when I was interviewed by the Selection

Officer to determine as to which lucky arm of the Services I was to be allocated. He was a pleasant sort of chap with the rank of major, and he asked me a lot of questions about my job, hobbies and interests. I made an effort to give a good impression, and told him of my interest in engineering, woodwork, radio, photography and entertaining. When he asked whether I would prefer to go in the Navy, Army or Air Force, I said I had no preference. He said, 'Then it will be the Army.' Extending his hand, he added, 'Good Luck.'

I thought that after all, the Army might be the lesser evil for me. Certainly I had no wish to fly, having no head for heights, and I reflected that in the Navy, one can never get away from the ship when off duty afloat, and anyway I couldn't swim. In this philosophical frame of mind I went home and told my anxious mother that I was fortunate to have been selected for the Army, that the Army was no less fortunate, and that Hitler's downfall was now assured.

A few weeks later I received through the post a bulky envelope bearing the ominous letters 'O.H.M.S.'. It contained a railway warrant and instructions to the effect that I was to join the Royal Corps of Signals training depot at Whitby on June the 13th 1940.

My first reaction was one of relief that I hadn't been assigned to the infantry, but to a technical unit. I assured my mother that the Royal Corps of Signals was non-combatant; a fact of which I was by no means certain, and which I eventually discovered to have been an optimistic guess.

During the next few days I set my house in order. I coated my tools with linseed oil to prevent rust while I was away, and sorted out my possessions. I informed the secretaries of the organisations of which I was a member that I would not be with them for the duration of the war, and said *au revoir* to my friends and relations. On the afternoon of the 12th of June, I collected what tools and possessions I had at work, and Bill Newsam, who had lost his left leg in the previous conflict, and whose son Rowland was also in the Royal Corps of Signals, took me for a drink.

Chapter 17
'You're in the Army Now'

THE MORNING of the 13th of June 1940 showed promise of another hot day. The family accompanied me to the station to see me off. I wore a grey suit—my second best—my working boots, well polished, my blue Rexine-covered gas mask was slung from my shoulder and I carried the attaché case that had formerly contained my concert party costume. We were all a bit strained and took it in turns to make stilted, reassuring remarks. Jack was waiting to go into hospital again for yet another operation, which was another worry. Eventually the train came steaming into the station, we repeated our last goodbyes, and I climbed aboard, leaving the anxious-looking little group on the platform, on my way to I knew not what.

Soon I was in conversation with the only other occupant of the compartment, a young butcher who was on his way to join the Army at Richmond. We parted company when we had to change at York, and I boarded the Scarborough train to find myself sharing a compartment with six cheerful chaps who were bound for the same destination as myself. Again we changed trains at Malton, and stayed together. It was a glorious day, and my misgivings about the future did not prevent me from enjoying the lovely scenery. We noticed that all the station names had been obliterated in order to give no help to any invading parachutists.

At Whitby the train disgorged a motley crowd of bewildered-looking young men. A corporal appeared and told us to form three ranks. Somebody muttered, 'You're in the Army now', and a nervous laugh ran around. We were then split into groups according to our religious denominations and addressed by our respective padres, after which we again formed three ranks and were marched to the Hotel

Metropole where we were issued with knives, forks, spoons and brass cap badges. I examined my badge with interest. It depicted Hermes, or Mercury, the messenger of the gods, with the motto 'Certa Cito' meaning 'Sure and Swift', the Royal Corps of Signals being of course concerned with communications. We were then conducted into a huge dining hall and given dinner.

The Hotel Metropole was the headquarters of the Signal Training Corps in Whitby, and we spent the rest of the day there, going through various examinations and receiving instructions. Everyone in the Signals is allocated to a trade, and a list of these trades was read out: wireless operator, telephonist, linesman, instrument mechanic, electrician signals, fitter signals, dispatch rider, driver mechanic, driver, and others. We were given forms on which we had to state which trade we would prefer to follow, to give details of any training or experience we had in that occupation, and also to write a short essay on our civilian occupation.

After a moment's furious thinking, I decided to put to use my early experience in my father's workshop, and wrote down 'fitter signals', adding some rather exaggerated claims regarding my engineering ability. Then we were allotted our service numbers by which in future we would always be identified. My memory does not easily retain numbers, but I shall remember 2346046 to the day I die, and will probably automatically quote it to St Peter when I arrive at the gates of Heaven hoping for admission.

Tea time arrived, and with it some savoury pasties, the ingredients of which were a vital secret, slices of bread an inch thick, jam and golden syrup. Sweet tea was dispensed from pails into tin basins from which we had to drink, as no mugs were available. After tea we were issued with palliasses containing a little straw, and four blankets (I managed to grab five) which we carried to our billet, a room in a big boarding house called Carlill in Royal Crescent, on the sea front. We laid our palliasses on the floorboards, and I was glad to be able to fold my extra blanket in two and arrange it so that I could lie on it for a little extra comfort. Having made our beds, we all settled down to writing home. After that, four of us went out for a walk and to post our letters, and completed the day by buying some chips. We had to be back in the billet by 9.30 pm, which was late enough for me as I had a splitting headache. Despite this, and the unaccustomed discomfort of my bed, I was soon asleep. That day, the Germans had entered Paris.

The next morning I woke early, and having noticed the scarcity of washbasins in relation to the number of men, I rose and managed to get my wash and shave before the rush began at 6.00 am. After breakfast we were paraded and marched from the Metropole Hotel right along the West Cliff seafront, and down to the old town near the harbour to the quartermaster's stores to be issued with our uniforms and kit. The items were thrown to us without any regard to size, and I was given a battle-dress which was far too small. I managed to get it exchanged for another which was a reasonable fit, except that the neck hung down like a horse collar, exposing my shirt with its too-tight-to-fasten neckband and tin button. One of the humorists who was issuing the kit said, 'If you find anything that fits, bring it back and we'll change it.' The only thing that actually did fit me was my greatcoat, which I retained throughout my service.

Wearing our battle-dresses, long-sleeved pullovers and greatcoats, and carrying a kitbag bulging with our equipment and our civilian clothes, we had to march in our heavy stiff boots up the steep cobbled hill that connects the old town with the West Cliff in the blazing hot June sunshine. Hardly had we arrived at the billet, thrown off our burdens and surplus clothing and collapsed exhausted onto our beds than a voice bawled, 'Everybody outside in five minutes in fatigue dress.' This meant carrying stores for an hour or two, then we had to do a rapid change back into battle-dress and spend the rest of the day marching and drilling. Then we received our rifles which had been stored in grease since 1918, and other long obsolete items of equipment, including leather bandoliers, circular mess tins, and old-type water bottles. We were the only World War II soldiers I ever saw who wore puttees, everyone else having gaiters. We looked like something left over from the Boer War, but of course it must be remembered that these were the disorganised days just before the retreat from Dunkirk when the British Army was being re-formed, and the authorities must have been scraping the bottom of the barrel for equipment. There was also a great shortage of NCOs. The draft that arrived at Whitby on June the 13th was divided into three squads: 94, 95 and 96, each of which had a squad commander, but only the one in charge of 96 was an actual NCO. Squad 94 was commanded by an old sweat named Paddy Ryan, who, although addressed as Corporal Ryan, had no stripes on his sleeve. Our squad was in the charge of a very nice lad named Don Levaliant, who was younger than we were, but had been in the Army for six months. He had been appointed Local Acting Unpaid Lance Corporal by virtue of the fact that he played the piano in the sergeants' mess. His inexperience proved to be a great disadvantage to us, as instead of always being drilled by the same NCO, we were drilled by whatever sergeant or corporal was available, and as some of them had been drafted in from other regiments where other procedures prevailed, we were often in confusion. Worst of all was the dreaded senior sergeant, Sergeant Kennedy, a regular who had served in India, where he must have got a touch of the sun.

On the first Monday morning we were ordered to parade outside the billet wearing our equipment and carrying our rifles. No one had shown us how the equipment should be assembled and worn and hardly anybody got it right. Sergeant Kennedy moved along the ranks shouting abuse and threats at man after man, ordering each one to fall out and have his mistakes rectified by the corporal, who soon had practically the whole squad to sort out. Having finally managed to get our webbing, bandoliers and various appendages into something resembling the correct order, we again formed three ranks, and the sergeant began to roar a series of orders relating to foot and arms drill which few of us even understood, as none of the movements had been explained to us. Throughout the morning he behaved like a lunatic, until every man in the squad was bewildered, terrified and completely demoralised. I can say with absolute conviction that during the years I spent in the Army he was without doubt the worst and most unreasonable NCO I ever encountered. He should never have been unleashed on new recruits.

Although we had done our best to clean our greasy rifles (I had begged some mutton cloths from a butcher to clean mine), they were declared to be filthy, and we were ordered to parade with them clean after tea. They were then inspected by the corporal, who was still not satisfied. 'Haven't you been shown how to clean a rifle?', he asked. 'No, corporal', we chorused. 'Give me a rifle', he said.

For once quick on the uptake, I leapt forward to hand him mine, which he proceeded to clean thoroughly, poking into every tiny crevice with a pointed matchstick. At the end of the demonstration he ordered, 'Parade again in an hour's time with your rifles as clean as this.' I sat on my bed for the next hour while my unfortunate mates endeavoured to emulate the cleanliness of my rifle. I was learning!

Life now became a ceaseless round of physical training, foot and arms drill, fatigues, gas drill, lectures and marches, with a few extra treats such as anti-tetanus and anti-typhoid inoculations thrown in. Just to add to our joy, German planes came over most nights on their way to bomb Middlesbrough and other industrial centres, which meant we had to get up and stand in the hall, sometimes for hours, until the all-clear sounded. One night when we were all down there, someone started to sing, and soon we all joined in, making our own harmony. When this began to flag, I sang a few of my concert party songs, and everybody was feeling in better spirits until a newly appointed corporal—another little Hitler—appeared and told us to shut up; he couldn't see anything to sing about.

One morning we marched to a schoolroom where the colonel gave us a pep talk, with considerable mention of 'esprit de corps', carefully translated for the benefit of those who might think it meant 'Blow you, Jack, I'm all right'. Then the captain read the Army Act, drawing attention to all the crimes and offences we must not commit, and the dire penalties that would be imposed if we did, such as death and other horrible punishments.

From the schoolroom we marched off to some other activities. After dinner, the squad paraded and there was a roll call, when it was discovered that a man named Morris of 94 Squad was missing. We marched back to the schoolroom for another lecture, and when the door was unlocked we went in to find Morris still standing to attention after three and a half hours. When a sergeant spoke to him he made no answer. The sergeant ordered us to sit down, which we did, except for Morris, who continued to stand to attention. 'Corporal' Paddy Ryan came in and bawled, 'Morris, sit down.' Morris sat down. Afterwards, the men of 94 Squad told us that Morris had been acting very strangely in their billet, telling them that they must obey Ryan and no other.

At the end of the lecture, Ryan gave the orders, and we formed three ranks outside. When we marched off down the road, whether by accident or design, Morris was in the front rank, and when we came to a traffic island, in spite of all the bellowing of the NCOs, instead of going round the island, he marched straight across it. Our destination was the Hotel Metropole, where we were to have one of our inoculations, followed by our tea. When we arrived there, Morris ignored the command to halt, and marched straight into the building and up the stairs, until Ryan rushed in and ordered him to halt, which he did.

After tea, the three squads which constituted A Company were to be marched back the the billets by Lance Corporal Levaliant, who made us fall in, in three ranks facing the hotel. When he gave the order 'Right turn', we all smartly turned except Morris, who continued to stand to attention at right angles to all the rest. Finding all his orders were ignored, Levaliant sent the senior soldier in search of Ryan, but as he was unable to find him, he returned with another corporal, who had no more success. Time after time all but Morris obeyed the orders: 'Stand at ease!'; 'Attention!'; 'Right turn!'; 'Left turn!'; 'Right turn!', until we saw with apprehension three sergeants approaching, one of whom was the dreaded Sergeant Kennedy. On being informed of the problem, he went up to Morris and asked him if he was all right. I didn't hear any reply he might have made. In an ominously quite voice Kennedy said, 'Now I'm going to give you the order "Right turn!", and when I say you will right turn, you will right turn. Squad, RIGHT TURN!' As a man we right-turned, and our hob-nailed boots crashed down on the road—except those of Morris, whose toe-caps continued to face the hotel. 'Left turn! Stand at ease!' roared Kennedy. 'Fall out two men—you and you . . .' . . . he pointed to the two biggest men he could see, 'Take him into the guard room!' When the two husky men seized him by the arms he remained rigid, and they had to carry him horizontally up the steps.

Afterwards we heard that in the guard room he kicked the medical officer and that he had been sent to a military hospital at York, and had been found running around that city naked. We never saw him again, and I often wondered whether his mind had in fact given way under the strain, or whether the whole thing was a crafty piece of acting which he hoped would lead to his discharge from the Army.

Each day, wet or fine, we went to a football field for physical training, and a comical sight we must have presented to the local inhabitants as we marched there. We were attired in white vests, blue shorts, grey socks and steel helmets, and carried our respirators, gas capes and plimsolls wrapped in a towel. If it was raining, we wore our greatcoats, which gave us the appearance of having forgotten our trousers. The training was very strenuous.

On Sundays I went to the Presbyterian church, where the padre was a retired minister named Dr Robertson. He told us a story about a new intake of recruits who were being separated into their various religious denominations by a sergeant. When the RCs, C of Es,

Methodists, Baptists and others had joined their respective groups, there was left one rather sad-looking man. 'Well, what are you?', asked the sergeant. 'Atheist, sergeant', was the reply. 'Not allowed in the British Army,' snapped the sergeant, 'Fall in with the Presbyterians!'

A letter from home told me that Jack, now fifteen, had been admitted to hospital. A few days later I received quite an amusing letter from him, which I answered as cheerfully as possible, and sent him a pair of cufflinks with the Royal Corps of Signals crest. I was very fond of Jack.

The next letter from Mother filled me with dismay. As I have already related, Jack's accident had left him with a ruptured bladder which many operations had failed to repair, and for a long time he had had a tube leading from his bladder through his abdomen to a rubber bag strapped to his leg. Now an operation was performed to re-route his urine through his back passage. Up to then, he had faced all his troubles with great courage and cheerfulness, but when he realised what had been done to him he became very ill, and seemed to lose the will to live. Mother asked if I could possibly get leave, as she though I might be able to arouse his interest. My application met with a blank refusal. The odious Sergeant Kennedy said we were on standby, and no leave could be granted for any reason. A couple of days later an even more desperate letter arrived. At that time I had not been in the Army long enough to know the ropes, and was handicapped by the regulation that I must go through the chain of command, which appeared to stop at Kennedy. Nearly beside myself with worry, I went into the empty church and prayed for Jack. Then I went and found another sergeant who I thought might be more kindly disposed, and asked if I might see an officer. When he asked why, I showed him the letters, and he immediately expressed concern and arranged an interview for me with a Lieutenant Booth. This young officer was most sympathetic, and indeed annoyed that I had previously been denied access to him. He immediately supplied me with a leave pass, with the proviso that I must be back by reveille Sunday Morning, as the unit was moving to Huddersfield on the Monday. This was Thursday afternoon, too late for a train that day. Sergeant Kennedy heard the news with ill grace, and ordered me to take all my kit and my rifle. I had then been in the Army just five weeks.

On Friday morning I caught the train to Sheffield and made my way home as quickly as possible. My heart sank when I saw the blinds were drawn. In the kitchen Mother greeted me emotionally. I knew I was too late, and would never see Jack again.

Although my short stay at home was filled with sadness, we were all glad to see each other again, and I delayed my departure the next day as long as possible, catching a train to York in the afternoon. There I transferred to the Scarborough train, but was told there would be no connection that day to Whitby. My problem then was whether to get off at Malton, or to carry on to Scarborough, and following the advice of other passengers, decided to get off at Malton. There I was told there was no train to Whitby that night, so I asked the advice of a police sergeant, who told me there was no bus or other means of getting there. However, there would be a milk train to Whitby at ten minutes to six in the morning, and he took me to a soldiers' reception hostel where I could spend the night. There I was given tea, bread and cheese and a chocolate biscuit, shown to a room where there was a pile of blankets, and lent an alarm clock. The sergeant there telephoned to my unit in Whitby telling them where I was, and that I should proceed in the morning.

I woke at exactly five o'clock, and arrived at the station at twenty to six, only to be told that I had been wrongly informed, and that the only train of the day had gone through at five minutes past five. Neither would there be any buses.

I stationed myself on the road to Whitby, and presently managed to cadge a lift on a big milk lorry as far as Pickering. There was very little traffic so early on a wartime Sunday morning, but presently along came a little car driven by clergyman who was going to preach in St Mary's Church in Whitby, and he took me as far as the harbour. Walking up the steep hill to the West Cliff I met Lieutenant Booth coming down on his way to church. He asked how I found things, and kindly expressed sympathy when I told him my brother had died before I had reached home. I apologised for being late back, but he said I was not to worry, I had obviously done my best, and having received the telephone call from Malton the previous night, he had informed the captain of the situation. I reflected that he was the second Christian who had helped me that morning.

Arriving at my old billet, I found it abandoned and empty, so I decided to dump some of my kit in the stores next door while I went to report at the company office. Unfortunately I was spotted by Sergeant Kennedy, whose voice was speedily borne to my ears, stating the fact that I was three hours late, and he made me carry my kit all the way to the Hotel Metropole to report. It was the worst he was able to do, as I knew well. He would have put me on a charge, had not the kind Lieutenant already cut the ground from under his feet.

The colonel was inspecting the billets that morning, and as there was no time to lay my kit out for inspection, I left it in the stores while I went to a house I knew of where I could get a breakfast for tenpence, as I was feeling famished. Just as I was sitting down to a plate of bacon and egg, a military policeman came in and told me to report at once to Sergeant Kennedy at the Hotel Metropole. I told him briefly where Sergeant Kennedy could go, and suggested that the MP have a cup of tea at my expense while I finished my breakfast. When in due course I arrived at the Metropole, my tormentor snorted and fumed, but was frustrated as the lieutenant and captain were there. The matter proved to be nothing more serious than the handing over of my pay, which Lieutenant Booth had saved for me. He saw me in the queue at dinner time, and asked me very kindly how I was going on. He was a real gentleman, and I'm pretty sure he had the sadistic Kennedy weighed up.

Next morning, those of us who had not already gone went to a camp at Berry Brow, near Huddersfield, and I never saw Kennedy again. We were under canvas, and of course it rained heavily all the time. Eleven of us, complete with all our kit, were crowded into bell tents that were intended for seven occupants. We were only there for a few days, at the end of which the colonel held a passing-out parade (on which nearly everything went wrong) and an inspection. Our basic training was then deemed to be complete.

Chapter 18
'2346046 Signalman Hatfield, C.F.'

OUT OF the three squads that had formed A Company, there was only one other man who was to be trained as a fitter: Tom Carter from Cantley, near Doncaster. He was five years younger than I, stood six foot one to my five foot eight, was as fair haired as I was dark, and was very much a ladies' man. Although we had very little in common, we paired up and were good friends throughout our trade training.

The men on the fitters' course were billeted in an old library in the centre of Huddersfield. There were no washing facilities, and we had to perform our ablutions in the public toilets. However, the Spartan living conditions were of insignificant importance compared with the advantages we now enjoyed in other ways. True, there were still parades, guard duties and route marches, but we were no longer terrorised, and most of our days were spent in the work-shops, which were situated in an old woollen mill which had been disused for many years before the Army commandeered it. Here we were doing practical work, which I really enjoyed.

Almost the first job we were given was to make a tool to clean the barrels of revolvers, a large version of the key that is supplied for opening sardine tins. Tom and I finished ours so quickly that we were assigned to teaching the others how to do it! Tom had first of all been a cinema projectionist, and then an auto-electrician, at which he was very proficient.

The trade training was very interesting. We attended lectures on all branches of vehicle maintenance, and learnt the theory of the petrol engine, gearboxes, final drive, steering systems, carburettors and electrical systems. Best of all were the practical classes, where we stripped down and rebuilt engines, gearboxes and back axles, and wired up the various electrical components of a vehicle, learning to locate faults. We were also taught engineering processes, and spent many hours filing steel to various shapes within very precise limits, tin smithing, soldering, brazing and forging. At last we felt we were doing something useful.

One weekend Princess Mary, who was Colonel-in-Chief of the Royal Corps of Signals, paid us a visit. Everything in sight had to be cleaned and scrubbed and polished. On the Friday she arrived she went round the workshops and saw us working; I believe I was tin smithing that day. On Saturday morning we had a parade, inspection, and march-past in the local park, and the Royal Corps of Signals Band from Catterick was in attendance. At the end of the ceremony, we marched out of the park to start our weekly route march with the band in front playing the Corps March 'Begone Dull Care'. The townspeople turned out to watch us marching smartly behind the band. We thought we were going to enjoy this route march, but when we reached the last pub in the town, the band fell out, and we were left to continue the march with no more musical accompaniment than the usual bawdy songs. On the return journey, the band fell in again at the spot where they had left us, no doubt suitably refreshed, to play us back into the town.

One morning, six of us found ourselves on fatigues for the day. The first job was to wash up after four hundred men had had liver for breakfast. The water was lukewarm, and we had no soap, nor had detergents been invented at that date. Worst of all to get clean were the tins and cooking utensils. Washing up finished, we spent the rest of the morning peeling potatoes, scraping carrots, bagging up the peelings and swilling the yard. After dinner came another washing-up session, then more 'spud bashing' until tea time, after which of course we washed up again and cleaned the area where we had been working. Just as we thought we had finished for the day, along came the sergeant major who ordered us to get shovels and shift ten tons of ashes.

As I have mentioned, Tom was a ladies' man, and never neglected any opportunity of chatting up the girls. One evening when we were out together, he entered into conversation with two girls in a café, after which we took them for a walk. To Tom's disgust and my surprise, the better looking one of the two attached herself to me. We arranged to meet them again the following evening.

The next day, on inspection, the sergeant noticed my haversack wasn't clean; it had in fact been borrowed by another soldier who had returned it dirty. Several of us whose equipment failed to meet the required standard were ordered to present ourselves for inspection with the offending items cleaned at eight o'clock that evening. The chap who had borrowed my haversack said he would take my place on the parade as I had a date, and with some misgiving I agreed. Tom and I took the girls to the variety theatre. When we returned to the billet that night, the guard who marked us in said, 'You're on a charge.'

It appeared that when the other men had arrived at the place where they were to be inspected, the sergeant wasn't there. They hung around for a while, and when he hadn't appeared, they dispersed. Of course the sergeant then arrived, and finding none of the men there, charged us all. In due course we were all taken under escort to be tried by a captain from another unit, and one at a time were conducted into his presence. My turn came. 'Prisoner and escort, quick march. Halt. Cap off!' I understand that the order to remove the accused's cap is always given at military trials because in the remote past some defaulter had the temerity to throw his cap at the presiding officer.

'2346046 Signalman Hatfield, C.F., you are hereby charged under Section 40 of the Army Act with conduct prejudicial to good order and military discipline, in that you did absent yourself from a place of parade at the time appointed. What have you to say?'

What I did say I no longer clearly remember. What the others said I didn't hear, but apparently the general defence was that we had waited until after eight o'clock by a clock that was on the wall of the room where we had been ordered to meet. The sergeant, however, said that this clock had stopped, and had not in fact been going for weeks.

Eventually we were all marched back into the room together, and the captain fixed us with a baleful eye. He said, 'I have examined the evidence, and there seems to be some doubt about the accuracy of the clock. I have therefore decided to give you the benefit of the doubt, but so that you will know that you must stay at a place of parade until you are dismissed, you will parade with the guard for five nights in full marching order.'

That was the only time I was ever on a charge, although I must admit there were occasions when I skated on thin ice. We never saw the girls again.

One of the jobs I had to do in the workshops was charging batteries from small portable generators. I didn't mind this, except that they were down in a basement, and the exhaust and sulphuric acid fumes were very unhealthy and made me cough. One humorist connected a wire from a spark plug on one of the generators to a bucket of water. Along came a sergeant. 'What silly so-and-so's left this bucket here for somebody to fall over?' He grabbed the handle to move it, and jumped about two feet in the air when the high-tension current hit him. Fortunately, when he had recovered from the shock he accepted the humour of the situation.

The trade training course lasted for sixteen weeks, and I greatly enjoyed the practical part. In those days I had excellent eyesight and steady hands, and having been accustomed to working with precision in the book finishing trade, I was very proficient at filing to fine limits and carrying out all the hand processes. I also went to great pains with my notebooks, in which I drew diagrams of all the electrical circuits of a vehicle in different colours, with explanations of all the functions. Tom also did very well, and having been an auto-electrician, he was able to re-wire vehicles without difficulty.

In one of the workshops there were a number of dismantled motorcycles, and I was assigned to reassembling a 500cc BSA. The engine, gearbox and other parts had been taken to pieces and all thrown into the same box. I sorted out the bits of the engine, put it together, and bolted it into the frame. I was told that I should not be able to complete the gearbox, as part of it was broken, and a new part was not available, but I regarded this as a challenge, and surprised everyone by making a new part and bolting it in. I succeeded in completely rebuilding the machine, and when the instructor had filled it up with petrol and oil, the engine started at the first attempt and he rode away. On his return he said the gearbox was functioning perfectly.

As we neared the end of the course, Tom heard that there was a chance of his being able to stay there on the cadre, as he was so useful with the wiring and fault finding. It struck me that it would suit me to do the same thing, as Huddersfield was so near to home, so I asked for an interview with our OC, Captain Beckett. He listened to my request, and then said, 'Actually we have something better than that in mind for you. I have a special report about you, and am going to recommend that you be sent to Harrogate on a junior NCO's course.'

The next day we passed our trade test, and went to another company at the other side of Huddersfield for a week's driving instruction, this being the last week of the course. On parade the next morning we were asked how many of us could drive, and nine of us who claimed to be able to do so went for a driving test, whilst the others went for instruction.

For our driving test, we went with a sergeant in a Guy 15cwt truck and took it in turns to drive. As I sat in the back, I noticed that everybody seemed to be having difficulty changing gear, and horrible grating sounds were coming from the poor gearbox. When my turn came, I noticed that the gears were the opposite way round to where they are on most cars, first gear being where one would expect to find fourth gear. This was exactly the same arrangement as on my father's Talbot in which I had passed my civilian driving test, and which also had no synchromesh. I engaged first gear, moved smoothly away, double-declutched and moved the gear lever silently through second and third into fourth. The sergeant said, 'Stop by that lamp post.' We came to a halt and he said, 'All right, you'll do!' I hadn't even driven round a bend!

At the end of that week, we went on our first week's leave. On our return, we scanned the orders to see where we would all be posted to. A Cornishman named Gerry Margo who had been with Tom and I throughout the course said to me, 'They've made a mistake. They've mixed you up with me.' When I was able to get near the notice board, I read:

Carter, T.; Cadre, No. 3 Workshop Company.
Hatfield, C.F.; 12th Corps, Tunbridge Wells.
Margo, G.; Junior NCO's Course, Harrogate.

Gerry was a nice amiable chap who had gone through the course just in an average sort of way, and he was as perturbed as I was. That day we moved to Shepley, where we were billeted in a church hall. I succeeded in seeing the officer in charge, and told him of Captain Beckett's promise to me, and how both Margo and I were convinced that a mistake had been made, but he said that whilst I had been away Captain Beckett had been promoted to major and had been posted elsewhere, and nothing could be done about it.

That was the only time I ever came within reach of any sort of promotion. At the time I felt very disappointed, but have since reflected that had I gone on the NCO's course, the training would have consisted of all the military activities I most detested. Furthermore, the subsequent chain of events would have been quite different, and my life would have followed a different path right down to the present day. There was a guiding hand at work.

I went to bed early that night as I was very tired, and presently was partly awakened by the others coming in, some of whom had obviously been drinking. I was soon soundly asleep again, but some time later awoke to become aware of a very unpleasant smell of burning. I got up and managed to locate a light switch, to find the room full of smoke. The kitbag a man was using for a pillow was smouldering at the top end, and so was the corner of his palliasse. Being unable to wake him, I dragged him off his bed and took his kitbag into the kitchen, where I put it in the sink and turned on the tap. Only one other man in the room awoke, and he put out the burning palliasse. We then put the still unconscious man back to bed and opened the windows to let out the smoke. Next morning, angry voices were demanding to know what b . . . . . . fool had opened all the windows on such a cold morning. The man who had been rescued was staring at his kitbag in stupefied bewilderment. The top part of the bag was completely burnt away, and some of the contents, including his plimsolls and underwear, were badly burnt, to say nothing of his palliasse. As we all moved away that day, I never knew the outcome, but according to Army regulations, he would have to pay not only for the damaged articles, but also for their replacement. He had, of course, had too much to drink the previous night, and gone to bed with a cigarette which had set fire to his kitbag.

Chapter 19
'Tunbridge Wells'

THAT MORNING a lot of us were taken in a truck to Huddersfield station, where we boarded a train for London. I was never to see Tom or Gerry again nor any of the men I had known up to then. A lance corporal, whose name I no longer remember, and I had been told that 12th Corps Signals in Kent required two fitters urgently.

The train wandered around Stockport and various other places picking up more soldiers, and took hours to reach London. Dinnertime came, and we were issued with a couple of fish paste sandwiches each. Eventually we reached Euston, where we stood on the platform for hours. It seemed that most of our party were destined for Weybridge, and twenty of us for Tunbridge Wells, and it was discovered that whoever was in charge of the party had a movement order for the Weybridge contingent, but not for·the Tunbridge Wells party. For some unknown reason we all boarded a train for Weybridge, where we twenty who were beginning to think of ourselves as the Legion of the Lost were marooned on the platform when the other lot departed for their destination. Darkness fell, and we became very hungry. Presently, searchlights and flashes in the distance told us that London was being bombed. At long last, we boarded another train and returned to London, where a heavy raid was in progress, and were billeted for the night on the top floor of the Hotel Great Central. No meal was provided that night.

Next morning we were given breakfast, our first real meal for twenty-four hours, after which we had to hang around outside for a very long time. The raid had been a bad one, and we saw a large unexploded bomb being taken away on a lorry. After a long delay, we boarded another train, and in the fullness of time arrived at

Tunbridge Wells, just in time to be too late for dinner. However, at about three o'clock in the afternoon, the cook achieved a meal of fried spam which we were glad to get.

The story we had been told about two fitters being urgently required there appeared to have been fictitious, as no one seemed to know why we had been sent. At the end of each morning parade, the wireless operators, linesmen, drivers and others dispersed to their respective duties, the lance corporal who had arrived with me was sent to supervise something or other, and I alone was left standing there. Each morning I was assigned to either cookhouse fatigues or billet orderly, which made me very disgruntled.

The Battle of Britain was then nearing its end, and we saw many air battles. The enemy planes came over in formation, and the Spitfires and Hurricanes dived onto them, trying to get them into disarray and picking off the stragglers. Planes came down in flames, and parachutes floated down. Although many bombs were dropped around

Tunbridge Wells, 1940

Tunbridge Wells, they appeared to do little damage: with the notable exception of one that fell on the Kent and Sussex Hospital, most fell on open land. Our billet was in a road called Mount Ephraim. On the other side of the road a little further along was another big house, also being used as a billet. One day all the soldiers moved out of it, and another lot were to come in the next day. During the night it was empty a bomb fell on it and totally destroyed it.

Being completely fed up with the menial duties I was performing each day, I kept complaining to the sergeant major, until he took me to the technical maintenance officer, to whom I explained that I was a trained fitter, and wished to be usefully employed in my trade. He told me to report to a line maintenance section, which had some vehicles, but no fitter. Thankfully I packed my kit and marched off to this unit which was billeted in the rather aristocratic district of Calverley Park.

I found this to be a small section of men who were practically all Londoners, and very nice friendly chaps they were too. The billet was comfortable, and the food excellent. I was not sorry to find that the vehicles had not been too well maintained, as that gave me some scope for showing what I could do.

One evening in December, we were talking in the billet, and one of the men asked me where I came from. When I told him Sheffield, he said, 'There's been a big air raid there.' A day or so later I received a letter from home telling me that this was true. The city centre had been gutted, homes and business premises in many areas destroyed, as well as a great many tramcars. Hundreds of people had been killed, including our cousin Alan Wolstenholme's wife Betty, a very nice girl indeed.

Our family had spent hours down in the air raid shelter. Dad had made an opening through one of the cellar walls so that the two old ladies next door could come in and take refuge in our shelter. They were Germans.

Christmas Day dawned, and according to Army custom the senior NCOs brought the other ranks a cup of tea. The Christmas dinner was far and away the best of the six I had in the Army: soup, turkey with all the trimmings, plum pudding and mince pies, all served by the officers. After dinner, we all sat round in a circle in one of the upper rooms, and the sergeant suggested that we should all take a turn at singing, reciting, or entertaining in any way we could. Everyone had a go, though some could only rise to the dizzy heights of telling a rude story. When my turn arrived, I recited one of Stanley Holloway's comic monologues, several of which I had committed to memory, and then sang a song. This went down very well, and the sergeant had me performing one item after another.

In the evening, some of the men had an invitation to a house party, and they insisted on my going with them. We went in an old Austin Seven. There were so many crammed into it that the doors wouldn't shut, and we went along in a highly dangerous manner reminiscent of the Keystone Kops. A large cake had been subscribed for, and this was ceremoniously presented to the long-suffering lady of the house, who was in fact a very jolly person. The evening passed in great merriment, and we didn't return to the billet, but slept fourteen men and a dog on the floor with blankets spread over us.

This was the best period I had so far spent in the Army. The sergeant and all the men were friendly, the living conditions were the best that could be expected, and I had a congenial job. I had been co-opted into the parish church choir, and must have looked very angelic in my surplice and hob-nailed boots.

A day or two after Christmas, the sergeant told me he had been given two invitations from a titled lady who lived in one of the big houses just down the road to go to a party at her house, and said he would like me to go with him and contribute towards the entertainment. We arrived at a beautiful mansion, and on being admitted were served with sherry by her ladyship's son, the Viscount. We passed a most enjoyable evening, though I was somewhat worried at the thought of what my Army boots might be doing to the obviously expensive carpet, though I noticed a number of other guests similarly attired who seemed to have no such inhibitions. I couldn't help reflecting on my meteoric rise from cookhouse scullion to one who could hobnob with the gentry, in spite of his boots.

However, pride goes before a fall, and a day or two later, the technical maintenance officer sent for me again. Without preamble, he said, 'Do you want to leave that mob you're with now, Hatfield?' 'No, sir', was the fervent reply. 'Well, I'm afraid you'll have to, because they aren't entitled to a fitter on their establishment.' Visions of more cookhouse fatigues swam before me. 'Do you know anything about battery charging?' he asked. 'Yes, sir', I replied, with what I hoped sounded like conviction. 'Well,' he went on, 'There's a signal section near Canterbury that needs a fitter, but they aren't entitled to any other technician, so if you go there you'll have to combine the duties of fitter signals and electrician signals. There would be a lot of batteries to charge. Do you think you could do it?' 'Yes, sir,' I hastened to say, 'I did battery charging on my training course.' 'Right,' he said, 'I'll arrange for you to spend a week in the instrument mechanics' workshop. Report to the corporal on Monday morning, and while you're there, ask all the questions you can.'

In the event, I spent a fortnight in the workshop, where the instrument mechanics were repairing radio transmitters and receivers and teleprinters. The corporal told me all I needed to know about charging batteries, and I made copious notes on that and any other electrical knowledge that might prove useful. I was very happy to be in that workshop, as there was a roaring fire, whilst outside was a lot of snow and ice.

Although I was glad to be going to a unit where I could follow my trade, I was disappointed to be leaving the line maintenance section where I had found such friendship. However, I have already mentioned the presence of a guiding hand in my affairs, and here was another manifestation of it. A year or so later, all those men were sent to the Far East. They arrived at Singapore ten days before it fell, and spent the rest of the war in a Japanese PoW camp.

Chapter 20
'Bishopsbourne'

ONE cold and frosty January afternoon, a young Scotsman and I were taken in the back of an open truck to the tiny village of Bishopsbourne, which is situated just off the main Canterbury–Dover road, four miles from the former, and eight miles from the latter. 'Jock', as he was inevitably called, had come from a farm in the remote Western Highlands, and had never been on a train before he had joined the Army, which had trained him as a lorry driver. His speech was so Scottish that at first few could understand him, so having always known a lot of Scots in the Presbyterian church, I acted as interpreter for him, though even I had difficulty at times.

Darkness had fallen by the time we arrived at Bishopsbourne, and on reporting at the signals office, we were interviewed by a lieutenant. He said they had been without a fitter for some time. They had had two previous ones, the first of whom was very good, but had been recalled to his civilian occupation, whilst the second had been no good, so they had got rid of him. 'And,' went on the lieutenant frankly, 'If you're no good, we'll get rid of you.' 'I'll do my best, sir', I replied. 'No man can do more', he conceded. He went on to tell me the company rules, which were reasonable, and what facilities there were. He was very straightforward, and I could tell I was going to like him.

A sergeant then took charge of us, and we were given a meal, after which we were shown to our billet which was at the other end of the village. It was a big rambling old house called Oswalds, and had been the home of Joseph Conrad, the novelist.

In the morning I washed and shaved in cold water, in the dark, and walked to the HQ where I had reported, a distance of about a mile. I was to get to know this walk very well over the next fifteen months. Close by our billet was the twelfth-century church, with its memorial to Richard Hooker, the theologian and writer who had been incumbent for a number of years until he died there in 1600. A little further up the village street on the left was the workshop of the wheelwright-cum-joiner-cum-undertaker, the blacksmith's forge and the village hall, which was a modern building bearing a plaque of Joseph Conrad. On the other side of the road was a row of neat old cottages, a tiny inn, and a general shop which was also the post office. On a side road there were a few more cottages, and the little school. Beyond the village there were pleasant views over open countryside, and a pair of gates stood at the entrance to Charlton Park in which our HQ was situated. I was told that the big house that had been requisitioned by the Army was owned by a titled gentleman who was the ambassador to Persia. Besides the company office, our cookhouse and dining room were situated here.

After breakfast, one of the two sergeants showed me my workshop. It was a fair-sized brick outbuilding containing an old oil engine, which before mains electricity had been installed had provided the power to drive a dynamo and charge a bank of batteries, drive a circular saw and pump water to a reservoir at the top of a nearby hill, whence it flowed by gravity down to the house. Near the door was the Army charging plant, consisting of a Lister four-cylinder engine direct-coupled to a fairly large dynamo, and which had a panel carrying a voltmeter, ammeter and field resistance control. Heavy cables snaked away from it to three charging panels on the wall, each equipped with fuses, switches, meters and various resistances to enable three banks of batteries to be charged simultaneously. What I was delighted to see was a sturdy bench with cupboards underneath, and a strong vice bolted on top. I was provided with a steel box of tools, and felt that at last I was in business.

It was evident that I should have no shortage of work. At that time there were sixteen trucks and eight motorcycles, though this number later rose to thirteen, and nearly all required some attention. My first task was to get the batteries on charge. There were about fifty to charge each day, and they were used to power all the communications receivers and transmitters in the East Kent area. First of all I connected all the 125-ampere/hour batteries in series and connected them to one of the charging boards, then the 85ah batteries to the second board, and the 16ah to the third board.

Having made sure that the engine was supplied with petrol and oil, I started it, and then spent a long time experimenting with all the resistance controls until the meters showed that all the batteries were being charged at the correct rate. The charging would go on for eight hours. This job took quite a long time each day, as the vent plugs had to be removed from all the cells, the electrolyte topped up with distilled water, and all the batteries connected to each other with wire.

The transport was in a sorry state, almost every vehicle needing some attention. Half the motorcycles were off the road, requiring spare parts. Some of these had been ordered, but had not materialised. A lot of the trouble was simply due to bad maintenance, like a truck that had three inches of play in the steering. This I speedily rectified by tightening the bolts securing the steering box to the chassis, after removing the mudguard to gain access. One driver complained that his truck was using an enormous amount of oil, and I found that this was simply due to the sump bolts being loose, allowing the oil to leak away. To cure this, I had to lie underneath the vehicle in the snow.

One of the dispatch riders had been in the Royal Corps of Signals Band in peacetime, and when hostilities began he was in the reserve, so was immediately called up. As everyone in the Signals had to have a trade, he had been designated a dispatch rider, but had never been one until he was recalled to the Army. He had little idea of riding, and none whatsoever of maintenance. When I had been there a few days, he told me he was going on leave, and would like to leave his machine with me for attention. To help my diagnosis of the trouble, he volunteered, 'It goes ch-ch-ch and stops.'

The bike came into my shop completely plastered in mud. It was so thick under the mudguards that the wheels would hardly turn. When I dismantled it, I found the following slight trouble: inlet valve spring broken; exhaust valve badly bent and guide broken; piston crown caked with carbon about an eighth of an inch thick; front brake lever missing; part of shock absorber missing; left foot-rest missing; electric horn missing and bracket broken; clutch cable frayed; clutch and rear brake requiring adjustment; spark plug gap too wide; and mud in the carburettor. Also the timing was incorrect.

We had now acquired a captain in addition to the lieutenant, and when these two officers came into the workshop I asked them to have a look at this candidate for the chamber of horrors. I suggested that I should use it for spare parts for the other machines, clean it up, and send it into corps workshops for a complete overhaul, and they both agreed to this idea with unholy glee. Some of the parts that had been ordered arrived, and with these and some parts I removed from the wreck, notably the magneto, dynamo and speedometer, I managed to get all the other machines back on the road. All the scrap parts were put onto the hopeless bike, and it went into the workshops. We received a new bike in exchange for it, but for at least six months the captain continued to receive angry correspondence regarding the matter, particularly in respect of the missing parts. When the rider returned from leave, he was asked (among other things) how he had lost so many parts. His reply was, 'I've got no lights—I can't see them drop off!' Shortly afterwards, for some unknown reason, he was posted to another unit.

The period I spent at Bishopsbourne was the most tolerable of all my time in the Army. True, I worked long hours, being usually the first to start work in the morning and the last to finish at night, but against this I hardly ever went on parade, and had no guard duties or fatigues. Most of the work was congenial to me, and I was held in some regard by our officer, Captain Caldicott, the lieutenant having been recalled to Tunbridge Wells and promoted. I had hopes that I might be promoted, as in addition to vehicle maintenance and battery charging, I had to carry out weekly inspections of the vehicles, and was in charge of petrol and oil issues to the dispatch riders. The captain would willingly have made me a full corporal, but he was unable to do so, as our unit was not entitled to a fitter NCO on its establishment.

With the approach of spring, the Kent countryside was revealed in all its beauty. My morning walk took me through fields where lambs were being born, and everything was fresh and green. Behind my workshop was a fairly high ridge of land which I climbed one day to find myself looking down into a railway cutting. The embankments were thickly carpeted with primroses. Then out came the apple and pear blossom, seas of white and pink, and golden cascades of laburnums.

The countryside was not always so peaceful. Enemy planes often came over, and one day when I was riding a motorbike, I saw one shot down by two of our fighters quite nearby. The pilot bailed out when he was almost too low for his parachute to open. He came down on the railway line and broke his leg. There were barrage balloons over Dover, plainly visible from Bishopsbourne, and we sometimes saw these being shot down by German aircraft. The Germans also installed a huge long-range gun on the French coast, and one day a shell from it fell in our vicinity every twenty minutes. Most of the shells fell on farmland, but one landed close enough to us for a splinter to go through the cookhouse roof, fortunately not injuring anyone.

However, two could play at that game, and on the railway we had two enormous twelve-inch naval guns, capable of firing a shell for many miles, known respectively as 'The Peacemaker' and 'The Sceneshifter', and one tremendous eighteen-inch weapon called 'The Boche Buster'.

Having heard that this giant was to be fired from the railway cutting behind my workshop one afternoon, I made my way to the top of the embankment and lay on my stomach peering down. A diesel

The 18" 'Boche Buster' gun at Bishopsbourne.
From the Sunday Graphic, *27th of April 1941.*

locomotive arrived drawing a coach containing a gun crew of twenty, a specially constructed van containing the ammunition, and the biggest gun I was ever to see.

The gun was mounted on a very long platform truck, which had an extension on which a bogey ran on rails to convey the shells from the ammunition van to the breech of the gun: a necessary device as each shell weighted twenty-two hundredweight. When a shell had been so conveyed through a door in the end of the van to the breech, the diesel moved the two vehicles some distance down the line away from the gun. The gun crew rammed the shell into the breech, and an officer measured the distance it had gone in to make sure it was fully home. The charge of cordite which was to propel the shell on its way went in next, and then the breech was closed. Direction and elevation were then adjusted, elevation by power except for the final stage of accuracy, which was obtained by two soldiers turning a large graduated wheel. When all was ready, the officer ordered all the crew except the sergeant who was going to fire the gun to move down the line towards the train.

The officer shouted 'Fire!', the sergeant pulled the lanyard, and there was an almighty explosion. The enormous projectile could actually be seen to leave the muzzle of the gun in a sheet of orange flame, to speed on its way across the English Channel. Not only did the great barrel recoil in the normal way, but the entire gun recoiled on its railway wheels a distance of sixteen feet with the brakes on. It was fired in the cutting to minimise damage to property from the blast, as when it had been fired on a previous occasion, in the presence of Winston Churchill, most of the windows in the neighbouring village of Kingston had been broken.

Sometimes on Saturday or Sunday afternoon I was able to go into Canterbury, either by bus or by hitching a lift. This was before the bombing had devastated that city, and I soon became familiar with the old walls, towers and lanes, and above all of course, the marvellous cathedral and its treasures. Like generations of pilgrims who had visited the shrine over the centuries, I gazed on the spot where Thomas à Beckett was murdered, and contemplated the tomb of the Black Prince with his armour hanging over it. The building itself was of course awe-inspiring, and I have never ceased to marvel at the vision, skill and resource of those generations of men who so long ago, without any of the mechanical aids of today, raised this huge magnificent edifice to the glory of their Creator.

If I went into Canterbury on Saturday afternoon, it was often in the company of one or more of my comrades. I was particularly friendly with the dispatch riders and the storekeeper, Doug Cairncross, who had worked in the City of Hull Surveyor's Office. There were two other men in the Section from Sheffield, as I had soon discovered when I heard a voice with a familiar accent say, 'Tha knows that's not reight.' We were soon conversing in my native tongue. On Saturdays we usually went to one of the three cinemas that Canterbury then boasted, and we had a meal in one of the Service clubs.

The local landowner was Sir John Prestige, an industrial baron, who lived in a big house in Bourne Park, which stretched from Bishopsbourne to the main Canterbury to Dover road near to the village of Bridge. In Bishopsbourne village were two old whitewashed cottages which had been knocked into one, and converted by him into a canteen and rest room for the soldiers. It was staffed by the local WVS, and nominally in charge of it (by virtue of which he hoped she might avoid call-up) was his daughter Rosemary, an attractive young lady of twenty-one, who together with her equally attractive sixteen-year-old sister Elizabeth, was anxiously guarded from the attentions of the licentious soldiery by the zealous ladies of the WVS. We were in fact very grateful to Sir John for providing this amenity, as there was nowhere else to go in the village. Rationing was not then so acute as it became later in the war, and for tenpence we could have an 'all-in fry' consisting of egg, bacon, beans, mashed potatoes and toast. A slice of bread and margarine cost an extra penny, a cup of tea a penny, or a cup of coffee three ha'pence. Upstairs was a quiet room where we could read or write letters in comfort. In spite of Sir John's efforts on her behalf, Rosemary eventually enlisted in the Motor Transport Corps.

On Sunday evenings the canteen was always full, and one soldier brought his piano accordion. We sang song after song, harmonising quite well, and one evening Mrs Morgan, one of the WVS ladies, brought along her husband who was the village church organist. He was so impressed that he said we ought to put on a concert in the village hall. Interest was shown in this idea, so Mr Morgan discussed it with Captain Caldicott, who not only welcomed the suggestion, but said his wife, who was lodging with him in the village, would be willing to act as accompanist. Some talent emerged among us, and we rehearsed and improvised until we thought we might risk putting on a performance. The captain surprised us by telling us that a very quiet officer who had recently joined us, Lieutenant Muir, was prepared to do a conjuring act.

We were assured of an audience, as there was never anything to do in the village, and almost the entire population, civilian and military, turned up for the concert. After the traditional opening chorus, the compère, who was one of the dispatch riders, John Copsey, cracked a few topical jokes, and the songs, humorous sketches and monologues began to follow each other. Some of the chaps were rather nervous, as they had never performed in public before, but all did quite well. Our dark horse, Mr Muir, proved to be a first-class conjurer and magician, and his act was a great success. I recited some of my comic monologues and sang, among other songs, the famous bass ballad 'Asleep in the Deep', going down the scale at the end to a sepulchral bottom D.

The next day we received many compliments and congratulations on the success of our concert. One of our drivers said to me, 'You and Mr Muir were the two surprisingest men I ever knew!' Another said, 'We only came to take the mickey, but we got a big surprise. Nobody knew you could do anything like that.'

Of the villagers, the one I most liked to talk to was the old blacksmith, Louis Milward. He lived in a cottage exactly opposite his forge, and was by this time semi-retired. When I first made his acquaintance, he was making the second of a big pair of ornamental gates. They were a wonderful tribute to his art, with their twists, scrolls and leaves skilfully hammered out of wrought iron, and I think few could match him in his craft. I found great pleasure in watching him work. An example of his skill can still be seen in Canterbury. Near the Westgate Towers is the Falstaff Inn which has a large signboard hanging from a very artistic ornamental wrought-iron bracket—the work of Louis Milward. Some years after the war I listened to a radio programme about Joseph Conrad, and among those who came to the microphone to recount their memories of the novelist was my old friend the blacksmith.

We were now being allowed to go home on leave for seven days every three months, and this of course was something to look forward to with keen anticipation. Also we could occasionally get a weekend pass, from after duty Friday to reveille Monday morning, and in spite of the distance to Sheffield, I thought it worthwhile to avail myself of it. I went by train to London Victoria, and the train from St Pancras to Sheffield often took five hours. All the seats would be occupied, and many passengers had to stand in the corridors. At night the train would be blacked out, the only light in a compartment coming from a small grey painted bulb. However, these discomforts never deterred me from snatching a few hours at home whenever possible.

Returning from one of these weekend leaves, I made my way by tube from St Pancras to Victoria to find I had missed my last train to Canterbury. At the enquiries office, I was told that my only chance was a milk train from London Bridge about 4.00 am, so I walked there through the blacked-out deserted streets, following the Thames. I scarcely saw a soul the whole way. About a week previously the area around St Paul's Cathedral had been bombed, the Cathedral itself having been considerably damaged, and I could see the devastation in the moonlight.

When I reached London Bridge station, I found the waiting room occupied by about half a dozen sailors who were unsuccessfully endeavouring to light a fire from the pages of a telephone directory they were tearing up. We had a long cold wait until the train arrived. It was a slow train, stopping at Rochester, Chatham (where the sailors got off), Sittingbourne and other places, until I left it at Canterbury to begin my four-mile walk to Bishopsbourne, where I arrived just in time for breakfast. After that I started on my day's work.

Towards the end of the year, bearing in mind the success of our village concert and the probability of our being asked to arrange another, I took back from leave some songs, sketches and other concert party material, also my make-up outfit. This proved to a prudent move, as the captain asked me if I could organise something for Christmas Eve. He had in mind a concert and dance, and as the date was only a week away, I had to take immediate action. There were only six of us who could really take part in the entertainment, and it so happened that three of us were Sheffielders. In addition, there was the captain's wife who accompanied my songs on the piano, and she and I had one or two practices in the afternoon at their cottage. One of the Sheffield men, Jack Taylor, a dispatch rider, had a very pleasant tenor voice, though he had no experience of singing in public, but with a bit of tuition I soon had him singing 'The Rose of Tralee' and 'So Deep is the Night'. Harry Roper, the other man from Sheffield had been a drummer in a dance band, and he could also do a comedy turn and impressions of film stars.

John Copsey, who hailed from London, was again to be the com-père, and he impersonated Jack Warner in 'I'm a Straightener-Out of Bike Wheels'. Sergeant Hope was to play a piano selection, Norman Charlotte (a chirpy little Cockney) to croon two popular songs of the period, 'Yours' and 'Russian Rose', and to take part with me in a comic sketch entitled 'The Singing Lesson'. I was to sing two bal-lads, and recite the Stanley Holloway monologues 'The Channel Swimmer' and 'Jonah and the Grampus'.

On Christmas Eve I was given the day off to superintend the preparation for the concert. Our instrument mechanic contrived a microphone, amplifier and speakers out of radio parts, and our entire stock of red and green signalling lamps was pressed into ser-vice for decoration. There was some consternation when we learned that our CO, Major Keith, was coming from Tunbridge Wells for the entertainment.

The party began at 7.00 pm. For a band we had two piano accor-dions, a drum kit played by Harry Roper, and the piano played by Sergeant Hope. Together they made a very fair dance band. A truck load of very nice WAAFs had been imported from Dunkirk near Faversham. I felt rather uneasy at the beginning, as many of our fel-lows had not turned up, and most of those who had couldn't dance, so the girls were sitting in a row like tripe waiting for vinegar. The major arrived with the captain, and they immediately repaired to the back premises where earlier in the day I had installed a quantity of beer, brought in some secrecy by one of the lieutenants and given into my safekeeping. This was not for the rank and file, lemon-ade being provided for them; the clergy had stipulated that the vil-lage hall was not to be used as a bar. The reason why so many men were missing was that they had gone to have one at the local, but soon they began to roll in and the party warmed up. In no time at all the girls all had partners.

The captain wanted me to put the concert on about eight o'clock, but one artist, Norman Charlotte, had not turned up. When a search party had failed to find him in the pub, I guessed that he must have gone to the 'Plough and Harrow' in the neighbouring village of Bridge. This proved to be correct, as presently he and his mates appeared wearing paper caps and carrying a red lamp and a red flag which they had purloined from road repairs, loudly singing 'The Red Flag'. This disturbance having been silenced, I propelled the somewhat inebriated Charlotte by the scruff of the neck to the regions behind the stage. To my relief, he had only reached the merry stage, and was not too drunk to play his part in the sketch. We were able to start the concert by 8.30, and fortunately everything went without a hitch. The audience laughed from start to finish at the sketch, Norman having improved his appearance with an old bowler hat and some other discarded civilian clothing, and his Cockney twang was a good foil to my Yorkshire accent. At the end, the captain went to the front to explain how little time we had had for rehearsal, and he sounded quite proud of us. Then I had the satisfaction of being personally congratulated by the major. Everyone said they had enjoyed the concert, and how well my little team had done, and we all felt highly elated.

The concert occupied exactly one hour, and then dancing was resumed until midnight. Refreshments were handed round freely— ham sandwiches, sausage rolls, mince pies, rock buns, etc. Our bacon ration had been replaced by sausages for many mornings so that we could have ham for Christmas! We had a jolly evening, and the Air Force girls left us with much merriment.

On Christmas morning, after a breakfast of bacon and eggs, we had a church parade, and then marched to the village church where the padre conducted a special service for the troops. A Royal Artillery driver played the organ, we sang well-known carols, the sergeants took the collection, I sang the solo 'Nazareth', and the padre gave a very fitting address. Those who wished stayed for communion, and we had the rest of the day free. Jack Taylor, John Copsey and I went through Bourne Park to Bridge, and called in a tea shop. I paid for the teas, which came to sixpence, and as we were given mince pies free, and mine had a threepenny bit in it, it was a cheap round.

Dinner consisted of chicken, roast pork, and all the usual Christmas accompaniments. Our plates were filled by the captain, sergeant major, and quartermaster sergeant; the sergeants and corporals waited on, and the lieutenant went round with a bucket of beer, filling mugs. In the evening, men drifted off in various directions, some to Canterbury, some to local pubs. A number of us went to the canteen and enjoyed the evening with the piano and a few games. Refreshments were provided free, and the quartermaster and one of the sergeants bought us all chocolate in an unwonted burst of generosity. Lady Prestige came in with her daughter Elizabeth and a very attractive auburn-haired girl. By request, I sang one or two songs, which the unknown young lady evidently liked as she entered into friendly conversation with me, to the envy of the other fellows. I must confess that this was only a flash in the pan, as I could never claim to be a ladies' man.

And so the year 1941 came to its end, and few were sorry to see it go. After two years of war, there was no sign of an end, and we had had few successes against the Germans. Gloomy news bulletins often contained the words: 'Our troops have made a strategic withdrawal'. Only against the Italians could we boast of any victories, having defeated their navy at the battle of Cape Matapan and sunk three battleships at Taranto; also our Western Desert Force had soundly beaten them in North Africa, taking thousands of prisoners. The German U-boats had taken a heavy toll of our shipping, and rationing was becoming stringent. Current recipes included such mouth-watering concoctions as carrot tart, lentil roast, and Lord Woolton pie, the ingredients of which I no longer remember. Many of our cities had been blitzed. German troops were advancing further into Russia. Japan had destroyed the American fleet at Pearl Harbour, and we had lost the battleships *Hood*, *Repulse*, and *Prince of Wales*.

The only ray of hope seemed to lie in the fact that America had now entered the war on our side. There is, however, much truth in the old saying that the darkest hour is just before the dawn.

Chapter 21
'Schemes'

IN FEBRUARY 1942 we were involved in a training exercise, or 'scheme', as it was called, in which we were supposed to be part of a defending force repelling an invasion by other units. Preparations for this meant a great deal of work for me, making sure that all the vehicles were in the best of order, and that all the batteries were fully charged.

I travelled alone in the back of a three-ton Bedford truck which was equipped with a canvas top, surrounded by all my gear and the spare batteries and charging plant. Besides my tools, there were jacks, chains, steel wire ropes, signal cables, twenty gallons of petrol, a large quantity of oil, spare ammunition, and a little bench I had contrived from a thick plank with legs lashed to the side of the truck. The roads were very treacherous in places, as there had been heavy falls of snow during the preceding days, and a sudden thaw the night before we started. Some of the drivers and dispatch riders had nasty skids, but fortunately there were no accidents. It was extremely cold and I was wearing most of the clothes I possessed, but I hit on the idea of obtaining additional warmth by starting the charging engine and sitting by the hot silencer, the exhaust fumes being carried away by a length of flexible pipe dangling over the tailboard. Every time the convoy stopped something seemed to be required from my collection, or I was called upon to rectify some minor fault.

Our route took us into Sussex, a county I had not previously seen, and for the first time I saw the charming old towns of Rye and Winchelsea, the Martello Towers which had been built as defences during the Napoleonic Wars, and the Hastings seafront which was completely deserted. A bitter wind was blowing a shower of sleet in from the sea. Some years later I was to enjoy seeing this resort under peacetime conditions and summer skies, but my first impressions were anything but favourable. At St Leonards we turned inland and established a position at the top of a hill, and were glad to find a billet for the night in a schoolroom.

The next day was bitterly cold, and I well remember having to dismantle and clean a distributor which an overenthusiastic driver had contaminated with oil, and the difficulty I had setting the contact breaker points gap to fifteen-thousandths of an inch with frozen fingers. A kindly lady came out of a nearby house and brought me a hot cup of tea, for which I was most grateful. Another vehicle which would not start was found to have a lump of ice in the petrol pump. It appeared that some water had found its way into the petrol, causing a lot of trouble for several days. The second night I was detailed to guard the vehicles from 10.00 pm to midnight, and from 4.00 am to 6.00 am. I made myself a hot drink by playing the blowlamp on a tin full of water and adding an Oxo cube. By this time, I had learned never to be without my own emergency rations.

The scheme was a complete waste of time as far as our section was concerned. All we did was guards and fatigues for the others, to our great disgust. The more interesting work was being done by the other two companies, and we had no active part. By appearing to be busy all the time on my own work, I managed to keep clear of fatigues, and only did guard duty once.

Our corps did not cover itself with glory. According to the umpires, the colonel disappeared off the face of the earth, nearly all the communications except those of our section broke down, our side retreated before the enemy (whom we never saw), and in theory we were driven into the sea and wiped out.

The active part of the scheme over, our disembodied spirits started on the return journey, going through Battle, and eventually crossing Romney Marsh which was covered in deep snow, and the ditch-lined roads treacherous with ice. All the motorcycles except one were loaded onto the trucks. One of our crack DRs, Ken Warren, alone tackled the job of escorting the convoy, riding ahead to direct the trucks at crossroads, then overtaking the whole lot when the last one had passed him and shepherding any stragglers. This was no mean feat on a road like a skating rink, as the trucks were travelling at about twenty miles an hour, and were spaced fifty yards apart. He was a marvellous rider, and his progress appeared to be one long controlled skid. However, when our captain had seen five military policemen fall off their bikes, he decided enough was enough for Ken, and had him and his bike taken aboard a truck, to everyone's relief. We were all glad to arrive safely back in Bishopsbourne, where we were overjoyed to find a hot meal awaiting us, and a fire in our room in the billet, thanks to an assistant cook who had remained behind and who shared our room.

A few weeks later our section moved to Ashford, Kent, where we were billeted in the Girls' High School in East Hill; the girls presumably having been evacuated, as in the event of an enemy invasion Ashford could expect to be in the front line. Behind the buildings on the other side of the road was a large open space which we were able to use as a vehicle park and parade ground, and on one side of this was a very large shed. A partition divided this, and one half became the stores, and the other half my workshop. A smaller adjoining shed became the home of the charging plant and batteries.

At times I had the help of a driver mechanic called Harry. He was a devious character who never spoke of his background, but I believe he came from Birmingham, and I strongly suspected he had been in prison. He often spoke in rhyming slang like this:

> I went down the frog and toad, knocked on the old one and four, and my trouble and strife opened it. After I'd had a steam tug of Rosie Lee, I went up the apples and pears, got into my jockey's whip, and laid my bobbin o' thread on the weeping willow.

For the uninitiated, here is the translation:

> I went down the road, knocked on the door, and my wife opened it. After I'd had a mug of tea, I went upstairs, got into bed ['kip'], and laid my head on the pillow.

My new workshop was excellent: well lit, and reasonably warm, and I was glad to have the noisy charging plant in the shed outside, as well as the batteries which emitted unhealthy fumes of sulphuric acid. When not actually engaged on vehicle maintenance, I made some items of equipment, starting with a wooden stand with a ramp at one end, onto which I could wheel a motorbike so that I could work on it at a comfortable height without having to bend my back so much. Next I made a treadle-operated grinder out of materials salvaged from the village rubbish dump. These included part of a sewing machine, a length of iron railing from which I made an axle and crank, a tricycle wheel, part of a bed, a telephone bracket, and part of a lavatory seat. My father had given me a grinding wheel. This incongruous collection of components made an excellent machine which proved extremely useful, and a coat of paint made it look more presentable than one would have imagined. I also made a drilling machine completely out of metal, the stand being made from lengths of the angle iron used in barbed wire defences. Making this involved many hours of hacksawing, filing and hand drilling. The captain was most interested in these fabrications, and always brought any officers who might be visiting to see them. On these occasions I always had to recite the list of parts employed, and there was always a roar of laughter when I reached the lavatory seat component. On the captain's desk was a table lamp I had made for him, the base being a brightly polished phosphor bronze bearing, the flexible stem a piece of speedometer outer cable with an iron wire inside to stiffen it, and a shade made from a painted tomato tin. From empty four-gallon petrol tins I made a mailbox, painted red, and an illuminated sign for the signals office.

In the stores adjoining my workshop the instrument mechanic Harry Balsillie had his bench. He was one of the most patient workers I have ever met, and spent all his time repairing communication sets with a very inadequate tool kit. The only soldering iron the Army had provided for his use was far too large for the class of work he was doing, and he was very grateful when I gave him a small one I had bought from Woolworth's before the war for the princely sum of sixpence, which also included a stick of solder and some flux.

One Monday morning, before starting work, I went into the stores to hand in my weekly laundry, and was standing beside the slow combustion stove chatting to the storeman, when we heard a plane coming over, flying low. The storeman went to the door, and called, 'Come and look at this!'

I had hardly reached the door when there was a tremendous explosion which shattered all the windows, and the glass from the skylight fell exactly where I had been standing a second earlier. Two German fighter-bombers had flown over Ashford, and each had dropped one five-hundred-pound bomb. My assistant Harry appeared out of our workshop with his hand cut by flying glass, although he had dived under a bench. Having attended to that, we sallied forth to see the damage. In the High Street, there was a Co-op butcher's shop, and the bomb had fallen on the rear premises of that, burying forty sheep that were awaiting slaughter by a different method, and twenty carcasses of beef. Access to this was up a lane at the side of the Baptist Church, whose schoolroom, which had been used as a Services canteen, was now wrecked. On the other side of the lane were some houses with weather-boarded fronts, which are common in Kent, and these were badly damaged. The boards were hanging off most of them, and the inhabitants were standing at their doors, looking shocked and dazed, some with cuts and bruises. Harry and I went from house to house, asking if anyone needed assistance, but no one appeared to have suffered other than superficial injury.

Later we discovered that an old lady had been killed in a very badly damaged house next to the butchery. Every shop window in the High Street and the upper part of Station Road was broken. The other bomb had fallen on an underwear factory at Willesborough, the district of Ashford in the direction of Hythe, killing a number of people. We soldiers spent all that day clearing up the mess. I was in the party that had to recover the meat from the rubble that had been the butchery. When we had got it all out, it was taken in one of the trucks to be examined by a food inspector to see if it was fit for human consumption. Another detachment was shovelling all the broken glass in the High Street into our three-ton lorries. Worst of all the jobs was the one given to the party detailed to deal with the Willesborough underwear factory. They were recovering the bodies of the people killed there.

There had been little more than the width of Station Road between our workshop and the spot where the first bomb fell. If the storeman had not called me to the door, I would certainly have been seriously injured by the shards of glass that fell from the shattered skylight just where I had been standing. I had great cause to thank God for His protection.

At Whitsuntide we were involved in another exercise, code-named 'Tiger Scheme'. As we were not far from the assembly area, and had vehicles to transport all our personnel and equipment, we started on the evening of the second day, whereas the infantry had a march of a hundred miles.

As darkness was falling, we arrived at the village of Frittenden, Sussex, where we had a meal. As we were simulating battle conditions, there were no billets, so some slept in lorries, some underneath them, some on the canvas roofs, and some in barns. My abode was a barn. Two of us lifted one of the doors off its hinges and laid it on the earth floor in the most sheltered corner, spread sacks on it, then our groundsheets and blankets, so we had a comfortable night. Through a grating in the wall, a large white pig in the neighbouring sty regarded us with interest. Over his head on the wall some pious soul had written:

> Blest is the man who ne'er consents
> In ill advice to walk,
> Nor stands in sinners' way, nor sits
> Where men profanely talk.

I don't know whether the pig or I was supposed to stand in need of this counsel. The only way for either of us to avoid 'sitting where men profanely talked' was to lie down or stand up. I was destined to spend three nights in the company of the pig, and conceived quite an affection for him. Little did he realise that I was thinking of him in terms of rashers, or in conjunction with apple sauce. The next morning I asked one of the local inhabitants to what Frittenden owed its fame and prosperity, and he solemnly answered, 'treacle mines'.

In one of the fields stood a rusting old Alvis car. I was regarding this with a speculative eye when along came the farmer. When I told him of the difficulty we had in obtaining spares, particularly small items such as nuts and bolts, he said I could take anything I wanted off the car, except the wheels and chassis, as he wanted these to make a tractor trailer. Two of us set to work and stripped it right down to the chassis, using a sixteen-pound hammer for the awkward parts. The farmer was pleased to get the job done, and I was pleased to get the spares, particularly the nuts and bolts. He also gave us an old Chevrolet engine and gearbox, and we had enough potentially useful spares to fill two sacks. The weather was warm and sunny, and we enjoyed working in the field, but later in the week when the scheme had actually started we were not so happy when it poured with rain.

On this scheme we were forbidden to buy any food locally, or to enter public houses. We were on field rations, with hard biscuits instead of bread. One wit suggested that a better use for them would be tiling a fireplace. On the third day of the scheme, our force (12th Corps) successfully attacked 'the enemy' (Canadian Corps) at midnight, and we made an advance which involved several moves. Our unit was maintaining communications between advance and rear units. We thought this scheme much more profitable than the one in which we had been engaged during the winter, and we learned some useful lessons for when we should have to face the real enemy. At the end, we had the satisfaction of being judged the victors.

Some time later, the Army abolished my trade description of 'fitter signals', and replaced it with that of 'vehicle mechanic'. As this was a higher and slightly better-paid grade, I applied for a trade test, and was sent to Aldershot for a ten-week course. Having heard many tales of the rigorous discipline of that military town, I went with a certain amount of trepidation, but actually had quite a good time in the vehicle maintenance school. We were billeted in the somewhat overcrowded Buller Barracks, next to the Army School of Catering, in consequence of which the food was the best I ever encountered in the Army.

Aldershot being a permanent military training centre, there were facilities for he troops seldom found anywhere else. One evening I went to the Garrison Theatre to see a variety show, during which there was a talent competition. Having seen what the entrants had to offer, I decided to have a go myself the following week. I sang a song and won the first prize. Prizewinners were not allowed to compete again, but they could participate in future entertainments, and I was regularly included in the programme during the time I was there.

The vehicle mechanics' course was most interesting and instructive, but unfortunately I was never able to finish it. News came that my unit was being mobilised for service overseas, and I had to have a medical examination to make sure I was completely fit in the event of being suddenly recalled. For quite a long time I had known that I was in need of circumcision, in fact for many months I had been awaiting admission to a hospital in Canterbury, and the MO decided that this must be done before he would pass me fit, so I was sent to Connaught Hospital, which was a military hospital in the grounds of Brookwood Mental Hospital, Knaphill, near Woking.

My stay there should have been very short, but the medical treatment I received after the operation was deplorable, and I was in hospital for several weeks. I was really miserable there. Once a patient could get out of bed, he was expected to polish floors and do all sorts of jobs. There was no argument, as the ward sisters had equivalent rank to a captain, and discipline was strict. The food was unappetising, and our only leisure occupations were reading and writing letters. Even when doing this we were often interrupted to do chores. As far as I can recollect, I was in the hospital for about two months, which was a ridiculous length of time for such a trivial operation. I became convinced that the fluid being applied to my dressing was actually preventing healing. At last there was some improvement, and I asked to be discharged so that I could return to my unit. Instead of this, to my dismay I was sent to a military convalescent depot at Silwood Park, between Sunningdale and Ascot, Berkshire. This was a new innovation, a convalescent depot being very different from a convalescent home. It was really for patients who were recovering from fractures, sprains, hernias, etc., and took the place of sick leave. Formerly such patients had been given twenty-one days' sick leave, and it had been found that they often spent the time sitting by the fire, with the result that they did not exercise the muscles that had become weak through inaction in hospital, so that they returned to their units unfit, and in need of further treatment.

At this depot, the entire mornings were spent on physical training, and there were remedial machines, heat treatment and massage. None of this would benefit me in any way, and I hated PT. It was by now the beginning of November and very cold, yet we had to wear shorts all the time. The Nissen huts in which we slept were cheerless in the extreme, surrounded by mud, and fires were not allowed, although one day we had to move eighty tons of coke, which seemed to add insult to injury. Presently it became so cold that we woke in the mornings to see icicles hanging from the corrugated iron roof where our breath had condensed and frozen.

Silwood Park, which covered many acres, surrounded a huge mansion, formerly the home of the proprietor of the pre-war product 'Bile Beans', whose name I believe was Lord Dolby. In the great house was a hall the size of a church. The building was being used by the Army as company quarters, medical officer's room, dental officer's room, message room, officers' quarters, sick bay, etc. We were accommodated in about thirty Nissen hits built behind the house, and a dinning hall, cookhouse, NAAFI, ablutions, lavatories and gymnasium had all been erected. A large area of ground was being cleared of fine mature trees, which had taken many generations to grow, to make a parade ground, football pitch, and assault course. This disgusted me.

Our general impression of the officer commanding the depot was that he must have been a sadistic lunatic. It seemed that everybody entering the place was automatically graded in medical category D, and to be discharged one had to be upgraded to category A, which involved having to do two twelve-mile route marches, and to go over the assault course. The latter was the most difficult and dangerous one I ever encountered in all my Army experience. One man who was recuperating from a hernia operation broke his thigh on the assault course and had to return to hospital. Each week we underwent a so-called medical examination, which was cursory to say the least. The MO asked how we were. If we said we felt fine, he took the view that we were only saying it to get away from the wretched place, and he was likely to keep us another week in the same category. If we complained of anything, we were likely to be accused of malingering, so we could hardly win. By saying I thought I was as well as I could expect to be, I managed to rise a grade each week, so spent the minimum of five miserable weeks there.

On the first Sunday morning I was there, three of us went to a Methodist church in Sunninghill, thereby swelling the congregation to fifteen, plus a few children. After dinner the sun was shining, so I went out and got on the first bus I saw, which happened to be going to Staines. I knew nothing about Staines, but one place was as good as another to me, and in the event I enjoyed the ride. The area was quite unfamiliar to me, and I was interested to see the great houses and estates of the aristocracy. Through the trees I caught a glimpse of Fort Belvedere, once the home of the former Prince of Wales, looking like a fairy-tale castle with its circular towers. On the other side of the road was the end of Windsor Great Park, which I understand is twelve miles wide. I also saw the estates of the Earl of Harewood and Lord Derby. Approaching Staines, I saw a huge brick building adorned with ornate towers and minarets, which I learned was Holloway College, part of the University of London, but at that time requisitioned as a training college for ATS officers.

I spent a while in Staines, mainly watching the small craft on the Thames, and then it began to rain so I decided to return, and boarded a bus with the same route number as the one I had gone on, but when well out of the town found to my dismay that it only went part of the way, and that the next bus to Sunningdale would not come for an hour. It was pouring with rain, and I found myself stranded at Virginia Water, which I considered to be appropriately named. There was not a vestige of shelter, and I had no overcoat. There seemed to be no sense in waiting for the next bus, so I had a four-mile work in torrential rain which soaked me to the skin, and also my boots were no longer waterproof. Not only had I no means of drying my clothes, but I had no others to put on, as my kit had been handed in to the stores at Aldershot before I went into hospital. The next morning I went on parade shivering in PT shorts, a shirt and borrowed pullover, with wet feet. For about the only time in the course of my military career, I was glad to go on cookhouse fatigues that morning. I was refused permission to dry my clothes in the cookhouse, but was allowed to dry my trousers in the NAAFI kitchen. By some miracle I escaped catching a cold.

A day or so later, I resolved to try to recover my kit from Aldershot. I thought of asking permission to go, but knew there would be some humbug, so decided to risk going without permission. My strategy was to go on the sick parade for a start, which wasn't really necessary, as the MO's orderly attended to my dressing, but the presence of my name on the sick report would provide a good alibi in my absence.

About 9.30 am I walked boldly out of the gate with a corporal who was also feeling like a day off, and the guard thought we were going on a job. When I reached the station, I found there was a train to Aldershot in about a quarter of an hour, so I tendered a ten shilling note for my fare, and received nine and fourpence change, which made it a very cheap ride, but I didn't argue. It was an hour's run, and when I reached Aldershot station I had no difficulty in getting past the only redcap on duty.

I went straight to the barracks, and taking the bull by the horns went to the RSM, who sent me to the stores. Having been so long away from my unit, I was 'Y-listed', which meant being liable to be posted to any unit, losing my issued kit, and being issued with new on arrival elsewhere. My kitbag was found, with the locked handle smashed. All my private property had been put into a small sandbag, and this I took away with me, along with my greatcoat, pullover, spare underclothes, socks and handkerchiefs. It was a great relief to have these once more in my possession.

At a little restaurant in a side street, I had an excellent dinner for a very low price, and spent the afternoon in the town. Arriving back at Silwood Park, I was relieved to find that my absence had not been noticed. That evening some of the other rebels in our hut chopped up the sweeping brush, pinched some coal, and lit a forbidden fire, so it was the end of a perfect day.

On the afternoon parade the following day, the sergeant asked for a volunteer for cleaning a few rooms, so I took the job. This was a good move, as not only was it an easy job, bit it got me out of PT, the everlasting parades, and wearing shorts in the bitterly cold weather. An added bonus was that when the coast was clear, I was able to enjoy the luxury of a bath in a very large blue-tiled bathroom, complete with white marble bath, heated towel rails, and a gorgeous washbasin of marble, glass and chromium plating. But despite so disporting myself 'mid pleasures and palaces' I was still longing for a sight of Home Sweet Home, as it was ages since my last leave.

As time went by, I was becoming increasingly despondent about my chances of getting back to my own section at Ashford. My friend Doug Cairncross, the storeman, wrote to say that Captain Caldicott said I must insist on being posted to 12th Corps, when he would apply for me. A letter from one of the DRs told me they had got a new fitter, so I didn't know what to make of it. In the end, I decided to apply for a pass to go to Ashford to try to get things sorted out.

The most the officer's generosity would allow was a pass from reveille Sunday morning to 9.45 that night, and I was strictly forbidden to go through London, although to go any other way would waste a great deal of my precious time. I have to confess that on this occasion I descended to the depths of bribery and corruption by presenting my cigarette and chocolate coupon to the corporal in charge of our hut in return for the favour of snatching my pass from the office on Saturday morning, and undertaking to mark me present at the 'Lights Out' roll call that night. Immediately after dinner I cleared off and caught the two o'clock train to Waterloo. Then for the first time I took a look at my pass and saw that it lacked the official stamp and officer's signature! Now I was in a tough spot because: (a) my pass was not valid; (b) I had cleared off half a day early; (c) I was going through London against orders; and (d) I knew there were more redcaps at Waterloo looking for just such miscreants as me than at any other station. Obviously I should have to use my loaf to avoid falling into their hands, and this was where my knowledge of geography came in handy. Instead of staying on the train right through to Waterloo, I got off at Richmond and took the tube to Charing Cross, where before catching the Ashford train I just had time for a hot meal at a cheap place I knew a bit off the beaten track. I arrived at Ashford at about 6.30 pm and walked away from the station without having encountered any redcaps.

My unexpected appearance at the billet caused quite a sensation. One of the few men in was Jack Taylor, the DR from Sheffield, who was just going out, so I went with him and we had a pleasant evening together. Then I went round to the stores and found my old friend Harry Balsillie, who slept there, just about to go to bed. He soon found me a palliasse and some blankets.

In the morning I went over to the billet where I found all my old mates, who thought they were seeing a ghost, but they were all delighted to see me. They didn't like the new fitter, and he didn't like the section. Although he had only been there three weeks, he had already been on four charges.

After a wash and shave and breakfast in the mess, I went to the section office, where the sergeant and lieutenant on duty received me with smiles and handshakes, gave me a seat in their office, and offered me cigarettes. I told them my story, and managed to get the position made clear. They were very anxious to have me back, especially the sergeant, who immediately got on the telephone to various higher officers, and set the machinery in motion for my return.

I thought it showed that one had to leave a place to be fully appreciated, but it certainly pleased me and stimulated me to find that everybody who knew me from the officer to my mates wanted me back. They said the new man was no good, and that he was a windbag. He hated the place, and had applied for a posting, so I began to think my chance of getting back was more rosy than I had dared to hope.

After dinner I had a walk with Doug Cairncross, who was going to his girlfriend's house. When we reached there, she came out and invited me in for a cup of coffee. She had once knitted me a pair of socks. Having drunk my coffee I left them, but met Doug again later as he was going on leave, and we travelled to London together. He had brought me a pasty from his girl. I shall have more to tell about this kind girl later in my narrative.

With some trepidation I left the train at Waterloo, where I had to change for Sunningdale. Two redcaps were standing at the barrier examining passes, but I created a diversion by asking the ticket collector for some unnecessary information about trains, thus causing an obstruction. I was told to 'move on there', and airily waving the invalid pass nipped past while some other victim was showing his pass. On the other side I saw two more redcaps at the barrier examining the passes of men boarding the Sunningdale train, so I awaited my opportunity, and when there was rather a crowd at the barrier I fell in beside an officer, trying to look as if I was with him, and by contriving to keep close to him so that he was between me and the MPs I slipped through again. There were no MPs at Sunningdale station, but I was over an hour late; in fact a clock struck 11.00 pm as I neared the camp, so I entered the perimeter through a hole in the fence in order to avoid the guard. My bed had been made by one of the convalescents, and my friend the corporal had marked me present again, so the whole operation came to a successful conclusion.

The events of this weekend had the effect of raising my morale a great deal. For the first time, the war news was also good, with the victory at El Alemein, and the failure of the Germans to take Stalingrad. I still had three weeks to remain in the wretched depot. Owing to my leaking boots and the constant wet weather, my feet were often wet, but the storeman refused to change them until they were completely worn out, so in order to speed them on their way, I had applied them to the grinder in my Ashford workshop.

Slowly the weeks passed. The two twelve-mile route marches were accomplished without undue difficulty, and then came the dreaded assault course. I had learnt from experience that the best way to approach this kind of situation was to start off with great apparent enthusiasm, avoid drawing attention to myself, and to try to keep with as many others as possible so as to bypass one or two of the most difficult obstacles without being seen. At the end came the most horrifying hazard. Between two trees at a height of about twenty feet was stretched a rope with a light line above it. The exercise was to climb the first tree, walk the tightrope holding the line, and descend by the second tree. Having no head for heights and a poor sense of balance, I knew I should never be able to do this, so I stood well back until some brave souls had accomplished the feat, and then while all eyes were on one terrified soldier who was wobbling dangerously on the rope, I sprinted smartly across to the rear of the ones who had done it, fortunately without being noticed. Otherwise I think I might have been there yet!

At last my release came, with seven days' leave, and orders to report to 12th Corps Signals at Tunbridge Wells. As soon as I was home, I wrote a very respectful letter via the CSM to the adjutant at Tunbridge Wells requesting an extension of leave, as it was so long overdue, and authorisation to return to my unit in Ashford instead of Tunbridge Wells. In reply I received a pass for a further seven days' leave, and a travel warrant from Sheffield to Ashford. This was probably the most welcome leave I every enjoyed. I wore my civilian clothes and had a complete rest, which did me a great deal of good, and I returned to my unit completely fit.

The unsatisfactory fitter had already been posted elsewhere when I arrived back, and I soon fell into my old routine. In my long absence the condition of the transport had deteriorated, and I found lots of work awaiting me. This suited me fine, as it was the kind of work that most interested me and I embarked on it with enthusiasm.

Chapter 22
'Lucy'

THE YEAR 1943 was to prove to be one of the most momentous in my life. The first months passed quietly enough, the most notable event being a dance organised by our section in a hall in Ashford High Street. Although not a dancer, I attended this, as any social occasion made a welcome change. At the end, I discovered a young DR who had recently joined us helplessly drunk and deserted by his mates. With great difficulty, for he was a heavy lad, I got him down the stairs and down the road until he fell asleep on my shoulder. Having dragged him the rest of the way (mercifully it wasn't too far) we were challenged by the guard at the gate of our billet:

'Halt, who goes there?'

'Friend.'

'Advance one and be recognised!'

'Sorry, mate, one can't advance, or the other will fall down.'

Having completed this ritual, I hauled the inebriated one into the building and succeeded in reaching the foot of the stairs, where I had to pause until help arrived. Two of us got him up the stairs and into his room. Of course, he just had to sleep on a top bunk, so one of us took his shoulders and the other his legs, swung him backwards and forwards a couple of times and sent him sailing through the air to land on his bunk. He never woke, and knew nothing about it in the morning.

Soon after that we changed our billet from the Girls' High School to Stanhope School in South Ashford. This had formerly been the Boys' Reformatory School, and was probably considered to be more appropriate for chaps like us.

The old charging plant had by this time worn out. The big end bearings had gone, and replacements not being available we had been issued with two charging panels working off the town mains. This was an improvement in most ways, as precious petrol was saved, as well as a great deal of time and attention, and there was no noise or exhaust fumes. A driver mechanic named Dennis Mullard was able to attend to the charging after I had given him some instruction, and this left me free to devote all my time to the vehicles.

I have mentioned Doug Cairncross's girlfriend, Lucy Wilkinson. The first time I had seen her was one evening when I had arranged to meet Doug on the warren, an expanse of rough, partly wooded country on the outskirts of Ashford. Nearing a large tree at the top of a rise, I saw a smiling girl approaching me. She said, 'Are you Charles?' When I admitted the fact, she led me to Doug, who was about to indulge in some revolver practice; shooting was his peacetime hobby. I have since taken a photograph of the tree under which Lucy and I first met.

Doug and Lucy had been going together for most of the time we had been in Ashford, and he had often told me of the kindness he had received from her and her parents. Strangely, some while after I had first met her, he began to behave in an offhand way towards her. In particular, his behaviour was discourteous to say the least when the Signals held a second dance, at which I was not present. Having taken Lucy, he left her high and dry for most of the evening in the dance hall, while he spent his time talking to other men in the bar. I was very surprised to hear this, as I had always known him as a very moderate drinker. She was very hurt, and it is not surprising that her feelings towards him cooled.

So I said to myself, 'What are you waiting for, Charlie boy?', and stepped into the breach. Doug then registered annoyance, and threatened to shoot me. Some of my pals who heard him were a bit worried about this, as he always carried at least one revolver and was a crack shot, but I doubted whether he would be quite so mad, so I played it cool and disregarded him. Lucy and I got on well together, and were soon 'going steady', as the phrase goes.

The question of my trade description was still outstanding, and I asked if it would be possible to return to Aldershot to complete the vehicle mechanics' course which had been interrupted by my admission to hospital. Instead, I was sent to Luton on another course. When I reached there, I was told to my consternation that it was to be of twenty-two weeks' duration. For more than one reason I was anxious not to be away from Ashford for so long, especially after my experience of the previous year.

The first twelve weeks were spent working in premises formerly occupied by a motor engineering firm called Dickenson & Adams. We were in civilian billets, and along with three other chaps I was assigned to the house of a Mrs Siddaway. It was a big old house, and also living there were Mrs Siddaway's daughter and her husband who was an ex-sailor, and their sixteen-year-old daughter and younger son. Mrs Siddaway was a crafty old crone who originally hailed form Yorkshire, and had the one merit of being a good cook. In order to get more meat than her entitlement, she fiddled the ration books in some way. One of her specialities was the delicacy known as 'Bedfordshire clangers'—a very substantial type of meat pudding which had a somnolent effect on us during the afternoon lectures. The house was none too clean and for the only time in my life I had to sleep in a bug-ridden bed. Fortunately, we were allowed passes most weekends, so I was able to visit Lucy. Her parents always received me very kindly.

The course itself was excellent. Most of the instructors were civilians, each of whom was an expert in some particular field. Not only were we instructed in every branch of vehicle maintenance, both theoretically and practically, but we were taught the skills of filing, soldering, tin smithing, bracing, forging, hardening, tempering, and grinding tools. By this time I excelled in filing, and a complicated handbrake knuckle joint I made entirely by hand, with one part filed to a cylindrical shape, was said to have been the best one that had ever been made since the courses had started. When checked with a micrometer, it was found that the only deviation amounted to no more than two-thousandths of an inch.

Every morning we had to assemble at 6.00 am (4.00 am GMT, as Double Summer Time was in force during the war) in shorts and vest. The roll having been called, there was a fairly brief period of PT followed by a cross-country run of about three miles. The fact that I had always been a non-smoker and as a singer had done a lot of breathing exercises gave me the stamina to finish these runs with less distress than some of those who were well ahead at the beginning. I was a steady plodder. After the run we returned to our lodgings to change into uniform and have our breakfast before beginning the work of the day. Apart from the PT there were no parades or other duties.

One of the instructors told us of a soldier who had earlier been on the course, and had proved himself to be hopeless. One day the instructor had been astounded to see him attempting to cut a steel bar by laying the edge of a steel rule on it and hitting that precision instrument with a hammer! This being the last straw, the instructor took him to the principal, to whom he related the story of this incredible performance. Having partly recovered form the initial shock, the principal asked him, 'Aren't you interested in this work?'

'No sir', was the answer.

'What was your job in civvy street?'

'I was a car salesman.'

'Well, any silly fool can sell a car when a clever man's made it.'

'That may be so, sir, but I can earn more money selling cars than a clever man can making them.'

'No doubt you can, and that's where the injustice lies. The craftsman is the most important member of any community. Without the craftsman you wouldn't have a car to sell, or a pen to push, a sheet of paper to write on, a desk to rest your elbows on, a chair to put your backside on, a garment on your back, or transport to bring you from your non-existent house, along a non-existent road to your non-existent work premises. Without craftsmen, civilisation would collapse. By rights, craftsmen should be the most highly regarded and highly paid of all workers.'

The car salesman was posted to the infantry forthwith. As a craftsman, I need hardly say that my sentiments have always coincided with those so ably expressed by the principal, although of course I appreciate that all workers are of importance, and that all members of the community are dependent on each other.

Our instructor in the filing class was a very quiet elderly civilian. One afternoon he had been out of the room for a little while, and on his return he went all round the class examining our work. Then he went to the blackboard and drew a design for a stud extractor, and two other objects. After explaining how to make the stud extractor, which he said we should find a useful tool, he said, 'There are two men who will not be making this. Two men who think they are cleverer than I am. Whilst I was out of the room, they took two exhibition pieces out of the cupboard, and exchanged them for their own inferior examples. They will be making these two pieces before they can continue with the rest of the course.' He then presented them with two rough scaly pieces of steel which they had to file flat on all sides, cut a one-inch-square hole on the centre of one piece, and file a lot of metal off the end of the other piece so that it would fit exactly in the hole. It was hard boring work, and led to them failing the course. One had been a military policeman.

After twelve weeks at Luton, we went to Chiswick to continue the course for a further four weeks at the premises of Lep Transport. This was a very spacious workshop with overhead cranes, pits, and all facilities. At the rear was a platform built over the River Thames from which it was possible to watch the river traffic. It would have given a grandstand view of the Boat Race in peacetime. This part of the course was entirely practical, each soldier being paired with an experienced civilian mechanic engaged in completely overhauling military vehicles. Having been given the choice, I elected to work on heavy vehicles in order to widen my experience. Some of these had searchlights mounted on them, the electricity to operate them being obtained from large generators powered by the vehicle's engine. All the vehicles were stripped down to the chassis, and the engines, gearboxes and final drives sent to specialist departments for reconditioning. The chassis and body were repaired if necessary and repainted. All the wiring was ripped out, and renewed by an electrician. Then we reassembled the vehicle, which after testing was issued to a unit in almost new condition. So important was this work considered to be that an official of the Ministry of Supply was stationed there to ensure that the necessary parts and materials were always available.

I enjoyed my stay in Chiswick. Along with a chap called William MacKenzie, but always known as Mac, I had a very comfortable clean billet with a nice landlady not far from Lep Transport, close to Chiswick Church. There were no parades or military duties of any kind. Once a week, a major and a sergeant came with our pay, weekend passes and NAAFI issue of cigarettes, chocolate, etc. It was hard to imagine we were still in the Army!

At this time I made up my mind to get married. Previously I had never considered it to be a good idea to marry in wartime, but having now made up my mind to marry Lucy, I thought we had better get on with it before distance might further separate us, perhaps for a long time, during which anything might happen. I was now twenty-nine years of age and thought it was high time I was married.

Having made our decision, we started on the necessary preparations. The date was largely determined by my father's ability to be away from work, so the 26th of July was decided upon. The major was helpful in granting me leave on alleged compassionate grounds,

Our wedding day, 26th of July, 1943

ten days in all, in return for which I forfeited my approaching seven days' leave.

The only Sheffield people present at our wedding were my parents. My brother Douglas, who should have been best man, was unable to go as he had a very bad foot, so this duty was undertaken by Doug Cairncross, who had luckily abandoned his murderous intent and returned to a friendly relationship.

We were married in Ashford Parish Church, on a glorious hot day. Lucy had been helping in a canteen that had been set up for the troops in the Congregational Church, and after the ceremony we came out of the church under an arch of canteen knives held up by ladies of the WVS, in recognition of my origin in the city of steel. Wartime rationing ruled out the possibility of a lavish banquet, but Lucy's family had done their best, and we returned to a nice dinner. We also had a wedding cake, the ingredients of which had been obtained with some difficulty.

For our honeymoon, we went for a few days to a cottage at Crowborough, the home of a jolly elderly character whom we called Uncle

Tom, the brother of one of Lucy's workmates, Miss Wickens. Tom was full of preposterous jokes, and he had been telling his pals he was having a honeymoon couple to stay with him, and he was going to take us to the White Swan and get me drunk. However, the next day he had to tell them that the laugh had been on him, for he was the one who went home a bit tipsy. The weather continued hot, and we enjoyed our little country holiday. We spent the last few days of my leave in Sheffield.

For the final six weeks of the course, we went to the North London Polytechnic, Kentish Town, again in civilian billets which proved to be very comfortable, and Mac and I, who had become firm friends (we still exchange Christmas cards), continued to stay there together. Here again the instruction, both theoretical and practical, was of a very high standard, and at the end of the course we were both graded A3 (my previous rating had been B2) and were now well-qualified vehicle mechanics. We also received an extra ninepence a day. When the course ended, we received a great shock. We were given seven days' leave and ordered to report back to the Royal Artillery Grand Depot at Woolwich, with the rank of gunner in the RA.

I went straight to Ashford, and made my way to the signal office with the news. Asking for Major Caldicott (his rank when I had last seen him) I was told that he had been further promoted to lieutenant colonel, and was now second in command of 12th Corps Signals at Tunbridge Wells. The corporal asked if I would like to speak to him on the phone. I said I would, and in a few moments my old OC's voice came on the line. I said 'Hatfield speaking, sir. Remember me?' He answered, 'I remember your voice!' When I imparted the news he said, 'So they've made you a gunner, have they! Well, I want you here at Tunbridge Wells. I want to put you in charge of entertainment. I'll do all I can to get you back.' But unfortunately he couldn't do anything, because it was a War Office posting.

Lucy and I spent my leave in Sheffield, after which we travelled together to London, she to continue her journey back to Ashford, I to Woolwich.

Off came my Royal Corps of Signals badge, on went the grenade of the Royal Artillery. Back I went to all the training routines I so detested: spit and polish, parades, guards, PT, fatigues, foot and arms drill, and now also gun drill. As often as possible Mac and I volunteered for work at Woolwich Arsenal, unloading railway wagons.

The barracks were miserable, and several times we had to leave our beds because of air raids, some bombs falling uncomfortably close one night. Twice I was on the Grand Depot Main Guard, which involved two days of preparation: polishing, blancoing all our webbing equipment, practising the guard-changing routine, and being inspected to make sure we were fit to be inspected.

The guard-changing ceremony was equal to that at Buckingham Palace. A number of guards were mounted simultaneously, the main guard in the centre, facing the imposing headquarters building where the colonel stood at the saluting base at the top of the steps. Every man's equipment gleamed, every drill movement was executed with perfect precision. The inspecting officers could find little fault. Finally we all marched past the colonel at the salute, and out of the parade ground.

After all this pomp and ceremony, I was disgusted to find that the purpose of our guard was to guard defaulters in the prison for the next twenty-four hours. Most of these were tough characters, and a lot of them were deserters. They tried continually to cadge cigarettes from the guards, who were forbidden to give them any, and when none were forthcoming they did their best to provoke us, knowing that we should be in trouble ourselves if we retaliated. The usual pattern of guard duty is two hours on and four hours off, but during the morning and afternoon a guard who would normally have been off duty had to stand just inside the narrow locked gate of the exercise compound, silently and motionlessly enduring the jeers and taunts of the prisoners. This was a great test of discipline for us.

We spent a few weeks at Woolwich, and then five of us who had been together on the vehicle mechanics' course were sent to Louth in Lincolnshire. Almost the first words addressed to us when we arrived there were 'Have you chaps had embarkation leave?' When we said 'No', the sergeant said, 'You'll go tomorrow then. You've missed a day of it.'

The next day was a Sunday, and no trains were running from Louth. One of us wanted to go to Manchester, one to Cornwall, Mac to Maidstone, I in the first place to Sheffield, and I forget the desired destination of the other man. Not wishing to waste the day, I proposed that we should all take a bus to Grimsby, where I was sure we could get a train to Sheffield, from where everybody would be able to get a rail connection. We did this, and all managed to get

home that day. My unexpected arrival on embarkation leave caused
a bit of consternation, but I allayed my parents' anxiety to some
extent by telling them that I was almost certain that we were bound
for North Africa, where the fighting was already over. This proved
in fact to be the case. I spent two or three days at home, and the
remainder of my leave at Ashford with Lucy. Of course we were
both very disappointed to think that I had to go abroad so soon
after our marriage.

Returning to Louth, we spent another week sorting out our kit,
being issued with tropical clothing, mosquito nets and other necessities. All my surplus possessions had been taken home. The unit to
which we were attached was an anti-tank artillery regiment. The
prospect of being opposed to enemy tanks filled us with no great
joy, but I had long since learned to accept each day as it came, and
to leave the future in God's hands.

Chapter 23
'Embarkation'

AT 10 pm on the 11th of November 1943 the unit boarded a train, upon which all the carriage doors were locked so that no one would desert. The blinds were lowered, and only a few dim lights glowed. During the night the train stopped several times, presumably to take on more troops, and we had no idea where we were. At 8.00 am we were surprised to find we had only reached York. From there we moved faster up to Edinburgh, with a stop at Waverley station, then on through Glasgow to Gurock on the Clyde, reaching there fourteen hours after leaving Louth. The carriage doors were unlocked, and we alighted to find ourselves on a platform immediately adjacent to the river, where a steamer was waiting to convey us to one of the troopships anchored in the estuary. We immediately boarded this vessel, which then proceeded towards a convoy of miscellaneous types of ships which was assembling. Coming alongside one of the largest of these, the *Cameronia*, we stepped from the smaller craft onto a gangway that sloped up the side of the former liner, now a troopship, and climbed up to the deck. I heard that in peacetime the ship had carried 750 passengers, and that now that the cargo space had been converted to mess decks it carried 4,000 troops.

Our quarters were in the very lowest of the ship, the former hold, now Mess Deck D. When we had slung our hammocks for the night, there was hardly any space between them, and some men had to sleep on the deck under them. Owing to the limited amount of fresh water the ship could carry, we had to wash and shave in sea water, which would not lather, even with the special 'sea soap' issued to us. The toilet facilities were disgusting. A canvas chute ran through the upper decks to a hatch for ventilation, but even so it was so hot at night that we lay in our hammocks with no other covering than our underpants, and this was in Scotland in November. We wondered what the temperature would rise to as we approached southern latitudes.

Each morning we had to parade on deck at our allotted stations for boat drill, wearing our steel helmets and Mae West life jackets, and with our water bottles filled. On the second day, one of the sailors told us that on boat drill the next day volunteers would be called for from the anti-tank regiment to comprise the ship's gun crew for the duration of the voyage, and that these men would have better quarters and would be exempt from fatigues, PT and all other duties. Sure enough, next morning these volunteers were asked for, and although Mac and I hardly knew one end of a gun from the other, ignoring the old soldier's golden rule never to volunteer for anything, we both took two paces smartly forward.

As soon as boat drill was over, we were told to hand in our hammocks, and were conducted to our new quarters above the water line, a spacious cabin with portholes with a view of the sea, comfortable beds with spring mattresses, and washbasins with a supply of fresh hot and cold water. We congratulated ourselves on having made a good decision when we volunteered. Even when our gun position was assigned to us our luck was in, as we were to be serving the twelve-pounder anti-aircraft gun on the port bow, which had a crew of four, one of whom was providentially a naval gun layer. Left to our own devices, Mac and I might have been as likely to sink one of the other ships of the convoy as to shoot down an enemy plane. Another advantage was that when on watch the four of us could chat, whereas those manning the Oerlikens had only their own company for four hours at a time, which must have been very dreary during the night. I can claim to have served in the Navy for a fortnight, as on this voyage we were under the orders of a naval gunnery officer, and we were issued by the Navy with thick duffel coats, for which we were presently very grateful.

That morning the convoy sailed. Once out of the Firth of Clyde the sea became very rough, and the movement of the boat caused many to be seasick. One man lost his helmet over the side, and a rather bombastic major lost his false teeth, after which we never saw him again. The situation was not helped by the diet that day: kippers for breakfast and greasy mutton stew for dinner. Mac started to be ill early in the day, and was unable to go on duty in the afternoon. One of our party of five vehicle mechanics, Reg Franks, was ill throughout the voyage. I was all right until I went on watch at 4.00 pm, when almost as soon as I had ascended the steel ladder into the gun turret I had one heave over the side. After that I had no more trouble throughout the voyage.

Our new friend the sailor was very amiable, and we enjoyed his company. He taught us all there was to know about the gun, and when we were well out in the Atlantic we had gunnery practice. Soon I had learnt to shove shells and charges into the breech at great speed, whipping my hand away as the breech block was slammed shut. Our guide and mentor also initiated us into the mysteries of some nautical terms and procedures, so that we no longer referred to the bow and stern of the vessel as the 'sharp end' and the 'blunt end'. Now we were to learn the meaning of 'dog watch'. In the Navy, watches are of four hours' duration, with eight hours off. If this routine were rigidly adhered to, the same men would always get the unpopular night watches, so to break the sequence there are the two dog watches: the first from 4.00 pm to 6.00 pm, and the second from 6.00 pm to 8.00 pm.

At night it was bitterly cold up in the steel turret, and I kept warm by wearing my long johns, battle-dress, overalls, pullover, scarf, greatcoat, woollen cap, duffel coat with the hood up, and gloves. During the night watch, a bucket of hot cocoa was brought round from which we filled our mugs. Everyone on watch was expected to keep a good lookout over his sector of sea for any signs of enemy submarines or surface vessels. At sea, the stars appeared to shine more brightly and to be more numerous, and I aired my not very extensive knowledge of astronomy by pointing out some of the stars and constellations of which I happened to know the names. After I had said 'That one's Sirius', the sailor referred to me as 'Old Serious'.

Learning that a concert party was being formed to entertain the troops on board, I went along for an audition and was accepted. There was a Welsh regiment on board, which of course was able to contribute a fine choir; a Lancashire lad who recited Stanley Holloway monologues; a guitar player; an impersonator of the comedians Rob Wilton and Tommy Trinder; and the medical officer who was perhaps the star turn as a raconteur of funny stories, also giving a hilarious impression of a Frenchman training a performing flea. The concert was performed after a couple of rehearsals, and was repeated throughout the voyage to audiences of different men. I sang twice in each concert, each time receiving an encore. One of my songs was appropriately 'Rocked in the Cradle of the Deep', sung swaying slightly to the roll of the ship.

There were cinema shows on board, and a NAAFI where there was usually a long queue for tea and buns, cigarettes, etc., and we of the gun crew were given priority tickets for this. As we proceeded further south, we saw flying fish, porpoises and dolphins. The convoy constantly altered course, zig-zagging in an attempt to avoid enemy submarines that may have been lying in wait. One day we came near enough to the troopship ahead to be able to read its name on the stern. It was the former Cunard line *Samaria*. When I was about sixteen years old our firm had organised a trip to Liverpool and New Brighton, and this had included a conducted tour around this very ship, *Samaria*. Once after a shower, there was a magnificent rainbow, the end of which appeared to come almost to the bows of our ship. At night, besides the display of stars, there was a phosphorescent light of the foam around the ship to watch.

One evening, Mac and I went on watch at eight o'clock just as we were approaching the Straits of Gibraltar. At that time of the year it was of course dark, but after years of blackout in England, we were fascinated to see the bright lights of Gibraltar on the European coast, and Tangier on the African coast.

Every morning there was boat drill, and sometimes the alarm bells would ring for action stations, when if we were below we would have to grab our equipment and dash to our gun, whilst the soldiers who had no duty on deck had to go below. After a number of these practices we were able to get to our stations very quickly. The morning after we had passed Gibraltar we passed Algiers.

About four o'clock that afternoon the alarm bells rang, and we rushed on deck to find that this was not just another practice, but the real thing. The convoy was being attacked by German bombers.

Orders from the gunnery officer came through the Tannoy speakers. The guns and rockets were to be fired at any plane that came near, even if there was little chance of hitting it, in order to discourage them from coming too close. Every ship of the convoy began to fire, and the noise reverberating from the surface of the sea was deafening. The men of the other watch and our sailor were manning the gun, so we three kept it supplied with ammunition, carrying the shells from the magazine and hoisting them up to the gun turret with a block and tackle. So many shells did this gun fire that the turret became cluttered with empty shell cases, and the crew had to heave them over the side. Our naval escort, consisting of four destroyers and a corvette, kept twisting and turning around the other vessels at full speed, with their anti-aircraft guns blazing all the time. They seemed to be actually chasing the planes.

The crew of the starboard twelve-pounder were working as hard as we were, and presently through the din of the guns we heard a cheer from our right, as their efforts were rewarded by the scoring of a direct hit on a bomber which came down in the sea. Between our gun and theirs, mounted on a superstructure, was a Hotchkiss gun sending forth a steady stream of shells. The sides of the ship were lined with Oerlikens, there were lots of rockets, and on a superstructure near the stern was a Bofors gun manned by Army officers. There was also an old six-inch naval gun mounted on the deck at the stern, but this was only for use in case of attack by surface vessels, and was of no use against aircraft.

That morning, two more ships had joined the convoy as we passed Algiers. One of these, an American cargo/passenger boat was almost exactly in line with our ship, about half a mile away to port, when we saw to our horror that it had received a direct hit amidships, and a cloud of black smoke was rising from it. Quickly one of the escorting destroyers laid a smoke screen round it. We heard next day that of 700 men on it, 400 lost their lives.

Presently a squadron of fighter planes appeared, and our hopes that they were the RAF coming to our aid evaporated when they proved to be Heinkels of the Luftwaffe.

I was going through an experience I shall never forget: the deafening report of the guns, the blinding flashes, the red tracers from the machine guns, the huge columns of water thrown up when the German bombs fell in the sea, the destroyers fighting with all they had, and laying smoke screens. Frightening as all this was, I was glad to be on deck taking part in the action, rather than below, where the troops lay helpless, hearing the din of battle but knowing nothing of what was happening. We all knew that should the ship be stricken, many of them would be trapped, especially my comrades down on D Deck, with little hope of being saved alive.

Mac and I had just lugged another load of ammunition out of the magazine and hoisted it up to the gun when I happened to turn my head, and saw the most terrifying sight of my life. I shouted above the din to Mac, pointing astern. A Dornier bomber, flying low, was coming over our stern, to fly straight along the length of the ship. Hypnotised, we waited for the bomb to drop, whilst I uttered the most urgent of all my prayers.

But no bomb dropped. As the plane had approached the ship, the officers manning the Bofors gun pumped a stream of shells into it, probably killing the crew. Immediately it had passed over us, the Oerlikens of a ship just ahead of us on the starboard beam fired at it as it lost height. It came down in the sea with a tremendous splash, cartwheeled and disappeared forever beneath the waves.

The battle lasted for two hours, when mercifully darkness fell. The gunnery officer ordered a cease-fire so that the gun flashes would not betray our position, and the convoy changed course several times. For a while we continued to hear the drone of the planes, but they eventually lost us and returned to their base, and silence reigned, except for the singing in our ears, which persisted for hours.

During the night Mac and I were again on watch, and seeing a light falling from the sky thought the Germans were back, but were relieved when we realised it was only a meteor.

Chapter 24

'Algeria'

WHEN I AWOKE the next morning, I immediately became aware that the ship was no longer moving. All was silent and still. I arose and looked out of the porthole, and stood spellbound by the scene that met my gaze.

The ship was anchored just outside a harbour, the entrance to which was barred by an anti-submarine net. On the hillside rising from the harbour was a town consisting of white buildings punctuated with the domes and minarets of mosques, surrounded by palm trees, with a backcloth formed by the range of the Little Atlas Mountains, a scene I had imagined only existed in picture books. This was the Algerian town of Philippeville. Algeria at that time had the status of a Department of France, but since independence Philippeville has received the Algerian name of Skikda.

After the anti-submarine net had been opened, we entered the harbour, but our draft did not go ashore till the next day. Our sailor friend (after a lapse of over forty years I am unable to remember whether his name was Fred or Frank) was tidying up the magazine, which had been almost depleted of ammunition during the battle. Over the Tannoy, the gunnery officer commended the gun crew for their defence of the ship. The convoy had lost two ships and shot down five planes, two of which were credited to the *Cameronia*.

Early next morning we went ashore, where we were immediately besieged by a crowd of Arabs, mostly in dirty ragged burnouses, offering for sale tangerines and cheap trinkets, and shouting rude English words, of which I suspect they didn't know the meaning. We bought some of the fruit, and ignored the obscenity. The African sun was blazing down, the temperature contrasting greatly with what we had experienced on our first nights at sea, and by the time we had marched with our kit to the railway station I for one was sweating profusely.

At the station we were each issued with a tin of bully beef and a packet of Army biscuits, our ration until the next day, and herded onto trucks which bore the legend '32 Hommes. 8 Chevaux'. By the time all the 'hommes' were on, we were hoping no 'chevaux' would turn up.

We had been ordered not to get off the train, but as the hours passed with no sign of an engine to provide the motive power, most of us got off to stretch our legs, and soon several coal fires had been lit to brew tea in biscuit tins. Along came a black Senegalese soldier in a shabby French uniform with uncared-for leather equipment to tell us in French that fires and smoking were not allowed on the station. Of course, everyone professed complete ignorance of the French language. A little later he came back with his instruction written in block capitals on a card, but the only response he received was an adjuration to march up and down in a soldier-like manner.

Presently an ancient locomotive of French origin appeared on the scene. It was in an advanced state of decrepitude, eaten with rust, and with steam escaping in all directions. When it was coupled to the long train, it failed to move it a yard, and was hastily detached before the boiler blew up. Some optimist had told us we should start at 3.00 pm, then it was to be 5.00 pm. Finally at 7.00 pm a powerful American locomotive arrived and the train at last got under way.

Someone had the brainy idea that we could take the fire in its bucket along with us to brew up on the way, so he wired it to one of the buffers. Unfortunately the train travelled in the opposite direction to the one he had anticipated, and he had hung it on the front. The fuel was railway coals, and the movement of the train through the air caused the fire to blaze up, lighting up the countryside and filling the truck with acrid smoke. We expected the truck to catch fire. By and by the train slowed down, so Mac jumped out and managed to get the bucket off, but just then we gathered speed again, and Mac caught his foot on a piece of metal which was sticking up out of the embankment and tripped up. The bucket went flying and rolled down the embankment. Mac managed to scramble to his feet, and we hauled him aboard again with nothing worse than a bruised leg.

There was nothing to sit on in the truck, and not enough room to lie down. As the train kept climbing to higher altitudes we were very cold and cramped. We thought the train must have had square wheels. We jolted and crashed to and fro in pitch darkness, stopped innumerable times, and sometimes even went backwards. We had been promised a hot drink when we reached Constantine, but this did not materialise. Dawn was breaking when we reached our destination, and we emerged stiff and cold to start making fires for tea, and getting out our rations of bully beef and biscuits. Then the sun arose over a hill and we suddenly felt an immediate and welcome rise in temperature. I found myself detailed for the officers' baggage party. One of the officers had obtained some hot water from the engine, and I managed rather adroitly to purloin enough of this to have a refreshing wash and shave.

Now it was daylight, I took stock of our surroundings. The railway consisted of a single line, and there was no station. The only building I could see was a nearby farm where some fowls of an unfamiliar breed were scratching in the sandy soil. I afterwards discovered that the name of this place was Château Dun. There were some barren-looking hills around, and facing us a great expanse of flat desert, on which about a mile away were rows of tents.

When all the baggage had been loaded onto a lorry, we climbed on top and had an interesting ride towards the tents. It was quite warm by now. We saw Arabs ploughing their fields of stony sandy soil, one with a donkey, and a shepherd tending sheep and goats. They looked like Sunday School pictures, and certainly brought the Bible to life for me. All these people seemed to be very poor, trying to eke out an existence from the unpromising soil. Their habitations were small huts. Later I saw some driving camels, and one day I saw two richly dressed Arabs riding on camels looking like the romantic sheiks of the movies.

As we arrived at camp, we found a sergeant major shouting 'Field artillery fall in on the left, anti-tank artillery fall in on the right!' As we five mechanics had been designated 'field' at Woolwich, we fell in on the left, and felt some relief when we had been documented and knew that we should have no further connection with the anti-tank outfit. We all managed to find accommodation in the same large tent.

Life in the camp was not too bad, but rather monotonous. Every morning there was a parade, and when it was called, the crowds of men milled around baahing like sheep until they sorted themselves into their respective troops. With the sun and wind, we quickly became sunburnt, and shaving was rather a painful business at the open-air ablution benches, as the water obtained from an artesian well was icy cold. We were about 2,000 feet above sea level, and one morning we awoke to find a thin cover of snow, which I had never expected to see in North Africa. The Arabs had a well from which the water was raised by a system of buckets attached to an endless rope running over pulleys, powered by an unhappy donkey which walked round the well all day turning a wooden bar.

The food came by the railway and was practically all tinned, but was nevertheless quite good. We had a lot of Maconochie's stew and some tinned steak and kidney puddings which I enjoyed. Biscuits took the place of bread, but they were a great improvement on the big hard ones we had on the Tiger Scheme in England, being more like crackers. We never wandered far away from the camp, as there was little to see but sand and stones. The only wildlife seemed to consist of a few lizards, which were exactly the same colour as the sand; the only entertainment was an occasional evening cinema show in a big tent. Owing to the necessity of travelling as light as possible, the only book I had brought with me was a pocket New Testament.

We knew that we were destined to be sent to Italy as reinforcements for the 8th Army which was fighting there, and were told that as complaints had been received about the lack of efficiency of some of the vehicle mechanics they had received we should have to undergo a test before we went there.

Mac and I reported to a very pleasant officer who was interviewing the mechanics in a big tent, and we must have made a good impression on him, because before he had tested our knowledge he gave us a job after our own hearts. He required a vehicle engine to be fixed to an angle iron stand in the tent for demonstration purposes. Outside was a dump of battle-scarred vehicles that had been collected after the desert fighting: British, German and Italian. From these we chose a Ford V8 engine that seemed to be in good condition, with its ancillary equipment, carburettor, dynamo and starter motor. Having removed this from the vehicle and thoroughly cleaned it, we built a stand and bolted it on, as well as a radiator, and for good measure lighting and other electrical equipment obtained from various vehicles.

All the time we were working, the officer was interviewing other mechanics, some of whom gave unsatisfactory answers which drew from him deprecating comments to us when they had gone out. After this had gone on for a few days, he called the names Hatfield and MacKenzie. 'That's us, sir', we informed him, ungrammatically. 'Oh,' he said, 'You've heard all the questions I ask, haven't you? Anyway, you both seem to be pretty competent.' When we told him of our previous training and experience, he had no hesitation in passing us. He was very pleased with the demonstration rig we had constructed. We then returned to our troop.

One morning our troop was taken out into the desert. The only object in sight was a burnt-out German tank, full of shell holes as it had been used for target practice by the anti-tank gunners. Shovels were issued to us, and we were told to dig a trench, 100 yards long, 4 feet wide and 4 feet deep. When this was done, rails were to be laid in the bottom, on which a trolley—to which was attached a silhouette of a German tank appearing above ground level—was to be pushed along by some luckless character crawling along the bottom of the trench while the gunners fired at it. This sounded so idiotic that one wondered if in fact it was a serious proposition.

We formed a long line and began to dig, but our efforts made little impression, as not only did the strong wind blow the sand off our shovels either back into the trench or into the next man's eyes, but every hole our shovels made was immediately almost filled again by sand that slid back into it. No one worked very hard, and after the middle of the day, when we had eaten the rations we had brought with us, we abandoned the futile task and sprawled on the sand.

Presently along came an Arab with a few eggs to sell. He asked me the price of five francs for an egg, whereupon I promptly offered him three francs. What followed was something in the nature of an entertainment. The Arab and I sat cross-legged on the sand facing each other, and argued for the next couple of hours; he in what seemed to be a mixture of French and Arabic, I in a mixture of diabolical French and Yorkshire, with the accent on the Yorkshire. In the end I got the egg for three and a half francs. Five Algerian francs were worth 6d. All the money was paper, down to the lowest denomination, and most of the notes were dirty, creased, torn, and mended with bits of sticky paper.

Whilst in this part of the world, I had another graphic reminder of the Bible when I saw an example of something which was forbidden by the Laws of Moses: namely the unequal yoking of an ox and an ass. Neither of these animals can accommodate its natural gait to that of the other, and this is an example of the common sense of the laws that were laid down in those far-off times. A lady doctor of my acquaintance once remarked, in another context, that Moses was the first medical officer of health.

Christmas was now approaching, and a number of turkeys were being fattened in the camp in readiness for our dinner. They were kept in a pen surrounded by barbed wire, watched over day and night by a guard armed with a tommy gun. One night Mac and I were crossing the camp when there was a loud report and a bullet whined over our heads. The turkey guard had accidentally caught his trigger on the barbed wire.

Our party was not destined to eat turkey for our Christmas dinner. On Christmas Eve we were back in the horse trucks returning to Philippeville. Being in daylight for much of the way, this journey was more interesting than our previous one. The country was wild and mountainous until we reached the more fertile coastal strip. We passed through the ancient city of Constantine which stands over 2,000 feet high on a rock, and has an impressive Roman viaduct.

We arrived in Philippeville after midnight, and in the darkness stumbled into our billet, an uncompleted Nissen hut with a roof but no ends, through which the wind blew from the sea at one end to the foothills of the Atlas Mountains at the other. The floor was littered with bricks, and clearing a space in complete darkness to put down our ground sheets and blankets gave rise to much profanity.

The morning of Christmas Day 1943 was warm and sunny, so having nothing to do Mac and I had a walk along the beach. At noon we had the usual 'M and V' (tinned meat and vegetables) and we thought this was our Christmas dinner. However, later in the day we had a more seasonable meal of roast pork with onion stuffing, tinned peas and tinned potatoes. Every man was given a bottle of Canadian beer, seventy cigarettes and two boxes of matches. My cigarettes were subsequently used for barter.

After dark we started a sing-song in the hut, and a bombardier who also came from Sheffield said to me, 'What about giving us a song, Sheffield?' I gave them several, and soon we had quite a crowd in and around the hut: Englishmen, Scotsmen, negro soldiers from Mauritius, New Zealanders, Indians and Italian prisoners. One of the Italians enjoyed it immensely. He cried 'Tank you, tank you', shook hands with me, and I almost feared he was going to kiss me! For his special benefit, I then sang in his language 'Caro mio ben', which sent him into fresh transports. Mac then requested Brahms's 'Wiegenlied', which he had previously heard me sing in German, but the Italian said 'No German! No Boche!', so we didn't have it. The Italians seemed to have no greater love for the Germans than we did at that time.

Our camp was about five miles out of Philippeville, and on Boxing Day Mac and I walked along the coast to the town, where we were pestered a good deal by the Arab boys who wanted to black our boots. I kept bawling 'Imshee!', the Arabic for 'Go away!', this being one of the few Arabic words I had learnt—hardly a propitious beginning to the learning of a language, but useful in the circumstances.

Philippeville proved on closer acquaintance to be a good deal less attractive than it had appeared when seen from a distance through the porthole of a ship, and reminded me of the Biblical phrase 'a whited sepulchre'. It was a dirty, ramshackle place of smelly streets, and buildings of disintegrating concrete in a flashy French style of architecture. We found a cinema, and saw an English film with French subtitles. After a cup of tea at the NAAFI we were fortunate enough to get a lift back to camp on a lorry.

In the evening we went to the beach, took off our boots and socks and soaked our feet in the Mediterranean. It was the only time I ever paddled in the sea on Boxing Day by starlight. An incoming wave nearly washed away our boots, socks and towels, and we had to chase after them.

Chapter 25
'Italy'

ON THE afternoon of December the 29th, 1943, we departed from the wind tunnel that had been our home for the past few days as part of a draft of a thousand men bound for Italy. We were taken to the harbour where we boarded ten LCIs (landing craft infantry). These craft were constructed of welded steel plates, and had flat bottoms and sloping bows to enable them to run onto beaches. We spent the night on board in the harbour, sleeping on bunks which consisted of canvas stretched over tubular steel frames which could be hinged back to the bulkheads, and were quite comfortable.

Next morning the flotilla set sail for Italy. We were not sorry to leave North Africa, although we had had interesting experiences there. The start of our voyage was not very promising, as the sun disappeared and the sea became increasingly rough. Soon four of the LCIs had to turn back for Bizerte: two were leaking and the other two had engine trouble. During most of that day we sailed eastward within sight of the African coast and inland mountains, but the next morning we saw no land until we sighted the island of Pantelleria with its high extinct volcano, now mist-capped. The enemy on this island had fairly recently been subdued by bombing, and it was now in British hands. It was evident that we were heading for a storm, and there was some signalling between the boats, which one of the crew told us was to decide whether to take shelter in the harbour of Pantelleria. The decision was to carry on.

During the night a very bad storm arose, and there was a twenty-foot swell. The boat rose on each wave, and then crashed down into the trough on its flat bottom, jarring the thin steel plates of which it was constructed and causing them to creak as though they were about to part company with each other. Thus we saw the New Year in, midway between two continents. I was fortunate to be one of the very few men on board, including the crew, who wasn't seasick, in spite of the fact that my bunk was immediately over the smelly diesel tank. We were afterwards told that it had been touch and go whether the boat went down, and I could well believe it.

When we went on deck next morning only one of the other vessels was in sight, so we were rather anxious regarding the fate of the other four. For our meals we had to ascend a steel ladder onto the wet slippery steel deck, which owing to the presence of a superstructure amidships was little more than a yard wide, with a single guard wire to prevent us from falling into the sea, proceed in single file past a doorway through which our mugs and mess tins were filled, round the stern where a good deal of the tea was blown out of our mugs by the gale, then back down by a ladder on the other side. Going down a vertical steel ladder with a mug of tea in one hand and a full mess tin in the other is no easy feat in a storm, but there were few accidents. The only lavatory consisted of a wooden seat with a hole in it built out over the stern, and using it was a wet and hazardous exploit.

In the afternoon we reached Sicily, and took shelter in the harbour of Augusta. Inland towered Mount Etna. Much of the lower part was shrouded in mist, and the snow-clad conical summit seemed to swim in space. Unofficially, some of us went ashore that evening, and half a dozen of us fell in with a party of Royal Marines who took us along to their base, and very hospitably treated us to a good supper.

The next morning we went ashore on a short route march, and soon noticed that the fertility of Sicily was in great contrast to the barrenness of North Africa. In the orange groves the fruit was in all stages of ripeness, and we obtained a good supply before returning to the harbour. On the way back it poured with rain, for which we had gone unprepared, and we got very wet. In the afternoon I hung my trousers up to dry and went to bed, where I read in the Acts of the Apostles the account of Paul's voyage in that part of the world.

Whilst in Augusta harbour we had a great laugh at the expense of the Italian Navy—at least what little the British Navy had left of it. Our boat was moored close to a floating refuelling jetty, on the other side of which was an Italian destroyer, a beautifully painted showpiece which put our shabby workaday vessels in the shade.

The Italian sailors were draped all over it, striking heroic poses and looking like the characters in a comic opera. There were plenty of gaily painted rafts and life belts to be seen, and scores of life jackets which the sailors all put on the minute they were about to put to sea!

When they had refuelled, the destroyer started to move out of the harbour, with some ropes still securing it to the jetty! When this was noticed, pandemonium broke out, with all the Italians afloat and ashore shouting, gesticulating and running about, to the jeers and derisive laughter of the delighted British. We had all heard that the Italian Navy was loath to leave port, but we had scarcely expected to see them attempting to take the port with them.

The following day it was considered that the storm had abated sufficiently for us to proceed on our voyage. There were still some heavy rollers, and there was plenty of seasickness. Throughout the voyage I spent as much time as possible on deck in the fresh air, and perched up in the bows with the chap who had been the comedian in the concert party on the *Cameronia* did much to enliven the spirits of those present with song and jest, until the sea again became so rough that the skipper ordered everyone below. Mount Etna remained in sight all day, the lower part still obscured by mist, and the snowy peak seeming to be suspended above the clouds. In the evening, when the mountains of Italy were also in sight, just before the sun sank into the sea the white cap of Etna was transformed to rose.

Another bit of excitement had been caused when a mine was sighted floating not far from one of the boats. Rifles were trained on it, and soon a bullet found its mark and the mine blew up with a tremendous explosion, sending a great column of water high into the air. After all the 'excursions and alarms' we were not sorry when we entered Taranto harbour and disembarked. To our relief we found that all the other boats had arrived safely.

From the harbour we were marched to Transit Camp X. The next day Mac and I were detailed to work in the officers' mess, which involved waiting on and some washing up. We found this job quite congenial, as we were able to get plenty of good food after we had served the officers, and we had quite a lot of free time. There were several cinemas showing English and American films, and as we were to find in other Italian towns, the local opera houses had been commandeered as a garrison theatre where ENSA parties performed.

We had noticed a great many funeral corteges passing our camp, with horse-drawn hearses of various types: sombre ones with black-dyed ostrich plumes at the corners of the roofs, and white and gilt ones with cherubs for children and young girls. One day we discovered the nearby cemetery, and what a gruesome sight met our eyes. Before the Allies had invaded Italy, the Americans had bombed the harbour, but some of the bombs had fallen on the cemetery. The wealthier Italians were interred in elaborate tombs, almost like little chapels containing a sort of altar with silver candlesticks, flower holders and portraits of the deceased. These dead were better accommodated than some of the living in the poorer parts of the town. The bodies of the poorer people were pigeonholed in high concrete erections, the coffins being slid in endways, and the opening sealed with a plaque bearing the name of the occupant, along with a flower vase and candle holder. These had been bombed, and the skeletons, many of them shattered, were exposed to view. One lidless coffin, standing upright, contained the skeleton of a little child. In one corner of the cemetery was an ossuary containing square caskets in the same pigeonhole arrangement, and in these were skulls and thighbones. This had also been hit by a bomb. In one of the cells that had lost its plaque, the end of the casket was also missing, disclosing a skull still adorned with long black curly hair, sprinkled with dust. In another corner of the cemetery we noticed a memorial inscribed in English, marking the resting place of some British sailors who had lost their lives in a submarine during the 1914–18 War. This had escaped damage.

The inhabitants of Taranto appeared to live by cutting each other's hair, for I have never seen so many barbers' shops. Mac and I patronised one of these establishments, where we received immediate VIP treatment, having our hair cut and shampooed, our nails manicured, and being given a supply of peanuts to sustain us during the proceedings. The obsequious barber made no fixed charge for his services, leaving the amount to the customer, and thereby receiving more than his own countrymen would have considered adequate.

At that stage we were of course ignorant of the language, which placed us at a disadvantage. We were, however, picking up odd words every day. I found I could deduce the meaning of a lot of words from observing notices. Thus, in the course of my subsequent travels, I noted that 'No Smoking' is in French 'Défense de Fumer', in Italian 'Niente Fumare', in German 'Rauchen Verboten', and in Flemish 'Niet Rooken'. This information was of course completely useless, as I didn't smoke in any language. We were also amused to see the women sitting outside their doors on the pavement combing the livestock out of their children's hair with a small-toothed comb.

After about a week we left Taranto and proceeded up the Adriatic coast by rail, not this time in horse trucks, but in carriages with wooden seats. At a transit camp near Bari we spent a couple of nights under canvas and then had another rail journey to yet one more transit camp on the outskirts of Foggia, where we were housed in a former maternity home. It had no doors or windows, and as the stairs were also missing we had to run up and down a plank with slats across, like so many tame white mice. We put some corrugated iron and cardboard up to the windows and made ourselves at home.

During the five days we were there, Mac and I went three times to the Garrison Theatre, as the opera house was now called. In the foyer was a bust of the composer Giordani, one of whose songs I sometimes sang. The first evening we were there, the show was just about to begin when all the lights failed. Nothing daunted, the producer came onto the stage with a flashlamp and shouted, 'Is there anyone here with a jeep?' Someone called out that he had one parked outside. The producer shouted, 'Will you drive it into the foyer and shine the headlights onto the stage?' In a few moments we heard the sound of the jeep's engine as the vehicle was driven into the foyer, the inner doors were opened wide, and with the improvised footlights the show went on. Another evening some RAF chaps put on their version of the pantomime *Cinderella*, using a lot of topical material. Of course all the female parts were taken by men, and the ugly sisters were particularly funny.

One day Mac and I had been out together, and when we returned to the billet found a list of postings on the notice board. There were now only four of us who had been together on the vehicle mechanics' course in England. Mac and I had been together since the course had started at Luton the previous April, and the other two, Reg Franks and a man whose name I now forget but whose appearance and quiet pleasant manner I well remember, had been with us since the Polytechnic at Kentish Town. Now, to the disappointment of all four of us, Reg and I were posted together to the 53rd Field Regiment, 8th Indian Division, 8th Army, and Mac and Reg's friend to some other unit.

The next morning Reg (a Cornishman) and I found ourselves back on the railway going northwards in a cattle truck. It was a slow journey, as every time we reached a station the locomotive was borrowed for shunting purposes. Leaving the train at last, we were taken by lorry to another transit camp where we spent a night under canvas, and arrived the following afternoon at our new regiment, which was in action against the enemy near Lanciano. As we neared our destination, we could hear the guns getting louder with every mile.

One of the first men we met on arriving at the regiment was making some temporary crosses out of packing case wood to mark the graves of four men who had been killed the previous day when a German shell had scored a direct hit on their dugout.

As we walked to a farm building which was being used as the battery office to report our arrival to the battery sergeant major, some anti-personnel shells burst in the air not far away, and everybody but Reg and I dived for cover. These airbursts were very dangerous, as the shrapnel flew over a wide area, but we didn't see what we could do about it, so just walked into the battery office. Unknowingly, we had established for ourselves a great reputation for cool calm courage, which was quite undeserved as we had merely behaved in foolhardy ignorance. Many years after the war, I accidentally met a man in a printing works in Bradford who had been present that day, and he referred to the incident with admiration. The regiment was in a spearhead position, which meant that by having penetrated the enemy lines, it now had the enemy on both sides, and one battery of guns was firing to the left, and the other to the right.

As it was too late in the day to start digging in, the sergeant major advised us to sleep that night in holes in the side of a haystack. As an added protection, I filled some empty ammunition boxes with earth and built a low rail of them in front of my burrow. Darkness was falling, and as I had no light, nothing to do and nowhere to go, I was just contemplating going to bed when a soldier came along and said, 'Are tha sleeping in theer? Tha's getten noa leet. Come in awr hoile for a bit. We've getten a leet and a fire.' Reg and I went with him across a field, down a slope, crawled through a hole in the side of a bank, and found ourselves in a dugout.

'Ah've browt some guests,' announced our host, 'Come thi ways in, lads, an' mak' thisens at hooam. Move up into t'corner, Joe, an' mak' a bit o' room at front o't'fire. Ha' about brewin' a sup o' tea?'

There was a fireplace made of old petrol tins with a wood fire blazing, and a chimney of bully beef tins joined together end to end. An ammunition box sunk into the wall on its side provided a shelf, and there was even a clock. It was quite home from home. We found that the nucleus of this regiment was the Bolton Territorials, and included the entire Bolton Wanderers football team, except for one man who had been killed in the fighting in Sicily. They had seen service with the BEF in France, had returned from Dunkirk, had been in Palestine and Iraq, and had fought in North Africa, including the victorious battle of El Alamein. They had participated in the invasion of Sicily and Italy, and had recently been involved in fierce fighting on the River Sangro. Having been abroad so long, they were eager to hear from us news of how things were back in England. We spent a pleasant hour or two swapping yarns, and then we returned to our refuge in the haystack, where in spite of the noise of the guns firing close by I was soon asleep and spent a comfortable night.

The sergeant major gave us the next day free to excavate a dug-out for ourselves, close to our new friends. Fortunately the soil was soft and sandy, so we soon had a sizeable cave. We found a lot of concrete posts that had been used for holding up wire to support vines, so we laid them over the roof close together, and threw on top the soil we had extracted, surmounting the lot with foliage for camouflage. Our attempt to make a fireplace was not very successful. I did make a lamp out of a small tin, but although it gave reasonable light it smoked so much that we emerged looking like a couple of chimney sweeps.

I soon found that I need not have worried about leaving the Royal Corps of Signals for the Royal Artillery, for a more friendly lot of men than those of P Battery, 53rd Field would have been hard to find. Battery Sergeant Major Charlie Banks, of whom I was to see a great deal, was one of the best. He was quiet, efficient, had a good sense of humour, and never asked anyone to do anything he wasn't prepared to do himself. The other vehicle mechanics were Lance Sergeant Willie Frame from Glasgow; Bombardier 'Happy' Appleton from Hartlepool; 'Pilky' Pilkington from Bolton; and Doug Porrit from Bradford, whom I met in the printing works in 1957.

The dialects of Lancashire and Yorkshire were a great deal in evidence. One day I heard a chap say, ''Arold, ah don't know ha' tha can cheek to write "On Active Service" on thi letters, for ah've never seen any action on thy part yet, except brewin' tea an' suppin' it.'

''Arold', one of the youngest in the battery, was one of the characters. He went around with a little bag scrounging tea, sugar and milk from the Indian soldiers who made up most of the division. They received extra rations of these commodities as they ate less meat than the Europeans. Several times a day he lit a 'benghazi' (a stove made from a tin full of sand soaked in petrol) and brewed up. He must have had an awful thirst. Appropriately, his job was driving the water wagon. He must have had a phobia against dirt, as he was always either stripping for a thorough wash down, or cleaning his teeth using an enormous amount of toothpaste.

'Curly' Taylor, so called because he was as bald as a bladder of lard, was probably the oldest of the gunners. One day we were sitting around on petrol tins eating our dinner when a gunner came up the field with the sun in his eyes and called, 'Curly, asta seen t'sergeant major?' 'Aye,' said Curly, 'He's reight o'er theer', pointing to the distant horizon. The sergeant major was sitting next to Curly. Pointing to him, Curly said, 'What dosta think this is, a bunch o' grapes?' The gunner blinked and said, 'Ee, I didn't know thi wi' thi 'at on, sergeant major.' 'He didn't know thi wi' thi 'at on,' said Curly, 'Tha'd better get it off and put thi owd night cap on agean so's folks'll know thi!'

The arrival of mail was always one of the highlights of our existence. Since leaving England, owing to my being of 'no fixed abode', my mail hadn't caught up with me, until one red letter day when I received no less than nineteen letters! Reg had twelve, and the rest of the troop about two among the lot. Sorting mine into chronological order and reading them passed a good deal of time quite pleasantly, to say nothing of the time to be spent replying to them by the light of my smoky tin lamp. I learned that Lucy had spent some time with my parents in Sheffield, but had now returned to Ashford, to prepare for the arrival of our baby, expected in April.

January and February seemed to be almost as cold in Italy that year as in England, and we had several snowfalls. One morning, when I had been sleeping in a derelict outbuilding, I woke to find my blankets covered in snow that had drifted in through the gaps. We lived and worked in a morass of mud. Reg and I had soon been found work to do on the vehicles, most of which were battle-scarred. One of our drivers, Sid Finney, came in one day looking rather white. A shell splinter had gone straight through one of his petrol tanks and punctured the one on the other side of the vehicle, fortunately without causing a fire. At first I was hampered by lack of tools, having only a pair of pliers and a jack knife, but after a few days, Sergeant Frame managed to get me a toolbox containing a meagre toolkit, which I gradually augmented by raiding knocked-out tanks and other abandoned vehicles, both British and German.

We seldom stayed long in the same place. One of our first moves was to a farm, where some of us slept in a dilapidated outbuilding. I laid an old door on four bricks for a bed, and when I moved it one morning, I found a scorpion under it. The farmer had a daughter named Maria, a rather odd-looking little squat girl, who would do our washing in return for a piece of soap, which the Italians were unable to obtain. Their usual method of washing clothes was to take them to a stream, where they would rub them and beat them against a smooth boulder. They always carried them in baskets balanced on their heads, often for considerable distances, and on the return journey, when the clothes were wet, they must have been very heavy indeed; in fact the women helped each other to lift them onto their heads.

One day I managed to obtain from the farmhouse a supply of hot water, and had a stand-up bath in a wooden barrel in a stable in the company of some sheep and two white cows. These animals regarded me with such interest in my role of Diogenes that they almost made me blush, and I quickly put my clean clothes on.

My knowledge of the Italian language was improving daily. In Taranto I had bought a little phrase book. It was badly printed on cheap paper, but nevertheless I found it very useful. My vocabulary increased at one bound when I realised that all the musical expressions I had learnt were everyday Italian words. Of course we were all trying to communicate in Italian, and we learnt a fair amount from each other. Very few of the Italians we met could speak English, but the farmer knew some French, and when my Italian failed, we managed to understand each other by interspersing some words of that language. I also found that Latin words were instantly understood, so bits of Beethoven's 'Mass in D' sometimes interlarded my conversation. For some reason, waving our arms seemed to aid communication.

Although the Italians had so recently been our enemies, our relationship with them was for the most part very good. They obviously much preferred British occupation to German, and we usually encountered a friendly attitude. Most essential commodities were in very short supply, and they were eager to beg or barter for anything the troops might have to spare, particularly soap, cigarettes or chocolate. When our meals were served, there were usually a few destitute people hanging round the cookhouse in the hope of being given any leftovers. We were as generous as our limited means allowed, especially to the children, of whom there were a great many. Mussolini had encouraged parents to have large families, as he had believed that a larger population was needed to expand his empire, and he had awarded certificates of merit to those who had excelled in this respect. Some of these certificates were to be seen hanging on the walls in the farmhouses, alongside the almanac which named a saint for almost every day of the year. Observing the fruits of their labours, it was apparent that many of them had earned not only certificates, but medals with bars and clasps. Another intriguing custom was that of hanging the chamber pot on a hook outside the bedroom window.

It was immediately obvious that the womenfolk were very much in the position of second-class citizens. On the farms they seemed to work much harder than the men, tilling the soil with mattocks and two-pronged hoes. Spades, which seemed to be less used, had long straight shafts with no handle. If anything had to be carried, it went on the heads of the women, balanced on a circular pad, and hardly ever held in place with the hands. Once I saw a woman carrying a great tree trunk in this way. Some months later, after we had pushed the Germans further northward, we saw some refugees returning down a mountainside to their home. A woman was carrying a Singer sewing machine complete with the stand and treadle on her head, whilst her husband merely carried a small bundle wrapped in a red neckerchief. During the winter, our gunners had raided a royal forest for firewood, and had a roaring fire going on the hearth of a farmhouse. The Italian men sat so close to it that they had to hold pieces of plywood in front of their shins to prevent them from burning, while their wives sat at the back of the room with small bowls containing smouldering embers, which they occasionally fanned, on the floor under their skirts.

Cooking was usually done on primitive stoves, with embers from the bottom of the fire on the hearthstone for fuel, and there was usually an iron pot hanging over the fire. Bread was baked in a communal oven out in the yard. The fire was lit under a stone slab on which the bread cakes were laid. The bread was dark in colour and heavy in texture. Once I had a meal consisting of a large slice of this and two eggs fried in olive oil, washed down with a glass of *vino rosso*, my feet resting on the back of a young pig that was lying under the table.

The farmhouses were usually of two storeys, the animals housed on the ground floor and the humans on the upper floor. The floors were usually tiled, and the windows were small for coolness in the hot summers. Farms appeared to be worked on the collective system, implements belonging to the community rather than to individual farmers. During the week, the garments of the women resembled Henry Ford's motor cars—any colour so long as they were black—but on Sundays when they went to Mass they arrayed themselves in more colourful clothing, bright red and green stockings being much in evidence.

Of the men, the peasants were much more industrious than the townsmen, many of whom seemed to be idle layabouts, pimps, scroungers or criminals. Some of the countrymen were very ingenious. One who worked quite hard on his farm had grown a crop of maize, and from the stalks he made a very neat fence and chicken house. In the evening he very cleverly made a pair of shoes for one of his children out of a piece of an old tyre.

We spent several weeks in the area around Lanciano. Owing to the bad weather there was a stalemate in the fighting, except for sporadic artillery activity. The Germans sometimes fired their 'Nebelwerfer' six-barrelled mortars which we nicknamed 'Moaning Minnies' because of the demoralising wailing sound the bombs made in their passage through the air. Our regiment was using the famous twenty-five-pounder field guns, which could be used for almost any purpose: infantry support, bombardment, anti-tank, or even anti-aircraft if propped up to give greater elevation. When our gunners were not firing high-explosive shells, they often fired propaganda shells which showered leaflets over the enemy lines, publicising Allied successes and telling the Germans how much better off they would be by surrendering to us. They had similar leaflets printed in English, but they didn't need to shoot them over—they just left them behind for us as they retreated. No doubt the great majority of them found the same use for ours as we did for theirs—in the latrine.

From our position near the farm we had a view of the distant sea, and in the opposite direction the mountains. Once we saw some white-clad Polish troops practising ski-ing down a mountain. Occasionally when there was a lull we were able to go into Lanciano. In the opera house there we saw a concert by an ENSA party which included Sandy Powell, the Rotherham-born comedian, whose familiar accents seemed to bring home a bit nearer. I bought some sweet almonds in Lanciano, and finding them good had hoped to be able to buy some more to send home, but we moved before I was able to go there again.

There was a very attractive little boy named Nicolo at the farm, of whom we all made a great fuss. One evening when I was on guard duty, the family were in great consternation because darkness had fallen and Nicolo could not be found. I joined the search, and at last found him in a distant farmhouse with some of the gunners, listening to an Italian lad who was playing an accordion. He and I went back hand in hand, to the relief and delight of his family, to whom I explained that it was all the fault of the 'soldati Inglese' who had taken him there.

Chapter 26
'The Gustav Line'

ON EASTER SUNDAY 1944 our unit left the Lanciano area and travelled south until we reached the River Sangro, beside which we camped. The rain poured in torrents, and I spent an uncomfortable night trying to sleep with a gun crew in the cab of a 'quad'—a gun-towing vehicle. The available space was quite inadequate for the number of men crowded into it and my place was on the steel floor, which abounded in bolt heads and other projections, curled in an arc around the gear lever. As if on a given signal, hundreds of bullfrogs began to croak, and kept it up all night, until as if someone had pressed a switch they all stopped as suddenly as they had begun.

During the next day a large tent was erected, and I was glad to get a space in that. In the evening a young fellow whom we called Claude, although it wasn't his real name, was reading Jerome K. Jerome's *Three Men in a Boat*, which was causing him great amusement. It was the last time I was to see him, as very soon after he was one of a party of men who were hit by a mortar bomb, and he and three others were killed. The only survivor was an officer, who although wounded managed to drive the truck back.

The Allied advance on Rome, by whatever route, had for a long time been barred by the heavily defended town of Cassino, backed by the dominating Monastery Hill. It was believed that the Germans were using the historic monastery as an observation post, though this has since been denied. In any event this eminence enabled the enemy to survey and accurately shell anything that moved on the surrounding plain, and already three fierce and costly battles had been unsuccessfully fought to dislodge them. We knew that we were being quietly moved to the other side of the Apennines to take part in another onslaught on Cassino.

From our position on the Sangro, we moved to a camp site near the village of Guglionesi. In the evening, Reg and I were standing by the tent talking when strains of music were borne to our ears. Going to investigate, we found two of our gunners, one with a cornet and the other with an old accordion. I joined in with my voice, and together we rendered a number of items. Among those who gathered around to listen was the battery clerk, Sam Howard. It turned out that he was a pianist, and he suggested to me that we should go into the village and try to find someone who had a piano that they would allow him to play. It seemed a good idea to me, so together we trudged off.

It was approaching dusk when we reached the village, which largely consisted of semi-ruinous medieval stone buildings and narrow steep flagged streets. Finding a piano there was like looking for a needle in a haystack, but we were a resourceful pair. A crowd of children was soon at our heels, as always, begging for chocolate, and for cigarettes and matches for 'papa'. There was one little mite whom the others said had neither mother nor father, as they had been killed by a bomb. I gave him half a bar of chocolate that I happened to have in my pocket. Then we saw a jeweller's shop, so we went in, and to gain an introduction Sam asked him if he could repair his watch, which could only be described as a lump of scrap, and had a case that appeared to be made of lead. The watchmaker gravely inspected it, and after condemning it as beyond redemption, tried to sell him a very old-fashioned lady's watch for a somewhat extortionate price.

Then Sam brought up the subject of a piano. The man said there were some in the village, but they were privately owned, and he wasn't very helpful, though polite. We tried the same game at another shop without success, and then we plunged into a labyrinth of back streets, steep, slippery and evil-smelling, where shady-looking characters cast sidelong glances at us. Next we saw two men coming out of a billiard saloon, so we approached them with an affable 'buona sera', and asked them if they knew where there was a piano we could use. They conferred together, and then one of them took us through more back streets to a carpenter's shop. By now it was dark. The carpenter had just finished work and was closing. The Italian who had taken us there explained what we wanted. The carpenter said he believed the family who owned a piano where having their evening meal. He left us for a moment, and when he returned we were taken upstairs, and to my great astonishment we found ourselves inside the best-furnished house I had seen in Italy. The walls were tastefully papered, and there was a modern dining suite in natural oak. We passed through this room into another, also well furnished, where our delighted eyes fell upon a lovely black German piano, a violin and a piano accordion.

The lady of the house invited Sam to play the piano, and whilst he was playing she showed me a book of music in Braille, explaining that it belonged to her son, who was blind. Presently this youth was led into the room. He was short and deformed, with a hunch back, and wore dark glasses. Having taken some music with me, I then began to sing a song in Italian, to Sam's accompaniment, and seldom have I seen a face light up as did that boy's. It was easy to see that music was his greatest joy. He begged for more, and kept asking for his favourite pieces, some of which we were able to render. As he spoke slowly, in standard Italian (not dialect), and his conversation was all about music, I could understand him quite well. Then he played himself, with many apologies for his deficiency, but we found that in fact he was an excellent pianist with a very fine touch.

At their invitation, we returned the next night, and Reg and 'Happy' (Lance Bombardier Appleton) went with us. I took all the music I had with me, and we spent a most enjoyable evening. The family had dressed up for the occasion, and treated us very courteously, giving us glasses of wine.

Leaving Guglionesi, we moved west across Italy to a position near the village of Mignano, to the south of Cassino. It was now April, and each day was hotter than the last. Our battle-dress had been discarded in favour of khaki drill shirts and shorts. As a precaution against malaria-carrying mosquitoes, an hour before sundown we had to change our shorts for KD slacks, roll down our sleeves and button our shirts up to the neck. Our hands and faces had to be anointed with anti-mosquito cream, and we had to sleep under our mosquito nets, or if we were in a dugout, with one sealing the entrance. As quinine was no longer available, the scientists had invented a substitute called mepacrine, and we had to take one of these each day for six days, missing a day before continuing to take them. They were yellow tablets, and tended to give us a yellow complexion. To prevent the mosquitoes breeding, all stagnant pools were covered with old motor oil. During the Sicily campaign, our Army had sustained more casualties from malaria than from the enemy, but owing to the precautions I have described, only one of our men had malaria in Italy. He was a water tanker driver, whose job entailed drawing water from any available source, after testing its purity and chlorinating it.

Our new camp site was in a deep ravine, and as the enemy were giving the area some unwelcome attention, Reg, Happy and I were not sorry to find an abandoned dugout in the hillside which had been dug by some Americans who had been there before us. We set to work enlarging and improving it, digging it out to a depth of about five feet. Although this did not give us enough room to stand upright, by the time we had reached this stage we were hot and tired with digging and slinging the earth out, and decided it would suffice. It was roofed with tree branches we had cut, and on top of those was a layer of sandbags, earth piled on those, then a waterproof sheet, and finally camouflage. There was a narrow entrance, which was covered at night with a mosquito net and a blackout sheet. A big bonnet rug served as a carpet, and we covered the walls with empty sandbags, secured with wooden pegs driven in to stop the earth from crumbling and falling onto our beds. Along one side was a shelf made of saplings lashed together with signal wire, and on this we kept our small packs, mugs, mess tins, books, a petrol stove for brewing up at night, and other odds and ends. Behind one of the sandbags was a secret hole where we kept our tea, sugar and tinned milk. Two ammunition boxes on their sides were fitted into other recesses, one of them containing the battery which could be connected to a headlamp bulb to supply our light, and a little clock. On the walls we had a calendar with a picture of Canterbury Cathedral, photos of our wives, and a picture postcard. It was quite a little home for us. As we lay in bed at night, we could hear a nightingale singing, its song mingling with the less pleasant sound of gunfire, which by now was so familiar that we paid about as much attention to it as to a clock ticking.

Some of our men, scorning a dugout, had pitched a tent at the bottom of the ravine. This was all very well until one night when the enemy guns found our range, and these chaps came flying head first into our dugout, landing on top of us. Our welcome was less than cordial, but in the circumstances we could hardly refuse them hospitality.

The next day, these gunners, stripped to the waist and brown from the sun, were digging themselves a dugout fairly close to ours, when we saw lying in the sun on the pile of soil they had thrown out the biggest snake I have ever seen. Someone went for a rifle, but the snake must have guessed his intention, for before he returned it had slithered away through the vegetation down the ravine, and we never saw it again.

In the late afternoon of the 30th of April, I was having a belated shave after a busy day when a telegram was handed to me. Quickly opening it, I read, 'Darling daughter born am well and fit Lucy Hatfield'. Christine Jane had been born on the 24th, and the telegram had reached me by the way of Cairo. It was a great relief to get it, as I had been wondering for some days how this matter was going. I subsequently learned that Lucy had not had an easy time, and we owed much to the skill of the doctor that we had a whole baby. We had rather expected a boy, as Christine was the first girl in the Hatfield family in two generations. The wives of both Reg and Mac were expecting babies about the same time, and I believe they both had girls. Naturally I was disappointed that I had not been able to be with Lucy and to see our child, but was somewhat encouraged by strong rumours that our regiment would soon be going back to England. Unfortunately this was not to be the case.

One of our Bren carriers needed a new engine, and accompanied by two driver mechanics I was sent to the Indian Division workshop to put it in. 'Indian Workshops' was a grandiose title for a field containing one or two large tents and a mobile crane. The job turned out to be fraught with difficulty, as the replacement engine was not of the right type, being designed for a Ford three-ton lorry. Both vehicles employed the Ford V8 engine, but there were many differences of detail.

There was a very limited time in which to do the job, as the carrier was required to participate in the coming assault on the Gustav Line. I was up at 5.30 on three mornings, and on one of the days I worked until 10.30 pm. I had to change the sump, oil pump, starter motor, exhaust manifolds, dynamo, fan assembly, carburettor and all controls, change oil and water gauges from electric to pneumatic, and alter the whole ignition system. The starter motor became a combination of two types, and had to be welded. An oil pipe was accidentally broken and had to be repaired. All the time, the sun blazed down and rivers of sweat ran down our faces, mingling with the dust that was blowing about to form a mask through which only the whites of our eyes showed.

The two driver mechanics helped to the best of their ability, and the Indian mechanics manipulated the crane, soldered the broken oil pipe, and drilled holes where necessary. Late in the afternoon of the third day, the engine burst into life, and we drove the vehicle back to our own lines, arriving in a cloud of dust, almost unrecognisable to our mates with our faces caked with sweat, dust and grease. The starter motor was still not fixed, and I fell to work on it the moment we arrived, while two of our fitters adjusted the brakes and the caterpillar tracks. I was struggling in the bottom of the Bren carrier trying to fit the rebuilt starter motor when the sergeant major of the Royal Electrical and Mechanical Engineers came to inspect our work, and seeing the state I was in, still soaked in perspiration, he said, 'For God's sake, lad, take a breather!' When he saw all the difficulties that had been overcome, he said he would recommend me for a higher trade rating. I succeeded in fixing the starter motor, tidied up the last details, and an hour later the carrier moved off with its crew exactly on schedule to take part in the big attack. It played its part, and returned safely with no casualties.

At 11.00 pm on May the 11th the attack on the Gustav Line had commenced, with the most terrific artillery barrage the 8th Army had ever inflicted on the enemy. Our own regiment participated, and there were some casualties among the signallers. The following extract from a contemporary issue of the *Indian News Review* gives a good account.

> The heroic part played in the fighting in Italy by the 8th Indian Division has added fresh laurels to the proud record of the Indian Army in this war. Full details have now been released of the Division's activities during the last eight and a half months, and the formation has been described as the 8th Army's crack division. Covering without break or respite the longest distance of any division in the 8th Army, in one month alone the Division advanced 220 miles. Tributes to this accomplishment are paid by Michael Reynolds in a dispatch to the B.B.C. He writes:-
>
> "Details have been given of the distinguished part played by the 8th Indian Division during the Italian campaign under the command of Major General Dudley Russell.
>
> "The Division, like all Indian Divisions, is made up of troops from the United Kingdom, as well as Indians. For instance, the Divisional Field Artillery, and one battalion in each infantry brigade

are British. Indian troops include Punjabis, Sikhs, Pathans, Gurkhas, Madrasis, Digras, and men of other races. Individual units served under Wavell in Egypt and Eritrea, but the division as a whole had not been in action before arriving in Italy last September.

"During the next month or two the 8th Indian Division fought its way slowly forward across the Eifurno, Trigno, Sangro and Moro rivers.

"It gained the respect not only of the rest of the 8th Army, but also of the elite German Paratroops opposing it. Friend and foe alike came to appreciate the skill in night operations and in mountain fighting, its aptitude for infiltration tactics, and its capacity for winkling out the enemy from house to house in strongly defended villages such as Tuffillo and Mozzagrogne.

"The winter came, and these troops from sun-scorched India surprised everyone by having a lower sick list than any other division in Italy.

"With the approach of spring the 8th Indian Division facilitated the regrouping of the Allied Armies by taking over from two other divisions a twenty mile stretch in front of the Orsogna area and another at Cassino. Then by gradual stages they themselves were moved to the western side of the Apennines; for some weeks General Russell had the unique experience of commanding one bridge in the Orsogna area and another at Cassino. But by April the whole division was concentrated between Cassino and the Liri river. Perhaps concentrated is the wrong word. At first General Russell held his front with a thin screen of troops, while his main strength was further back training for the coming assault on the Gustav Line, and in particular learning how to row. Luckily the Division included a good many men who had grown up by the great rivers of India. They formed the nucleus of the splendid crews which took the assault craft across the Rapido. One of the chief factors making for the success of that crossing was the Division's skilful use of concealment and deception. Indian troops entered whole-heartedly into this. You could hear them chuckling to themselves at the crafty way they had hidden their vehicles and ammunition.

"When on the night of May 11th the blow was finally launched it became obvious that the enemy had in fact been taken by surprise and had no idea how much strength had been piled against him. His confusion was aggravated by various feint attacks and demonstrations for which he fell very thoroughly.

"Nevertheless the fighting was very severe. Divisional engineers, all Indian, did a splendid job during the battle, indeed it was they who built the first bridge across the river. General Leese himself has said that this was an action of decisive importance."

Once the Rapido had been crossed, the full might of the Allied Armies was hurled against the ruins of Cassino, and the Germans were finally driven out. The honour of taking Monastery Hill fell to Polish troops.

Our regiment entered Cassino shortly after its fall. It is impossible to describe the state of the town, which had been completely annihilated. Not a single building had escaped destruction. The ruins of some were still blazing. Some of the buildings on Monte Cassino had been so pulverised with bombs and artillery fire that it was difficult to distinguish the material of which they had been built from the natural rocks and boulders. On the summit stood the famous monastery. The immense strategic value of the monastery was obvious, for its commanded a view of many square miles. Whilst it has since been denied that the Germans used it as an observation post, it was very difficult at the time to believe that this was not so, as they had directed damaging fire on Allied troops for many weeks.

Bulldozers had cleared a semblance of a road through the rubble, and filled in the worst craters so that vehicles could pass. Two of these that had recently been hit by shells were still burning, and had to be dragged off the road out of our way. Deep bomb craters were full of water. The atmosphere was pervaded by a smell of stagnation, of burning, of cordite, and of death and decay. Notices stating that there were mines and booby traps had been placed at frequent intervals by sappers. Bits of equipment strewed the roadsides. German sandbagged defences were still in place. A pall of dust was raised by our wheels. No one lingered on that road, for it was still under spasmodic shell fire, as was shown by the two burning trucks. It was a spectacle to arouse awe and horror in the most hardened, and thoughts arose of the hundreds of lives of both friend and foe that had been given in the four bitter battles fought for this vast heap of rubble. Hereabouts lay their mortal remains, as shattered as the miserable buildings for which they had striven.

Past the town we turned to our left and proceeded down a country road where many other evidences of the conflict remained. Wagon lines were established, and preparations for the night being made when the sergeant major announced that he needed eight guides to go with ammunition wagons up to the guns, which were some miles forward, and I had the ill luck to be one of those chosen for this duty. As none of us knew the way to the gun position, it was rather a case of the blind leading the blind, but as the drivers of the trucks were all Indians, it was necessary that an English-speaking soldier should travel on each wagon. I was about to experience the most hectic night of my life.

From our lines we travelled in the back of a covered 15cwt truck, in the dark, to the ammunition point, so we had no idea where we were or what route we had followed. Eight three-tonners had been loaded with twenty-five-pounder shells and charges, and in pitch darkness we climbed aboard. Only sidelights were allowed at any time, and these were covered with a tin disc with an $\frac{1}{8}$" hole punched in it to make the vehicle just visible to oncoming traffic. At the rear there was a small lamp that directed some light forward onto the axle casing which was painted white and carried the unit's number. The sergeant major rode in the first truck, and I had been assigned to the last truck of the convoy with the world's worst driver, a Maharatta with a big black moustache. He knew about as much of my language as I knew of his, so conversation was difficult to say the least.

We had not gone a mile when he took a wrong turn, and by the time he was back on the road the rest of the convoy was out of sight, so we were on our own. Every time we stopped, the engine stalled, so we were soon far behind the rest of the convoy. After a time we found the road blocked by a long stream of traffic, and during the next couple of hours made very little progress. I dismounted from the truck and found a distracted MP who told me we were on the right road, but far behind the rest of the convoy. The various convoys were inextricably entangled.

We turned off where I had been directed, and followed an ambulance along a dreadful track where I fully expected the truck to overturn at any moment. A small white patch of light that I saw ahead on a bad bend proved when we came to it to be the axle light of an overturned ambulance. No one was in it. It was more by luck than management that we were not in the same plight, as it was inconceivable that a worse driver could exist. On one occasion the wheels dropped into a hole from which he was unable to remove them, and I found it necessary to take the wheel and get the vehicle out myself. Knowing the sensitivity of the Indians, I was anxious not to offend him, and realising his reluctance to let me drive his vehicle, I moved back into the passenger seat and tried to resign myself.

One of the worst moments of that nightmare journey came when we reached a bridge that had been partly demolished. It was the blackest of nights, and here was this bridge, with a missing parapet, half the roadway gone, a hole, a hump, and two right-angle bends all together. A good driver in broad daylight would have had difficulty in negotiating it. I prepared to jump out, but found myself on the edge of a sheer drop. By some miracle, another Indian then materialised out of the darkness, and he began calling instructions. We made two or three false moves, trembled on the brink, the engine raced, and then by the grace of God found ourselves safely over. Why we escaped crashing into the river below I still regard as one of the miracles of the age.

I had been told to look out for an officer who would tell me where to turn off. There had been no sign of any officer, and I began to think that we must be on the wrong road, as nothing else was in sight now. It was not a very cheerful thought to be lost with an incapable driver and a truckload of high explosive on an atrocious road in the dark, with mines everywhere, making towards the German lines.

At last we came to a group of men, including an MP, standing at a crossroads. I asked them where I was, and to my dismay found that I had bypassed my own regiment and had arrived at the gun position of the 3rd Field Regiment. As no less than three trucks which should have brought ammunition to this regiment had not arrived, the officer asked me to leave my load with them. My position was difficult, as I was responsible for the load being delivered to its correct destination. On the other hand, it was now practically impossible to get it there before dawn, and if daylight should find me still in this area I stood a grave risk of being shelled, as this road, known as Route 6, would be an enemy target. Here was a regiment of our division, short of ammunition for the barrage which I knew was to be fired next morning, whilst I had about three tons of the stuff, liable to be blown up with any stray shell. Besides, there was always a chance that their missing trucks had arrived at our regiment's position, being as lost as I was. Turning to the officer I said, 'Make that an order, sir, and I'll leave it.'

After being directed down a dark narrow lane, we found a bombardier who was fed up with waiting for the ammo. He, a gunner, the Indian and I had just started to unload the shells when enemy aircraft appeared. We immediately became the centre of anti-aircraft activity. At any other time I should have dived for shelter, but too weary to bother, we just jammed on our tin hats to guard against falling shrapnel, and carried on with the job of unloading the heavy boxes of shells and charges and stacking them at the roadside. The long streams of red and green tracers and flak provided a pretty enough spectacle, but none of the spectators were in any mood to enjoy it. The heavy crunch of falling bombs was too near to be pleasant.

By the time our load was off, the fireworks display had abated. I asked the bombardier how to get back onto the main road, as the lane was too narrow to turn the vehicle. All I could get out of him was a gruff 'I don't know. Good night', with which he disappeared into a hole, wherein no doubt was his bed.

I took a walk along the road to see if there was any place suitable for turning, and found a large gateway. In spite of my directions, the Indian was unable to accomplish the manoeuvre, so we had to proceed further, in the direction of the enemy. It was with relief that I managed to see a large courtyard on the right where we contrived to turn. Returning down the narrow lane, we had the atrocious luck to meet three other large wagons coming in the opposite direction, also driven by Indians. An attempt was made to pass, but we jammed against the side of the leading vehicle. This was the last straw. Ignoring the jabbering Indians, I got out and sat down on the bank to watch the performance. After each had made an unsuccessful attempt to pull free, the two drivers made a concerted effort, raced their engines, let in their clutches, and with a rendering of metal and canvas tore themselves apart, my chariot charging precariously upon the opposite bank, regardless of the danger of mines. Here it was at least out of the way, and the other trucks were able to pass. Not until the truck was safely back on the road again did I resume my seat.

A system of one-way traffic was in operation, so we could not return by the way we had come. At the crossroads the MP directed me to the correct road, and thence I had to find my own way. At every junction the Indian asked me which road he was to take, and I just had to make a blind decision. At one point I made a mistake, and to get back onto the right road my bright driver drove straight across a triangular piece of ground which had been taped off because it had not been cleared of mines! My hair stood on end.

A bit further on, we reached an open space where the road seemed to divide into a number of tracks. Dawn was just beginning to break and looking around I recognised Mount Cairo which I had seen the previous day, and which enabled me to establish some sense of direction. I told my driver to turn round and follow a certain apology for a road which seemed to lead the right way. In the middle of this wide open piece of ground stood a solitary truck, and with ·all that room to turn, we had to bang into it.

My hunch proved to be correct, as the way I had chosen presently brought us into the ghastly skeleton of Cassino. The valleys were full of mist, from which rose hills looking like islands in a white sea. Cassino had looked terrible in the red light of the night before; it looked even worse in the cold grey light of dawn. The house on the corner that had burnt so brilliantly was burning still, but dull red and sullen. Half a broken hotel sign hung from a shattered fragment of wall. A few sappers were about already, starting on their dangerous tasks among the ruins. A party of military police came along in a jeep and asked who we were. When I told them, one said, 'You're the chaps we've been looking for all night.' I replied, 'I wish to goodness you'd found us', and asked them if they knew where 53rd Field's wagon lines were, but they didn't. As we had by now almost passed through Cassino, I told Jehu to turn round, and as we approached a side road he suddenly became excited, and indicated that he had recognised the way.

Soon we had reached the ammunition point, and he was back in his own unit, but I still had to find my way back to our wagon lines—no easy matter as my movements the previous night had been in the dark, and there was nothing I could recognise. Setting out on foot, I had not gone far when I saw a jeep coming towards me containing some Canadians and a fat soldier whom I recognised as one of our gunners. They stopped, and grinning broadly Fatty explained, 'Now I'll be able to find my way! This is one of our chaps.' He had been out on the same job, and was also lost. Wearily we trudged along together, vainly trying to recognise some feature that would guide us back to our lines. There were many signs of the recent battle around: graves of friend and foe, German jackboots, rifles, ammunition and all kinds of abandoned equipment. Shattered tanks, Bren carriers and guns were also plentiful. By now the sun was rising and the unsavoury smells that a battle begets were beginning to be in evidence.

Somehow we found our way, and at last trudged into camp exhausted and unshaven. Breakfast was just being served, and a mug of tea was never more welcome. After that I just crawled into my blankets and 'died' until late in the morning when someone woke me to say the sergeant major wanted to see me. Naturally he wanted to know what had become of my load of ammunition. When I explained, he said that one of 3rd Field's wagons had turned up at our gun position, and he had commandeered their ammunition, so everybody was even.

Shortly after this hair-raising episode, the Gustav Line was broken and the 8th Army moved forward to attack the Adolf Hitler Line. This was a formidable line of defence where the mountainous nature of the country was of the greatest advantage to a defending army. Concrete gun emplacements had been constructed, and in some places tanks buried except for the turret for use as artillery. Field Marshall Kesselring was given no time to regroup his defeated armies after the Gustav Line breakthrough, and the invincible 8th Army pressed on with such vigour and in such strength that this much-vaunted line very rapidly shared the fate of the Gustav Line. From here our advance along the famous Route 6 was practically unchecked. The RAF pounded the fleeing German columns, smashing bridges to delay them while our pursuing artillery brought down barrages on them. Long stretches of road were strewn with the blackened twisted wrecks of shattered and burnt-out vehicles, tanks and guns, including many of the self-propelled guns our enemy had been using for harassing purposes. The aerodrome at Aquino with its wrecked hangars became one of our gun positions. At this time the enemy were fleeing so fast to escape total destruction that they rapidly drew out of range of our guns, and we had to make almost daily advances. After we had passed the picturesque castle of Roccasecca on its high hill, we reached Arce, which was an important road junction on the way to Rome. Here, as at many other places, the artillery was in action only a few hours after the Germans had left the town. In this area we were met by crowds of refugees returning from hiding in the mountains to what remained of their homes. They clustered round our improvised cookhouse begging for food. They carried on their heads the possessions they had contrived to save from the clutches of the robbing Germans, ranging from pitiful little bundles to sewing machines, which were much prized, and handed down from mother to daughter.

One of our 15cwt trucks had been badly damaged at the front by a bomb, so we had removed the cab and power unit, and had the chassis side members bent towards each other at the front, and a towing attachment welded onto the apex of the triangle thus formed, converting the truck into a very useful trailer on which we fitters carried our tools and spares. One morning, Willie Frame and I were unloading the trailer before breakfast. We lifted out a very large spare wheel which bounced out of our grasp and ran away down the field, straight towards the tent occupied by our CO, Captain Knibbs. We raced after it, but were unable to reach it before it scored a direct hit on our respected commander's habitation and brought it down rounds his ears. Fearing he might have been killed, we were relieved to see him disentangling himself from the wreckage in his pyjamas, under the impression that his tent had been hit by a shell. Fortunately he had emerged unscathed, the only damage being to his Primus stove, which I then spent most of the day repairing.

All along the line of our advance the devastation was appalling. Very few buildings were left intact, and many were completely destroyed. Villages were reduced to mere piles of rubble. Everything of value had been taken away by the Germans, and some things that they had been unable to remove they had wantonly destroyed. Hundreds of civilians were left destitute. We soon became familiar with the universal story in the pidgin Italian we had learned to comprehend: 'Niente mangiare, niente vino, niente scarpi, Tedeschi portare tutti.' In other words, 'No food, no wine, no shoes, Germans have taken all.'

Much of this ill-gotten loot never reached its intended destination. More than once I saw the ruined relics of some Italian's former possessions scattered around a burnt-out German vehicle. The number of enemy war vehicles destroyed was almost incredible; their twisted remains lined the verges for miles. Many of them had been pushed off the roads and had rolled down precipitous hillsides. When a motor stopped because of a mechanical breakdown, it often happened that the Allied Army was so close that there was no time to rectify the trouble and the vehicle had to be abandoned. Before leaving them the Germans usually tried to render them useless to us. Sometimes they set fire to them, and at other times removed and smashed vital parts. Nevertheless, so swiftly did we advance that in a few cases vehicles were left intact and undamaged. These were sometimes overhauled by our fitters and put into commission.

We were somewhat elated when we found one of these vehicles abandoned with only a missing battery and a punctured radiator, which I temporarily repaired with chewing gum. It was the very thing we had been needing for a workshop truck. Formerly it had been a mobile cookhouse, and had a huge caravan-like body. Soon we had fitted a battery and installed a bench and two vices and all the tools and equipment formerly carried on the trailer. The name of the make was 'Büssing Nag', which gave rise to many quips. Its one great fault was that the radiator was in the habit of boiling when climbing the Apennines. This was due to the fact that our repairs to the radiator had considerably reduced its cooling area. The heat of the country also had its effect, and consequently we had to carry gallons of water and to stop at frequent intervals to fill the radiator.

Some time later, we found an abandoned Citroën truck, which was a superior type of vehicle, and we were anxious to reclaim it. An Italian told us that only half an hour before we arrived, the truck had stopped there, and after the German occupants had tried feverishly to get it going again, they had dismounted the gun it carried, thrown it down a bank, fired revolver bullets into the tyres, and smashed the distributor and carburettor; after which they ran away down the road just in time to escape the Indian infantry. We decided to tow it away with the Büssing Nag in the hope of being able to obtain suitable spares later.

On a long steep ascent which caused our radiator to boil, we were held up by a long convoy of Bren carriers driven by Indians, and some vehicles of the Argyll and Sutherland Highlanders. The jam was caused by a one-way traffic diversion where a bridge over a river had been blown up, and realising that we should be there for some time, we got out to stretch our legs. The road at this point was a ledge along a hillside, and on our left the land fell away steeply to the valley below. We became aware of an aeroplane flying along the valley at a little above our own height. It was a British plane, and when it was almost level with us, we were amazed suddenly to see puffs of black smoke from the wings, and to hear the sound of the plane's cannons. A burst of shells hit the bank in front of our two trucks, narrowly missing a Bren carrier. We realised with horror that the pilot must have seen our two German trucks, which still had the original paint and markings, and believed them to be part of an enemy convoy! There was mad rush away from the road, and we flung ourselves down under what cover we could find. The plane circled around, and the pilot must have discovered his mistake, for he departed without firing again.

All efforts to obtain a distributor for the Citroën having failed, we were soon obliged to abandon it, after having removed a few parts that we thought might be useful. Our morale was very high as our advance continued unabated for 220 miles in less than a month, as was mentioned in the extract from the *Indian News Review*. We entered Spoleto four hours after our infantry had driven out the enemy. Their withdrawal was not a retreat—it was a rout. The Italians had decorated the town with bunting, and received us with great enthusiasm, lining the streets and clapping their hands with shouts of 'Viva!' Some of the women threw flowers to us, and some handed us bottles of wine.

To delay the pursuit, the enemy tried to destroy all bridges behind themselves, but so rapidly did we chase them that more than once their engineers were caught at their task by our advance units before they had time to complete it. Where the bridges had been destroyed, our engineers quickly erected Bailey bridges, or made diversions with bulldozers. They performed some marvellous feats.

Once when a company of American engineers had built a bridge over a river, they erected a notice stating the length of the bridge and the number of hours in which it had been completed by X Company US Army Engineers. Shortly afterwards a bridge of similar length was built by a company of South African Army Engineers who erected a notice carrying the same information, to which was added 'There is nothing remarkable about that'.

Some while later I went on guard at midnight beside a similar river. About a hundred yards away were the ruins of a bridge which had been blown up that day. At about quarter past twelve I heard a number of lorries arriving, and a great clatter of steel being unloaded, so I went to investigate, and found that a company of British engineers had arrived to erect a Bailey bridge. By the time my spell of guard duty ended at 2.00 am the bridge had been completed some while, and transport and guns were rolling over it. The Royal Engineers didn't bother to erect a notice.

Our northward advance brought many changes of scenery, which became increasingly beautiful. One scene which lives in my memory was the great waterfall cascading down the precipice at Tivoli, gold and red in the rays of the setting sun.

Chapter 27
'A City of Silence'

ONE SUNNY June morning we were approaching the village of Bastia. Not for the first time the mind found a fitting application for the line so often sung in the calm atmosphere of an English church: 'Where every prospect pleases, and only man is vile'. Only four hours before the Germans had been in the village through which we were passing. A couple of houses were still burning, and as our column proceeded, we saw the wreckage of our enemy's equipment: shattered and burnt-out tanks, trucks and self-propelled guns which had been dragged to the sides of the roads out of way. Here and there lay mules and horses, stiff and rigid, already the prey of swarms of flies, and lying face down in the gutter the body of an unfortunate civilian.

There was a side turning along the road, marked by a finger post bearing the direction 'Assisi'; I tried to remember what I could about Assisi and St Francis, but I could only recollect that a famous hymn was ascribed to him. We left the main road, and camouflaged our vehicles by driving them as nearly as possible under the olive trees. Our camp was in the midst of the vast plain that lies in Umbria, bounded by foothills and mountains. In front of us, at a distance of perhaps a couple of miles, a large white church with a fine dome rose above the olive groves in what seemed at that distance to be splendid isolation. This, I was to learn, was the church of 'S. Maria degli Angeli'.

But there was an even more imposing sight than this. Slightly to our right rose the great hill of Mount Subasio, itself dwarfed by the mighty range of the Apennines in the background. An ancient ruined castle crowned Mount Subasio, and at a somewhat lower level of the slopes extended the picturesque and historic city of Assisi. At its extremity on our left stood a strange and vast edifice with rows of Romanesque colonnades, and a square-towered church superimposed. The grey buildings of the medieval city were cleanly divided from the steep olive-clad slopes below by an ancient encircling wall. The towers and domes of several other churches rose from the compact huddle of houses with their old grey walls and old red roofs. Assisi has been described as a city of silence, and this epithet certainly matched my first impression of the place. Not a sound was heard from it, nor could we see any sign of life, except that at intervals the sound of church bells was borne on the air. Surely this old city must have been deserted by its inhabitants in the Middle Ages, and left there unaltered and unspoilt, with only the ghosts of the bell ringers remaining. The dominating edifice on the left of the city proved on closer acquaintance to be the Basilica and Convent of St Francis of Assisi. A large building at the other end of the city had a huge red cross painted on the roof, and had been used by the Germans as a hospital. Both sides had respected Assisi as an open religious city, and as no fighting had taken place there, it was completely undamaged.

No sooner had we pitched our camp in the olive grove than it became apparent that a storm was approaching, and we hastily dug a channel round our tent to carry the water away. Barely had we completed this when we were assailed by a thunderstorm of almost tropical severity, and the rain continued for two days, the first we had had for weeks. Our gun emplacements were waterlogged, and the enemy took advantage of the respite to establish defences, which checked our advance.

After a couple of days we moved our wagon lines even nearer to Assisi, and I had several opportunities to climb the steep slope of Mount Subasio and to enter the city through one of its ancient narrow gates. About this time there was a lull in the fighting as far as we were concerned, and I rejoiced in this opportunity to enjoy the unique atmosphere of this calm place, which has been described as the Nazareth of Italy.

My first visit was full of surprises. Since my arrival in Italy I had never been in a single place on which the war had not left hideous scars. Here was the first exception. Assisi's sanctity having been respected by both sides, and being just off the beaten track, its ancient streets had not known the clatter of tanks and guns. For once we saw shops stocked with a reasonable supply of goods, moreover at reasonable prices, as the better-paid Americans had not yet been there. The inhabitants were for the most part well dressed, and there were many pretty girls to be seen. The shops were soon thronged with our men buying souvenirs for wives, mothers and girlfriends. One shop near the Basilica was full of carved wooden figures of Christ, Mary and various saints. Whilst these were of course of special interest to the Roman Catholics among us, all had to admire the excellence of the craftsmanship and the fine details of the carving of these exquisite figures. I chose an effigy of St Francis with his hand on the head of a sheep: every minute detail perfectly carved even down to his fingernails and a twist in his girdle. It cost me the Italian equivalent of £1.12½ at the prevailing rate of exchange, and was the cheapest and the best souvenir I ever bought. Carefully packed in a box I made, and protected with cotton wool and shavings, it reached home safely and is still admired as it stands on our mantlepiece.

My steps inevitably brought me to the Church of St Francis. It was a church upon a church, each of the stature of a cathedral. The lower church, vaulted like a crypt, was adorned with frescoes painted by such old Italian masters as Simone Martini, and built in the Romanesque style. It was a place of silence and peace. Near the great altar with its high sconces stood a papal throne, under a canopy covered in cloth of gold. Above the altar was a masterly painting depicting St Francis ascending into Heaven. Perhaps most beautiful of all were the paintings in the little side chapel of St Martino. Several times I returned here to hear the robed friars chanting their vespers, as they and their predecessors had been doing at this same hour for hundreds of years. Unfortunately I was never able to gain access to the upper church, which by all accounts is even more impressive than the lower, and has frescoes painted by Giotto.

Assisi had other ancient sanctuaries, the churches of St Clara, St Ruffino and others no less remarkable for the artistry lavished upon them. In the big square stood Assisi's most ancient building of all: the pre-Christian Temple of Minerva. What changes the centuries had wrought since its classical columns were first raised by the early pagan inhabitants of Assisi, yet they still stood, battered but intact; though the building once devoted to the worship of Minerva was now dedicated to a Christian saint.

Standing near the Church of St Clara, I gazed over the city wall across the beautiful plain of Umbria. Seldom can a lovelier scene have been painted by nature. Clear-cut in the unique golden light of that region was the distant line of hills bounding the plain, and beyond mountain peak on mountain peak, rising higher and yet higher, stretching away to infinity. At my feet lay that vast fertile plain known as the Vale of Spoleto, richly clad in a chequered pattern of golden cornfields, olive groves and vineyards. In the midst, like a pearl adorning a rich robe, lay the white marble-domed church of St Mary of the Angels.

St Francis must have been contemplating this view when he was inspired to write his 'Canticle of the Sun'. From the din of the conflict and the Hell of war, I had found, if not a glimpse of Heaven, a haven of perfect peace.

As evening approached, every breath of wind sent a ripple of silver along the dark green of the olives that clothed the hillsides, as their leaves were turned to show the silvery undersides. Then, as the day died in glory, the roseate hues of the sinking sun coloured the distant mountains, and threw into picturesque relief every detail of tree, hill, tower and castle before the coming of the purple starlit Italian night.

Chapter 28
'Rome'

BETWEEN Assisi and Perugia the enemy began to offer more resistance and there was some very fierce fighting, but after a few weeks our regiment was withdrawn for a very welcome rest. We returned past Assisi and through Foligno to a rest area near Trevi. Our camp was on farmland in the vale I have described, and behind us rose a high steep conical hill on top of which was the little town. From the valley, this looked most picturesque with a church tower crowning the summit, terraces of medieval houses, and several other towers piercing the skyline. From these towers was borne at intervals the sound of bells.

A visit to Trevi soon convinced me that distance lent enchantment. The streets were incredibly narrow and steep, paved with rough cobbles, and I failed to find much of interest to repay me for my toiling climb up the steep hillside. Two or three of my acquaintances took quite a liking to the place because they had formed an attachment with certain *signorinas* there, and had access to their homes and supplies of *vino*. For myself, I preferred to remain in the valley below and contemplate a scene which looked for all the world like a page out of a child's picture book.

Here I was content to write my letters and read my books in comfort, and in the evening to fry my supper of newly dug potatoes, with sometimes an egg from the farm. Occasionally I joined one of the parties that left in trucks each evening for Foligno, Spoleto, Assisi and Montefalco, where various forms of amusement were to be found.

It was from Trevi that I had a day's leave in Rome, an order having been issued that all the troops who had participated in the capture of that city should have an opportunity of seeing it. The party left early in the morning in a three-tonner, carrying our blankets and haversack rations. A few miles short of Rome we reached a rest centre where we were to spend the night before continuing our return journey. Here we left our blankets, and were provided with a mug of tea to wash down our sandwiches, after which we continued on our journey to the capital. Entering the city, we proceeded alongside the Tiber with its artistic bridges, and past great blocks of modern flats. The vehicle was parked, and we were left to spend the rest of the day as we pleased.

The first striking feature I encountered was the vast Victor Emmanuel II Memorial. Dazzling in the brilliant sunshine, the great white marble edifice with its pillars and sculptures in marble and bronze, gilt overlays, and colourful national flags was a sight to create an impression of splendour. Centrally placed was the tomb of Italy's Unknown Warrior, and in the foreground a massive equestrian statue of King Victor Emmanuel. The statue was lavishly decorated with gold leaf, and was flanked by standards bearing the red, white and green flag of Italy. The memorial entirely fills one side of the great square known as the Piazza di Venezia, where crowds assembled to listen to the speeches of the Fascist dictator Mussolini from the balcony. Above this building now floated the flags of Britain and America.

Impressive as are the buildings of modern Rome, it is of course the relics of her ancient glories that compel the most interest, and on which her fame chiefly depends. Short as my stay was on this occasion, I managed to visit the Forum, the Colosseum, the Pantheon, and most of the more famous ruins. In the afternoon I went on a conducted tour, which included the catacombs where the early Christians sought refuge from their persecutors, and where many were finally laid to rest in niches in the walls. There we were shown the tomb of St Cecilia, patron saint of music. Our guide told us that her tortured body had lain for hundreds of years beneath the spot now covered by a beautiful white marble effigy of the martyr, and that when it was disinterred for reburial, it was found to be incorrupt. Here, deep down in the earth, remain the altars where the Christians used to worship in secret, and where services are still occasionally held. On the plastered walls of these chapels the colours of ancient frescoes are still well preserved, as we could see by the light of the tapers we carried.

The catacombs were well outside the city, on the famous Appian Way, along which St Paul journeyed to Rome to be tried by Caesar. That day was just about the hottest I have ever known, and on emerging from the catacombs I was glad to find a fountain from which I refreshed myself with a drink of icy cold water. In the evening I visited a theatre where I saw a play with an American cast, after which I made my way back to the truck which conveyed us back to the rest centre where we had a hot meal and stayed the night, returning the next morning to Trevi.

Our three weeks' rest at Trevi came to an end, and we returned to action, passing through Foligno, Perugia, and the interesting old city of Siena, which had just been taken by French troops. We were now in the Chianti country, famous for its fine wines (which we had many opportunities of sampling) and also for its scenery and medieval castles. Near Certaldo we found cool and safe billets in some large wine cellars which had been dug out of a hillside.

One battery of our regiment lost a cook at this place. Seeing a large field full of fine growing tomatoes, he went to pick some to augment the rations, and was severely injured by the explosion of a mine which had been wired to the plants by the Germans before their retreat. Another man who went to his assistance unfortunately set off another mine which badly injured him and killed the cook.

As we spent a couple of days at Certaldo, I took the opportunity of doing some maintenance on our ex-German workshop truck. The cable-operated brakes were of bad design and had become inefficient, so I jacked up the vehicle with all four wheels clear of the ground, and spent a long time adjusting the brakes until they all operated evenly. The wheel nuts had developed a habit of working loose, so I replaced the studs and nuts with Morris parts. The same afternoon, our unit received orders to move, and we set off with Happy driving and Willie Frame and me in the cab beside him. Happy remarked that the truck was now better than it had been since we had acquired it.

A few minutes after he had said this, we passed a train of mules, and then suddenly the truck went out of control. In spite of Happy's desperate efforts, it veered across the road, plunged down a bank, and overturned on its side in a field. We three piled on top of each other, but except for a slight cut on Happy's forehead were unhurt, and managing to open the door which was now above our heads, climbed out. The cause of our mishap was soon obvious. One coil of a steel tow rope which had been wrapped round two projections on the front of the vehicle had sprung loose, and caught itself round one of the front wheels.

On opening the rear doors, a scene of utter chaos met our eyes. Tools, crowbars and spare parts lay in confusion, a vice still bolted to the bench had crashed through the roof, the lid had come off a seven-pound tin of black grease, and the squashed contents of a bowl full of tomatoes had anointed everything. It was a mercy no one had been riding in the back.

Some of the contents of the vehicle were transferred onto another one, and I was left behind to guard the remainder. Nearly every passing vehicle stopped and the occupants dismounted to investigate, and had I not been there a good deal of our property would have disappeared. As darkness fell, the traffic ceased, and I set about making myself comfortable for the night, and arranged my bed on a board inside the overturned truck. As soon as I had succeeded in getting my board level, I got between the blankets and slept soundly until morning, when a couple of our fitters arrived on a Harley Davidson motorcycle. One of them relieved me, and I was conveyed on the back of the bike in the direction of much-needed ablutions and breakfast.

The old Büssing Nag was emptied and hauled away by the recovery unit, but it was declared to be beyond repair. We were told, however, that we could have an old Ford three-ton ammunition truck to replace it, on condition that we immediately converted it to a workshop truck. At my suggestion, we adapted the body of the German truck to fit onto our new chariot. This was by no means easy, for it was necessary to reduce both the length and the width of the body by a few inches, but we succeeded in making a very good job of it. The top was repaired and rendered waterproof with a covering of canvas, and an overall coat of battleship grey gave it a tidy appearance. Inside we were well equipped for working and sleeping when the weather was bad. At this time we were near Empoli, and temporarily attached to the 5th Army.

The struggle to break through the Gothic Line had now begun, and we moved constantly from one part of the front to the other, always in the mountains. Soon we were overlooking Florence, which was still in German hands. The scenery of the mountains was often very lovely, but we found the narrow, rough precipitous roads very trying for our transport. Often our guns had to be hauled to incredibly difficult positions. The terrain greatly favoured the enemy in their defence; at one place they had a self-propelled gun concealed in a railway tunnel. At intervals they brought it out and fired a few rounds, taking it back into the tunnel before our guns could be brought to bear on it, but they did this once too often, and it was destroyed.

In August my turn for seven days' leave came round, and with several others I went to Rome. Having received short notice that I would be going, I had to wait until the signora who had been bribed to wash my khaki drill uniform had finished ironing it, and was the last to get on the truck, so had to perch on the spare wheel which was mounted in an upright position between the cab and the body. I had actually ridden hundreds of miles in this way, as it was a good vantage point for viewing the countryside, and in the event of the truck overturning, I would have had a good chance of being able to jump off in time. On this occasion we had a pleasant and uneventful journey through wonderful scenery under a blazing sky, and I considered I had the best position on the vehicle.

We were taken to the 8th Army Rest Camp in a suburb of Rome. It was a large modern building of the Fascist regime, and had been renamed the Dorchester Hotel. In contrast to the dugouts and derelict outbuildings we had inhabited during the past months, this was the height of luxury. We had brand-new beds and mattresses, and a big dining hall with tablecloths, cups and saucers, and Italian waiters. The meals were excellent and plentiful. There was a lounge, library, billiard room, barber, shoeshine, laundry, photographer, music room; in fact almost every possible facility.

Every hour a truck left for the city centre, a distance of about five miles along the Appian Way. Not having seen St Peter's on my previous brief visit, I joined a party being conducted there in a ramshackle Italian bus. On entering the largest church in the world, I was awe-stricken by the size and the grandeur. There was so much to observe in detail that I soon became oblivious to the well-rehearsed patter of the guide, and was left so far behind by the rest of the party that I never saw them again, and must have been there for hours after they had left. The nave was big enough to accommodate several football crowds. Although the walls and the floor were of white marble, there was no impression of coldness, for there was colour everywhere. There were huge mosaics, some of which resembled paintings, some tapestries, all consisting of tiny pieces. The work of immortal artists such as Raphael and Michelangelo abounded. Magnificent sculptures amazed the eye and confounded the imagination. One of these depicting a bygone Pope interposing between Attila the Hun with his army and the inhabitants of Rome was carved out of a single block of Carrara marble. Each of the many chapels had its own altar, all of great beauty, but the high altar, which I understand is used only by the Pope, was adorned with real gold ornaments of inestimable value. A star-shaped window with panes of amber diffused a soft yellow light from behind the golden altar. Incomparable paintings were to be seen on all sides, as well as overhead, those in the small domes being particularly beautiful. I was interested to see the tombs of the Stuarts who were the last Pretenders to the throne of England, namely James the Old Pretender, Charles Edward the Young Pretender (Bonnie Prince Charlie), and Henry, Cardinal York. These ended their lives here in exile, and the inscriptions on their tombs tell us that they were known to the Jacobites respectively as James III, Charles III and Henry IX.

Like most visitors to St Peter's, I ascended to the great dome, which like our own St Paul's has a 'whispering gallery', where a person speaking softly on one side may be distinctly heard by anyone on the opposite side. From this great height, the people down below looked no bigger than flies. Set in the walls of the stairway were tablets bearing the names of royal personages who had ascended. Returning to ground level, and knowing that I had long since lost the party with whom I had arrived I simply tagged onto another party and returned to the city centre in their bus.

Italy is the land of opera, and ever since I had entered the country it had been my ambition to visit an opera house where an opera was being performed. Now in Rome I had my chance, and I was able to see 'Aida' at the Royal Opera House. I was thrilled both with Verdi's music and the lavish presentation. The singers lived well up to my expectations, particularly the leading tenor, whose name was Renato Gigli, which caused me to speculate as to whether he was related to the great Beniamino Gigli, whom I had heard sing in our own City Hall. The following night, which was Sunday, I again went to the Royal Opera House when the programme consisted of orchestral works and two scenes from different operas. During the week I saw 'La Bohème' well performed at another theatre.

I also found pleasure in some less classical entertainment, and paid several visits to variety theatres where both British and Italian artists performed. These shows varied both in their entertainment value and their quality of performance, but they afforded relaxation. The weather was very hot, and I found the excellent Italian soft drinks very cool and refreshing, and occasionally I had a glass of the local wine or vermouth. Some of the shops were interesting, though the prices were generally beyond the reach of my pocket, but I bought a few small gifts and souvenirs. All too soon my leave came to an end, and back we all went to the regiment.

Rome 1944

Chapter 29
'You Are Now Under Enemy Observation'

ONE MORNING I was riding beside the driver in a cab of a command vehicle (not that I was in command of anything or anybody) when the convoy of which we were part came to a halt. Curious to know the reason, I opened the observation hatch in the roof and stood on the seat with my head out. In front the road curved to the left up an incline, and I could see that round the corner a great fire was blazing, the flames rising to a great height, above them a column of dense black smoke. I remarked to the driver that it looked like a petrol fire.

After some delay, the column moved slowly forward, and when we turned the corner, a scene of horror met our eyes. One of our large tanks had been blown up by mines, and was lying on its side blazing like a furnace. One of the crew, who must have been navigating, had been blown out of it, and was lying dead in the middle of the road, stark naked. He had been a fine tall young man, probably an officer, and I could see no marks on his body. The blast must have killed him instantly and blown off his clothes. We shuddered to think of the fate of the other crew members who had perished in the inferno, and could only pray that their end had been instantaneous and painless.

Another day we heard a loud bang, and saw that a mine had exploded under one of the Bren carriers. We hurried over, and were relieved to find the crew unhurt but badly shaken. The carrier was somewhat damaged and one of the tracks had been blown off.

Another of our Bren carriers was hit by a shell, fortunately when no one was in it, and for quite a time the ammunition in it continued to explode, bullets flying out in all directions. Two of us were working on a vehicle in the same field, and as the German shells fell, we dived under the truck. It was some minutes before I realised that I had taken refuge under the petrol tank, which was hardly likely to improve my chances of survival. After one bombardment, one of our sergeants confessed that he had tried to take shelter by covering himself with straw! One night, one of our ammunition dumps was hit by a shell. There was an almighty explosion, followed by many others as the shells kept on exploding and flying around for a long time. Luckily there was a convenient ditch into which we threw ourselves with all possible speed.

In a dugout one night, we discussed the question of fear. All agreed that anyone who said he was never afraid was a liar. What we were most afraid of was being seen to be afraid. Whilst we took reasonable precautions, everyone seemed to get on with his job calmly. Only one man lost his nerve and deserted, but he was soon brought back and placed under the care of the medical officer. The MO was a member of the Oxford Group Movement, and he actually seemed to do more active Christian work than the padre, whom we seldom saw.

Even at the altitudes at which our division usually operated, the weather continued to be very hot throughout August. A spanner left in the sun soon became to hot to hold, and we had to remember to lay them in the shade of the truck on which we were working. Our swift advance had ended, as the enemy was now firmly entrenched behind the Gothic Line of formidable defence, and taking full advantage of the natural obstacles afforded by the mountains. An Indian soldier of our division was decorated with the Victoria Cross, and some men of our regiment received the Military Medal for acts of bravery.

Morale continued to be high, and there were many humorous episodes to brighten the days. One day a gun sergeant was airing his views. He was saying that we could clear the Germans out any time we wished, only somebody hadn't made enough money out of the war yet. 'This lot we're up against are only a bunch of cripples', he affirmed. Not long afterwards a load of German shells came whistling over. 'Hey, sarge,' shouted a gunner, 'Can tha hear yon cripples throwin' their crutches abaht?'

Some of us had pets that travelled around with us. On our truck we had a little brown rabbit of which I was very fond. When we moved, he rode under the driving seat with a bit of greenstuff, and when we stopped we just laid him on the grass beside the truck and he never went far away from us. One of the drivers had adopted a little goose called Donald. It was a comical little beggar, rather weak on its pins, and often fell over. One chap had a sparrowhawk until he lost it. Answering a distress call, I came across him late one night with a broken fan belt. Looking the picture of misery he moaned 'What a day! First I lost me sparrer'awk, then me back axle went. I changed trucks, and now me fan belt's gone, and I shan't get in for me grub.' He got his grub, because I put him a German fan belt on out of my stock of 'loot', but I didn't get any, because my day's supply had been given to me early in the day, and having no clock but my stomach, had eaten it all by about half past three in the afternoon. Exploring my kit, I found four biscuits, a bar of chocolate that had melted in the sun and set again, and a packet of chewing gum.

The Gothic Line, behind which the Germans had now retreated, was a line of naturally strong positions formed by a lateral barrier of mountains north of Florence, running roughly between Rimini in the east and Pisa in the west. Our enemies had constructed a chain of pillboxes and other defences, and this line proved to be the toughest nut we had to crack in the whole Italian campaign. After some stubborn fighting Florence fell to us and our troops crossed the Arno. As part of a mountain division we had our full share of work to do, and were constantly on the move from one gun position to another. We were now fighting with the 5th Army instead of the 8th.

After a time, a system of day leave was started, giving me an opportunity to visit Florence. Having already seen Rome, my first impression of Florence was rather one of disappointment, as I had heard so much about the beauty of the city. The streets were narrow and unimposing, and most of the shops were closed. The Germans had destroyed all the bridges over the Arno with the exception of one, the ancient and romantic Ponte Vecchio, which is lined with houses, and there was little of the picturesque about the utilitarian Bailey bridges that had replaced them. The great cathedral certainly presented a striking appearance with its ornate exterior of intricate marble sculpture, but its interior, plain to the point of barrenness, was an anticlimax after the glories of St Peter's, and I thought it was redeemed solely by its fine proportions. To my further disappointment, the famous art galleries were at that time closed.

As a centre for relaxation, however, Florence proved adequate, and after dinner in a Forces' restaurant, my two comrades and I went to a cinema. After passing the afternoon there we had another meal and went on a further exploration of the city, finishing up at the NAAFI, where we seated ourselves at one of the outside tables to sip vermouth and to listen to an excellent Italian band which was playing on a dais in front of the building. All in all, we had a very enjoyable day.

Most of our days, however, were far from enjoyable, like the one when it was reported that one of our trucks was broken down at an observation post with a fractured brake pipe and bolts missing from the back axle casing. The sergeant major sent Happy and I do to do the necessary repairs, with many earnest warnings about the dangers that lay ahead of us, and strict instructions to wear our steel helmets. We set off in a 15cwt truck, Happy driving. The road we had to go down was known as 'The Mad Mile', and a series of warning notices, each more dire than the last, did nothing to cheer us on our way. They read respectively: 'Is your journey really necessary?'; 'This road under shell fire'; 'For dust's sake go slow'; 'You are now under enemy observation'.

The road was full of shell holes, and Happy did his best to avoid the worst of them, driving at a moderate speed to avoid stirring up a cloud of dust which would advertise our presence. We were travelling along a hillside, and on our left lay an expanse of open country at a lower level where the enemy lay. After we had passed the last notice a shell came our way, so it was evident that we had been seen, and as there was now nothing to lose, Happy put his foot down and we bumped and bounced along as fast as we could. Presently we turned off at the ruins of a village, a place known as 'Hell-Fire Corner', where the remains of a Calvary stood. These wayside shrines are common throughout Italy. All that remained of this one were three crosses of steel girder, which must formerly have been covered with some ornamental material, probably marble, of which no vestige remained. And there, of all places, was a military policeman in his red cap signalling to us to stop. 'What are you chaps on?' he asked. We told him the nature of our mission, and he said that we must only drive another quarter of a mile, and then park the truck behind a ruined wall, and proceed the rest of the way on foot. He urged us to get on with it, as a shell landed at Hell-Fire Corner every twelve minutes. 'How do you go on then?' I asked curiously.

'I just get down in a slit trench and wait till after the shell's landed', he replied.

Lingering no longer, we followed his directions, and having parked the truck close to the most substantial stone wall still standing, we set off on foot carrying our tools, and soon found our OP party in what remained of a building. They were not sorry to see us, as they were marooned there until the truck was repaired. It was decided that Happy should attend to the comparatively simple back axle job whilst I tackled the split brake pipe, for which of course we had no replacement.

I removed the pipe from the vehicle and thoroughly cleaned it with emery cloth all round the area of the split and for about two inches beyond it each side, and tinned it with solder. Next I scraped bright a length of copper wire and wound it closely and tightly around the fracture. Having applied a generous coating of solder to the coiled wire all over, I played the flame of the blowlamp onto the repair, slowly turning the pipe round, until all the solder had melted and filled every crevice, thus forming an oil-tight sleeve. The pipe was then re-fitted, and the brake master cylinder replenished with fluid. Happy, who had completed his part of the job, then helped me to bleed the system. Having had our mid-day meal with the OP party, we returned to the truck and once again ran the gauntlet of 'The Mad Mile', arriving safely back at battery HQ to the obvious relief of the sergeant major, not to mention ourselves.

October is the wettest month of the year in Italy, and not only did we find ourselves in the wettest part of the country then, but it was abnormally wet. One afternoon we had to move to another position, and in order to avoid the attention of the enemy we had to make a detour round the mountains. As one of the ammunition truck drivers had no mate, I was glad to ride with him in the cab instead of perching on the outside of the fitters' truck in the pouring rain. The driver was glad to have me to get out and direct him round some of the bends which in some cases were so acute that it was necessary to reverse when halfway round and have a second try. One false move would have ended in disaster, with the truck plunging down the mountainside.

At one point we were following some tanks when we came to a stretch of road which had been blown up by the Germans, and later roughly filled in by the Pioneers, who were Basutos. Each tank dislodged some more of the makeshift road, and the one immediately in front of us only just managed to get across when the road collapsed and we had to stop. Everyone jumped out of the trucks and formed human chains to pass boulders and stones up the steep mountainside to rebuild the road. There were no NCOs around until an officious Irish sergeant major of another battery appeared, and to our utter astonishment called us to attention! How he imagined anyone could stand to attention on a precipitous stone-strewn mountainside whilst holding a half-hundredweight boulder was beyond comprehension. Then it dawned on us that the reason for this lunacy was the appearance on the scene of the commanding officer of the division, General Dudley Russell. Giving the sergeant major a withering look he said, 'For God's sake, man, don't stop the work!'

As soon as we had sufficiently restored the road, we continued on our way until we reached the mountain village of San Benedetto in Alpe, where the trucks were parked in a field on the lower side of the village. Then a DR rode in with bad news. The fitters' truck, which was always at the end of the convoy in order that we could render assistance in the event of any vehicle breaking down, had itself come to grief. One of the front wheel hubs had smashed and the wheel had rolled down the mountainside into a river far below. Fortunately the truck itself managed to remain on the road. This was a calamity for me and several others, as our blankets and eating and washing requisites were on the truck which had broken down several miles behind.

The village had been totally deserted by its former inhabitants, and in the nearest house I managed to find a glass mug and a small basin which I borrowed, and having my knife, fork and spoon wrapped in a rag in my map pocket, I was able to eat my meal. All the time the rain poured in torrents, and darkness had already fallen when we had arrived in the village. One driver was carrying four blankets that had belonged to a man who had been killed, so we borrowed them. Four of us got down for the night in the back of a covered wagon, sharing the blankets and our greatcoats on the cold steel floor, uncomfortable but at least dry. Also I had to thank God that on this occasion I had not been riding on my usual perch on top of the spare wheel, as I could well have been thrown down the ravine when the wheel came off our truck.

When morning broke, the rain was still pouring down, the mountains were enveloped in mist, and the all-pervading mud was nowhere less than ankle deep. After a damp breakfast, we accomplished the filthy task of fitting skid chains, and one by one the vehicles wallowed through the deeply rutted mud back onto the road—a few by their own efforts, but most with the assistance of winches, as it was almost impossible for the wheels to grip in the mud. As the weather made any kind of activity extremely difficult, billets were commandeered for us in the deserted village, and our vehicles were now parked there on firm ground.

It was a picturesque village of steep narrow twisting streets, commanding on a clear day extensive views of magnificent mountain scenery. Our first day there was very far from clear, and only the nearer hills, shrouded in mist were visible. A bombardier named Harry Fletcher and I installed ourselves in a house where there was a huge bed with a spring mattress, and a worm-eaten writing bureau, both of which we put to good use. We were still much handicapped by the absence of our kit, especially as our feet were constantly soaked and we had nothing else to put on. Some miles forward, our guns were in action, and twice I had to go there helping to feed them with ammunition, as bereft of my tools I was unable to do my own job. All my clothes were wet through. On the evening of the second day our bedding and essential kit was brought to us, so the situation became easier, though for days I never had dry feet.

We stayed in San Benedetto in Alpe for about a week. One morning I was sitting at the old bureau in the billet writing a letter, when who should walk in by my cousin Ted Milner, whom I had last seen in a field near Cassino. He was in a counter-battery RA regiment and was billeted in the same street. During the next couple of days we were able to see quite a bit of each other, and we spent two pleasant evenings together in his billet which had more amenities than ours, being illuminated with hurricane lamps, and quite cosy. The truck he drove was in a state of neglect and dilapidation that would never have been allowed in our unit, and I tried to sort it out for him. I believe he had been on a charge for allowing it to get into that condition, but Ted was so easy-going it would make no difference. Our MT truck presently arrived having had a new front axle fitted at the roadside, and the runaway wheel was recovered from the river.

After leaving San Benedetto we occupied several positions in the neighbourhood of Marradi. The only remarkable thing about any of them was the amount of rain that fell and the amount of mud through which we had to struggle.

An article which appeared in our paper, *Eighth Army News*, is worth quoting. It was entitled 'About this Weather you are Having' and reads:

> The weather conditions under which the Allied Armies in Italy are fighting have frequently been mentioned in general terms.
>
> Here are some detailed notes on recent rainfall which may give a fuller conception of the conditions in which our troops continue to press forward in Northern Italy.
>
> Even in normal weather the rainfall on the present battlefront is two to three times heavier than in the greater part of all the rest of the country.
>
> A basic comparison might well be made with London's average annual rainfall of 24.5 inches. Against this, Florence's normal yearly rainfall is 32.7 inches, while the normal fall at San Benedetto in Alpe, on the road from Florence to Forli, computed from five years records is 69.2 inches per year.
>
> Autumn, in any case, is the wettest season in Italy, where one third of the year's rain falls from September to November. At Firen-zuola, for example, near the Florence–Bologna road, where the annual rainfall is 54.6 inches, the average seasonal fall is:- Autumn, 18.4; Winter 122.9; Spring 14.7; Summer 8.6.
>
> This present Autumn, which found the Allies in the wettest region at the wettest time of the year, has indeed been abnormally wet. At Fiesole, just north of Florence, the average October rainfall of 3.07 inches was eclipsed by a fall of 7.49 inches, while the normal November average of 2.68 inches already looks small against the 4.56 inches that fell in the first 15 days of November this year.
>
> The climax of the present season's abnormal rainfall in the battle area was reached at the junction of the two months, on the night of November 31st.
>
> There was a cloudburst, and rain fell continuously for ten hours. In that short period, 8.47 inches were recorded at one place.
>
> With such a combination of abnormality—wetness of region and of season—small wonder that the River Arno rose throughout its length to within a few inches of Bailey bridges, and almost to the top of the arches of the Ponte Vecchio, the only Florence bridge the enemy left standing.
>
> Rivers flooded their banks, roads and bridges were washed away, walls collapsed on roads, diversions became impassable, and fields disappeared under water or became swamps.
>
> Throughout it all, operations continued along the Allied front, with Engineers, Signals, Supplies, and other services working steadily for 24 hours a day.

The above extract mentions the cloudburst on the night of November the 31st. Three of us were sleeping in the MT truck at the time, and the sound of heavy rain and rushing water woke me during the night. When we looked out in the morning, we were amazed to see that the road running alongside the field in which we were encamped had become a river, in fact a raging torrent. On every hand, streams raced down the hillsides, uniting in the valley to form a strong river, cascading in waterfalls and roaring along with a great noise. A great deal of our gear was out of sight under the mud and water, and our toolboxes were completely filled. For days, any attempt at work meant a soaking.

Nevertheless, the war still went on, and the transport had to be maintained, although it was impossible to get underneath any vehicle. One of our trucks was running so badly that I had to dismantle the engine and fit a new cylinder head and valves, working in a field in pouring rain.

I have mentioned that the REME sergeant major had recommended me for a higher trade rating when I had done the job on the Bren carrier just before the Rapido crossing. News now came that Reg Franks and I were to go to the Indian workshops to undergo a test for A2 grade. On three successive days we went there on a motorbike over an appalling road that had become a river. The 8th Indian Division MT Workshops consisted of a morass of deep liquid mud and a few tents. My leaking boots had now been supplemented with a pair of Wellingtons, but the mud sometimes even came in over the top of these. The rain still came down like stair rods, and for a fortnight we never had a dry garment.

For our test, we had to replace the engine of an ambulance with an engine we were to take from a damaged truck. This truck had been brought in by an Indian driver for a minor repair. On seeing it, the workshop officer had said to him, 'Yes, but where's the body?' Then only did the driver notice the empty space to the rear of his cab! As the Germans had retreated they had cut pieces out of the railway lines. Our engineers had then thrown the rails and sleepers down the embankments, levelled the ballast, and the tracks had become roads. Coming through one of the tunnels, which were lit by current supplied by portable generators, the body of the truck had struck a projection in the wall, and been torn from the chassis. The driver had never noticed! It had been decided to scrap the truck and cannibalise it for spares. Almost up to our knees in mud, with no respite from the incessant rain, Reg and I changed the engines satisfactorily, were deemed to have passed our test, and received a small increase in pay.

Everybody at this time was singing a song called 'Stuck in the Mud at Marradi' which had been composed by some unknown wit to the tune of 'Deep in the Heart of Texas'. Occasionally we had opportunities to go into Marradi to see films and shows at the Garrison Theatre—another commandeered opera house. Even more valued was the installation there of mobile baths where we could at last wash away the filth and change our clothes for clean dry ones.

About this time, our troops were beginning to use 'artificial moonlight'. This device consisted of employing batteries of searchlights to blind the enemy, whilst at the same time light reflected from the clouds assisted our infantry when they attacked. One night, a party of us were going in an open truck to see a film show when the rain began to fall. To our astonishment, we saw the phenomenon of a rainbow at night, caused by the artificial moonlight.

With the approach of Christmas, a pantomime was staged in Marradi by some members of an Army unit, and it was just about the most entertaining I have ever seen. The dresses, scenery and presentation were up to professional standards, and the material was all original and topical. There was a line of glamorous chorus 'girls', and the leading 'lady' looked and sounded most authentic. A man impersonating an Arab caused great mirth every time he crossed the stage, although he never spoke a single word.

One day our MT sergeant, Willie Frame, came into our workshop truck with a gloomy expression on his face and a broken metal object in his hand. It was a Lockheed transverse bisector, part of the hydraulic braking system of an armoured car which was used as a mobile observation post from which firing orders were conveyed to our guns by field telephone.

'The scout car's off the road,' he said, 'There isn't one of these parts to be had anywhere in Italy. I've tried every possible source. They say we'll just have to scrap the scout car, and the OP party will have to use a Bren carrier, and there's no protection in those.'

I looked at the component, which had one of its fixing lugs broken off, and said, 'That can be repaired.' Willie said, 'Workshops say it can't be. The RSM in charge of divisional workshops says it can't be repaired.' I replied, 'I say it can be.' Looking sceptical, Willie continued, 'It can't be welded.' I said, 'I'm not talking about welding.'

'Can you repair it?' asked Willie. 'I'm willing to have a go', I answered. Willie handed me the part, shrugged his shoulders disbelievingly, and went off to tell the sergeant major that I was proposing to achieve the impossible.

I had noticed that behind the damaged part there was an aluminium plate which only served as a packing piece, and calculated that if this were dispensed with, there would be sufficient room to substitute a steel plate to which the bisector could be riveted. I found a good piece of mild steel of the right thickness, marked it out, and began the laborious task of cutting it to shape with a hacksaw, files, and a breast drill borrowed from the sergeant gun fitter. A hole an inch and one eighth in diameter was cut by drilling a circle of small holes almost touching each other breaking out the centre, and filing the hole to a perfect circle. Two ⅜" holes in the fixing lugs I had formed, and two more holes for rivets were drilled. Two corresponding holes had to be drilled in the original part, which was very hard work with the hand drill, and then I made rivets from high-tensile steel bolts, made them red hot with the blow lamp, and riveted the two parts firmly together. When it was bolted onto the vehicle, and the hydraulic system bled, the brakes worked perfectly, the reward of two days' hard work. To the crew of the scout car I was regarded as a hero, as they had been dismayed at the thought of having to do their highly dangerous job in an open Bren carrier, which was in every way a poor substitute for their modern scout car with its armoured protection. The workshops RSM who had said it was impossible to repair it inspected it and said it was a marvellous job. Another success of mine was the redesigning and altering of the linkage between the accelerator pedal and carburettor on a Dodge truck that was causing trouble. This was considered to be such an improvement that I was asked to carry out this modification to all the Dodges.

As our regiment had been in action without respite for six months almost to the day, it was decided that we should have a break of ten days, which included Christmas. Leaving the snow-capped mountains, we came by Borgo San Lorenzo to Antella, about four miles beyond Florence. The peaceful conditions we found there were in great contrast to those we had left behind in the wintry mountains. At this lower level the weather was so warm and sunny that we seemed to be in another country, and we could no longer hear the sound of the guns. Every olive-clad hill was crowned with a picturesque castle or villa.

It had been planned to make our stay at Antella as nearly as possible a complete rest, after the rigours of our long spell in action under such severe climatic conditions. For the gunners it was indeed almost a complete holiday, while those of us who had essential work to do, such as cooks and fitters, contrived to have our afternoons free, or to relieve each other so that we had as much free time as possible. A 'bus service' was started, a three-tonner travelling every hour between the camp and Florence for our convenience.

Florence was by now almost back to normal, and possessed many amenities for the soldiers, such as theatres, cinemas, the opera, and perhaps most valued of all, the Robertson Club. This immense modern building, a product of the Mussolini regime, had been transformed into a lavish club for the British soldiers. It housed a theatre, a restaurant, library, swimming pool, three snack bars, writing rooms, gramophone rooms, and a host of other amenities such as a news room and a billiards saloon. Every evening we dined in the restaurant, enjoying both the food and the music of the Italian orchestra. The cellist was a girl, and from time to time she abandoned her instrument to sing such well-known local songs as 'Mama', 'O Sole Mio' and 'Oi Marie'. The programme was the same every evening, so we knew what to expect.

There was also a canteen run by the Salvation Army, which possessed an orchestra and a tenor singer with a very fine voice, who also sang the favourites, his speciality being 'You are my Heart's Delight'. Though the songs were hackneyed, the rendering made amends, and half an hour in the Salvation Army canteen was always well spent. One evening, in one or other of these canteens, I recognized a familiar face at one of the tables. It was none other than my old friend Mac, whom I had not seen since we had parted at Foggia many months earlier. We were very pleased to meet again, and were soon relating our experiences to each other. Mac didn't appear to have been too happy in the regiment to which he had been posted, and had been involved in the terrible Anzio landing. We parted with mutual good wishes.

The original intention was that our unit should spend ten days at Antella, which would just give us time to have our Christmas dinner there. A concert had been planned, in which the more talented were to perform. Imagine our surprise and disgust when we were all awakened at 5.00 am on Christmas Eve and ordered to prepare to move. Many of us in fact thought it was a practical joke and stayed in our beds until the sergeant major disillusioned us. There was much bad language as we ate our breakfast in the dark and stowed away the cheese sandwiches that would be our dinner. Several vehicles were under repair and not in a condition to move, so we fitters were more than busy, but thanks to our efforts, everyone moved off at 9.00 am. So unexpected had been the move that one sergeant who had decided to stay out the previous night for reasons that I needn't go into was caught napping, and hearing the sound of heavy traffic, looked out of a bedroom window in the village to see our guns going by! His section of signallers pulled up and waited for him, and the gallant sergeant scrambled aboard with his boots in his hand. He had been awarded the Military Medal at Cassino, but he would have been awarded something less glorious for his exploits had he missed the truck.

We were moving up to the 5th Army front, where the Germans had pushed back some coloured American troops and retaken two villages. Emboldened by their success, they planned to take Lucca and Pisa. But they had reckoned without their old adversaries, the 8th Indian Division, which they believed to be still deployed on the central sector north of Marradi, where in fact part of the division still remained. We sped north along a good road, one of Mussolini's more commendable projects, the autostrada, through Florence, Pisa and Lucca. Much of Pisa we found to be in ruins, but we were all looking for the famous leaning tower. Soon we had a distant view of it through the ruins, and eventually passed close to it, though outside the high city wall.

Our mission was to stop the German advance, but just as Drake of old found time to play his game of bowls before defeating the Spanish Armada, we found time to celebrate Christmas before going into action. Having passed through Lucca, another old walled city, we made a detour and arrived in the village of Marlia, where we pulled up in a big square in front of the church. As it was Christmas Eve, the villagers were dressed in their best clothes, coming and going from the church, and congregating idly in the square, where our appearances as the first British troops caused great interest. A curious crowd had soon gathered around our wagons. They displayed a great interest in the unloading of the wagons and the preparations our cooks were making for our evening meal. There were a couple of wine bars in the village, which those interested lost no time in finding. We soon found billets, as there were many unoccupied houses, owing to the war being so near. That night I slept in a deserted watch repairer's shop, surrounded by a variety of incomplete timepieces.

In the morning we were awakened by the sergeant major in the time-honoured Christmas Day style, with the conventional greeting and a mug of tea apiece. After breakfast I found I had to overhaul the petrol system of one of the trucks, and I note this fact as being the only occasion in my life when I have worked on Christmas Day. It was not a big job, however, and I had ample time to wash and change before sitting down to the Christmas dinner our efficient and resourceful cooks had prepared under difficult conditions.

In a corner of the square was a fair-sized hall belonging to the church, and it was here that we had our dinner, through the kindness of the priest. Three long tables had been placed in position and covered with borrowed linen tablecloths, a seldom-encountered luxury for us. The cooks had done their best, and had produced a very enjoyable dinner consisting of turkey (tinned), roast pork, and the usual accompaniments, followed by that time-honoured seasonal sweet, plum pudding. The tables were also graced with quantities of cigarettes, sweets, oranges, nuts and beer. The Christmas custom of the officers and senior NCOs waiting on the men was of course observed. At the conclusion of the meal a piano was dragged in, and a sing-song started. Some of the songs were of a type exclusive to military circles, though interspersed with others of a more respectable nature, and once again I was able to contribute to the entertainment.

After a while the party broke up and we went to see a football match played between B Troop and Battery HQ. The game was characterised by humour more than skill, and a shell hole in the middle of the pitch proved to be a stumbling block for the unwary. As I was in B Troop, but attached to BHQ, I was in the happy position of being able to shout for both sides. The honours went to B Troop to the tune of 5–2, but BHQ had the disadvantage of having one of their players injured early in the game when he fell in the shell hole.

Whilst we were in Marlia I took a look inside the church. It was of a size and grandeur truly astonishing, considering the smallness of the community. Above the west door was a magnificent organ. A series of tableaux occupied the south side, depicting the Nativity with the adoration of the shepherds; the approach of the Three

Wise Men with their servants, camels, horses and gifts; and the slaughter of the innocents. The figures were about three-quarters life size, and realistically dressed. A woman was showing the tableaux to her little boy, and explaining to him the evergreen story. On Christmas Eve people came from miles around to attend midnight Mass, and some of the soldiers who were Roman Catholics also went.

On Boxing Day we proceeded on our way north, our guns going into action near Bagni di Lucca. A few days later we again advanced, with the result that the enemy were not only checked, but forced back beyond their original starting point and forced to give up the two villages they had taken. Once again our Indian infantry fought with skill and aggression, and recaptured a lot of war material that had been taken from the Americans.

Whilst we were in this area, a serious accident occurred. One night a number of our vehicles were taking ammunition to a new gun position when the driver of the leading truck, peering into the darkness, suddenly saw to his horror that immediately in front of him a bridge had been blown up. He instantly applied his brakes which fortunately stopped the truck in time to prevent it from ploughing through a barbed wire barricade. Not so fortunate was one of our motorcyclists who failed to see the obstruction and overtook the stationery convoy, with the result that he crashed through the barbed wire barricade and plunged over the edge of the broken bridge, landing on the tumbled masonry far below. The ammunition party climbed down to him, and when they had carried him back up the road, laid him on the back of a 15cwt truck from which they had quickly transferred the contents to the three-tonners, and took him to a dressing station with all possible speed. His condition was critical, as he had extensive injuries including a fractured skull and a broken thigh, but the wonder was that he was living at all, as the bridge was about forty feet high.

The next morning we went to recover his motorcycle, which was not as badly damaged as we expected to find it, although someone had stolen one of the wheels during the night or early morning. The boulder on which he had struck his head was covered with hair and blood, and when we saw the height from which he had fallen, and the amount of blood he had lost, we marvelled that the rider had not been killed outright, and were of the opinion that he stood very little chance of recovery. Enquiries were made at the dressing station where he had been taken, and it was stated that if he could survive the journey to hospital there was a chance that he might recover. Later we heard that he had arrived safely at a hospital in Florence, and in what seemed a surprisingly short time he was back in the regiment almost as well as ever, and again riding a motorbike. His recovery was nothing short of a miracle.

Chapter 30
'1945'

ON THE EVENING of January the 5th 1945 we witnessed for the first time an Italian peasant custom much resembling from the children's point of view our own Christmas Eve: namely the annual visit of the Italian equivalent of Santa Claus. His visit was not attended with the same secrecy as that of his English counterpart, as he came at about eight o'clock in the evening, dressed in a white robe and flowing beard, visiting in turn each house in the hamlet distributing parcels to the children. The young ones had never known conditions of peace and plenty, and there was terrific excitement when the pathetic little parcels were opened, disclosing sweets, chocolate, biscuits, nuts and oranges. We recognised the sweets, chocolate and biscuits as having been part of our rations, bartered to the poor peasants for eggs, and carefully hoarded by them for this occasion. We had not realised the purpose for which the stuff was being collected, and when we saw the delight of the children over their meagre gifts we all wished we could have given them more, and began to search through our kit for anything else that we could contribute. There was a big fire in the house where I had found a billet, and the people pressed us to partake of quantities of hot roasted chestnuts, as well as sweet cake and red wine. Songs were sung in both languages, and general merriment and goodwill prevailed. A young woman with a fine strong voice sang 'Mama son tanto felice', a great favourite all over Italy. Everyone thoroughly enjoyed the evening, and I went to bed wishing that the lunatics who had dragged us into this war that nobody wanted could have been there to see how the ordinary people of different races could mix so happily together. On Twelfth Night as I take down our Christmas decorations I still think of those friends.

Four days later we left Bagni di Lucca, and I have occasion to remember the drive, which was at night, as I rode in a jeep which had a rather alarming wheel wobble as the result of a recent accident. Another slight accident took place that night, as one of our trucks ran into the muzzle end of a gun which was preceding it in the convoy, and badly damaged the radiator. This move took us well away from the scene of action to the village of Pisano, near Pisa, and we stayed there about a month. Almost all the time we could hear the sound of distant bells being rung discordantly and conforming to none of the recognised rules of tune or time.

After we had been there a few days, I had the opportunity of going to Pisa, which I found, as I had expected, to be a place of great interest. After entering the city by one of the ancient gateways that pierce the wall, I soon made my way to the group of historic edifices that comprise the cathedral, or duomo, the baptistry, and the campanile—the famous leaning tower. There had also been a famous library here, but unfortunately this had been destroyed by a stray British shell. The interior walls had been decorated with frescoes painted by famous artists. When the library had been destroyed by fire, the paint was burnt off the walls, but the preliminary charcoal drawings remained, and were of great interest to scholars.

The appearance of the leaning tower is of course familiar to all. In the bright sunlight it reminded me inevitably of a many-tiered iced wedding cake. Laboriously I climbed its interior spiral staircase, noticing the steel tie bars which had been inserted years before by a British firm in an attempt to arrest the slowly increasing lean. At different levels it is possible to emerge onto the balconies which encircle the tower, and venturing onto one of these, I found I was on the side to which the tower leaned, contemplating a sheer drop to the ground below, so having no head for heights, I quickly returned to the stairs, and continued my ascent until I reached the top.

Now I saw the reason for the cacophonous jangle of bells we had been able to hear in Pisano. In Italy, bells are not rung from ground level with rope as in England, but up in the belfry itself by means of wheels or levers attached to the pivot. Here, great wooden levers were used, and each one was being swung up and down by a soldier. When the man swinging the biggest bell of all relinquished it, I took his place. Soon I had the great bell swinging sufficiently for it to start sending forth its deep sonorous chime, and at each swing the lever rose higher and higher, until my feet left the floor of the bell chamber and I was carried upwards on the end of the lever at each stroke of the bell. Not everyone can boast of having rung the biggest bell in the leaning tower of Pisa!

Recovering my breath after my exertions with the bell, I gazed out at the extensive panoramic view. Around Pisa is a level plain spanned for miles by an ancient aqueduct which once carried water to the city from the distant hills which provided such a picturesque background to the scene. Far away beyond them rose higher mountains, their snow-capped peaks tinged by the rays of the sun. A silvery ribbon marked where a river meandered over the plain to the sea.

Once on terra firma I had a walk round the old city, observing much of interest. In the shops were many beautiful *objets d'art* made of alabaster and marble. I bought an elephant, a pair of book ends and an ashtray to send home. The next time I went into Pisa was to watch a football match between our team and another field regiment, played in a big modern stadium. Our team won 4–0, and it was a very one-sided game. We could have fielded almost a complete team of professionals, but on this occasion I believe only two of the ex-Bolton Wanderers played, Ernie Forest and Stan Hanson, and they ran rings around their opponents.

Following the football match, some of us went to a variety show where we were treated to the antics of some mis-shapen chorus girls who compared very unfavourably with their English counterparts, both in appearance and expertise, and a duet sung by a six-foot-two soprano and a five-foot-four baritone.

Somebody had liberated an old piano from a wrecked building, and this was carried around on the cooks' truck. It was hopelessly out of tune, and some of the notes wouldn't play, but I made a wrest so I could tune the strings to some semblance of the right pitch, and fastened up the loose bits with adhesive tape and wire so that the battery clerk could knock a few tunes out of it. It wasn't exactly up to Steinway standards, but it served for a sing-song, and when the lads had imbibed a few glasses of vino, they were not very critical. The name of the house where Lucy and I now live is 'Holly Dene', and as it is not graced with a holly tree, I have often thought of changing it to 'Nellie Dean' in memory of the most popular song of those now-distant days.

The men of our regiment were on the whole friendly and good hearted, but generally speaking were not quite as intellectual as many old pals in the Royal Corps of Signals, who were now fighting in Normandy. Conversation was endlessly of sex and drink. One who had followed the civilian occupation of cat burglar was always regaling us with stories of his exploits in the pursuit of that calling. A gun sergeant was said to have earned his living by stealing clothes from washing lines and selling them back to the unsuspecting owners. The cat burglar was supposed to be our equipment repairer, and he was undoubtedly the idlest man in the regiment. Every morning he would lay out all his tools, survey them, and say, 'Tomorrow, I'm going to repair . . . . .', but tomorrow never came.

On the other hand of course, the great majority were very decent chaps. One good friend of mine was Harry Fletcher, a bombardier who had been a joiner in Leeds. He was quiet, humorous, good tempered, and always willing to lend a hand. Like me, he had a child at home whom he had never seen. Another lad I liked very much was Ray Smith, a driver, whose boyish face and short stature caused him to look younger than he was. He came from a remote village in North Yorkshire, where there was no employment, and he had had to cycle ten miles to and from a market garden where he had worked each day, sometimes arriving home so tired that he had fallen asleep over his meal. He hoped to be able to get a job in a garage after the war, and I helped him to pass a driver mechanic's trade test. After the war, I lent him all my motor maintenance manuals and textbooks, and he succeeded in getting a job in a garage in Blackpool. Willie Frame, who had been a bombardier when I first joined the regiment but had been promoted to lance sergeant, was a very decent type, conscientious and hard working, but lacking the technical training and experience of some of us. The battery sergeant major was probably about the most intelligent man with whom I had regular contact. Before being promoted to BSM he had been quartermaster sergeant, and I heard how he had led a party of men carrying heavy backpacks through shell fire to get rations to the gunners during the River Sangro battle, bearing a load with the rest. His rather subtle brand of humour was lost on some of the rougher element.

When it became known that we were about to leave Pisano, the Italian family with whom we were billeted insisted on all the chaps in their farmhouse having dinner with them. In our honour, they had set the table in unaccustomed style, with a tablecloth, plates and glasses. The menu consisted of macaroni bolognese, fried greens in batter, pieces of rabbit and fried potatoes. There was of course wine, which accompanies all their meals.

Having said farewell to these friends, we travelled for two days eastward through some very picturesque scenery, and in glorious weather. Once again we crossed the Apennines, and rejoined the 8th Army near the Adriatic coast. At last we had left the mountains where we had spent so many months, and were on the Lombardy Plain, which reminded me of Lincolnshire. Part of our route lay through what appeared to be paddy fields, which were flooded, as was indeed the road, and our vehicles were at times axle-deep in water.

One Sunday morning towards the end of February, I was just going for my breakfast when I was asked, 'Do you want to go on leave to Rome this morning?' I quickly replied in the affirmative and without delay packed a few necessities into my small pack, stowed the rest of my kit, underwent a medical inspection to make sure I was not carrying any disease, and drew my pay. By twelve o'clock I was on my way in the back of a truck with nine others, with £10 in one pocket and three mutton chops between two slices of bread in another. As one of my comrades remarked, 'Whoever thought of making mutton chop sandwiches must have been wrong in the head, for owing to the bones, there's nothing harder to chew.'

During the afternoon we passed through some picturesque country that was new to me, and I saw for the first time the great seaport of Ancona. Further on we stopped at a railway station, where we were given a hot meal. I was amused to notice that although I had brought the minimum of kit, I was about the only one who had remembered to bring his knife, fork and spoon. One chap had brought almost enough gear to equip a regiment, but had omitted to bring the essential 'eating irons'. We boarded a train as darkness was falling, and I made myself a place to sleep on top of a pile of kit that was in a corner of the carriage, but though I spent a comfortable night there, the draught from a window that was without any glass gave me a cold.

We reached Rome at about 6.30 am and were taken to the rest camp where I had been the previous August. This time I was in a wing that had been named 'The Savoy Hotel'; on the previous leave I had occupied 'The Dorchester Hotel'. Having dumped my blankets on my allotted bed, I washed and shaved, breakfasted, collected my ration of cigarettes, soap and air mails, sold the cigarettes, and then attended a lecture by the CO of the camp who explained to us the amenities and amusements, and gave us the customary advice regarding vices and dangers. This practically occupied all the morning, so I stayed in camp for dinner, which was served in a pleasant dining hall by Italian waiters.

After dinner I went into the city, where I saw a Bing Crosby film, and then went to the Alexander Club for tea. This club was a huge modern place similar to the Robertson Club in Florence, with a restaurant, snack bars, wine bar, gift shop, reading and writing rooms, information centre, in fact almost everything one could wish for. In the evening I went to an entertaining variety show.

Having seen the ruins of ancient Rome on my previous visits to the Eternal City, I spent a good deal of this leave enjoying contemporary entertainment, of which there was a surprising amount. Some of the shops had interesting displays, but the prices were extortionate. One evening I went to the Royal Opera House to see 'Rigoletto'. This, like so many Italian operas, has a crude and somewhat sordid plot, and ends in tragedy, but is more than redeemed by Verdi's superb music. The singing and acting were of the high standard one would expect to find in the home of opera, though the leading tenor (who sings the famous 'La donna e mobile') was a substitute for an even greater artist who was indisposed.

The Royal Opera House itself is an imposing building of great size, with an exterior of carved stone. Even the foyer is almost like a marble palace, with great mirrors on the walls, and lit by the scintillating light of cut-glass lustre chandeliers. The auditorium is horseshoe-shaped, and the stage immense. All the furnishings were crimson, and a vast amount of gold leaf had been used in the decoration. The domed ceiling was adorned with a painting depicting a scene from ancient Roman history, with a procession of slaves, soldiers, chariots and the usual conquering hero. The balcony in which I sat had boxes at each end; below me were three tiers of boxes extending right round the theatre, and above me was the gallery. The pit seemed to cover acres, and for those occupying the more distant seats, opera glasses (which were on hire) must have been almost a necessity. At intervals guards of the Carabinieri stood in their picturesque uniforms, embroidered with scarlet, wearing swords, and Napoleon-type tricorn hats decorated with a large red, white and blue cockade with a silver badge in the middle.

One morning, I went on a motor coach tour of ancient Rome, and saw much that I had missed before, and found it all very enjoyable and interesting. The party visited the famous Pantheon, which before the Christian era was the Temple of Jupiter, and is one of the oldest buildings in the world still in its original state. It was built by Agrippa in 27 BC, and it became a Catholic church in 609 AD. It consists of a circular hall with a colonnaded rectangular entrance. The huge dome in the centre of the roof is pierced by a hole which admits the only light, and directly under this is a drain in the floor to carry away rainwater. Round the walls are niches and embrasures in which are the tombs of the Italian Royal Family: Victor Emmanuel II, Umberto I, Margaret of Savoy, and also the tomb of Raphael. It was a marvellous sunny morning, and we went up a hill called the Janiculum from which we had a glorious panoramic view of the truly beautiful city of Rome. The coach broke down whilst we were climbing this hill, so we all sat and enjoyed the view while the driver sorted out the trouble and the guide pointed out buildings of interest. Presently we drove along one of the banks of the Tiber, eventually arriving at Vatican City, and of course St Peter's. It was well worth a second visit.

On the Sunday morning I attended a service in a Presbyterian church which I had been surprised to find existing in this most Roman Catholic of all cities. It was crowded with British soldiers of all ranks. This was the first Christian service I had been able to attend since arriving in the country.

The other occupants of the room in which I slept at the Savoy Hotel were all South Africans, who I found to be very agreeable company. They were most interested to hear that my wife had been born in South Africa. My stay with them was most enjoyable.

When our leave ended, we travelled by train to the Adriatic resort of Rimini, where we had a long wait at the station until a truck arrived to take us to our regiment, which had now moved to the north of Ravenna. The war had now reached a fairly static stage, but we knew that a big spring offensive was being planned. Anti-tank gunners were practising slinging their guns across a river on wires, and the infantry were practising with flame-throwers, horrible weapons that would send a stream of blazing fuel the length of a field. At night, we carried tons of ammunition to dumps which were then camouflaged, so close to the enemy that strict silence had to be maintained. Our infantry were positioned along the River

Lamone, which reminded me of the drains in which we used to fish near Boston, having high artificial banks. German troops occupied the other bank, and occasionally threw hand grenades over. On our side was a basketful of grenades with a note that read 'Please take one', so anyone could return the compliment.

During this period, the Argyll and Sutherland Highlanders had established a rest camp at Ravenna, and as a mark of gratitude for the support our artillery gave them had invited our battery to send two of our men at a time there for three days. To decide who should go, all our names went into a hat, and the first to be drawn out were mine and that of a gunner named Morgan. This came as a great surprise so soon after my leave in Rome, but was none the less welcome. I was glad to have an opportunity of seeing something of this historic city. There were many fine old buildings there, but unfortunately the war had caused a lot of damage to some of them. Although Ravenna was rich in sculpture, it was chiefly renowned for its mosaics, which possess the subtlest of tints and the richest of colours. Morgan was a man with whom I had had no previous contact, and we soon found ourselves in disagreement on almost every subject as he was both a communist and an atheist. We argued about everything from the Government of India to the chocolate ration. By the time we parted, the only thing he had managed to convince me of was the truth of the saying that empty barrels make most noise.

The only point of accord was our mutual love of music. At the Ravenna Opera House we attended a performance of 'The Barber of Seville'. Whilst this fell far short of the superb standard of Rome, it was still very good, and it is an opera I enjoy. We also went to a symphony concert. When it ended we went to a canteen, where we found a lot of drunken commandoes fighting and smashing bottles and glasses, so we beat a hasty retreat to a more peaceable tea and cakes emporium. During my service in Italy, I often longed for a camera, but the security regulations did not encourage us to have them, and films were almost unobtainable. There were so many picturesque scenes and interesting buildings that simply asked to be photographed. After returning to our regiment, Comrade Morgan and I had no further contact, and I was soon immersed in my job of maintaining the vehicles.

For a few weeks the war remained in this static phase, punctuated with occasional artillery duels. One day I had to repair a hole in the petrol tank of one of our Dodge trucks. Needing a piece of brass to make a patch, I went over to where our guns were firing, and picked up a twenty-five-pounder cartridge case. Taking it back to our truck, I put it in the vice, sawed off the base, sawed the cylinder down its length, and flattened it. From this I cut a patch about three inches square, which I shaped to fit the rounded corner of the damaged tank. This I had removed from the vehicle, emptied, and laid in the sun without its filler cap to allow the last traces of petrol to evaporate. When I judged it might be safe to apply a blowlamp to the tank without too much risk of explosion, I soldered on the patch and completed the job successfully.

A day or two later, I was tidying the workshop truck when I picked up the base of the cartridge case and saw that this could be made into an attractive ashtray. Not having much else to do that day, I filed the sawn edge smooth, fitted four channel-shaped rests for cigarettes, and in the centre fixed a lighter made from an anti-tank rifle cartridge case, with a cap made from a brass nut and the front of an RA button. When this was completed and polished, it was much admired, and I had many offers for it, but I still have it. Later, I made another one with a matchbox holder instead of a petrol lighter, and this was decorated with the 8th Army shield with a cross imposed, cut from a bit of brass. This one I subsequently gave to my father.

Chapter 31
'Fight the Good Fight'

THE SPRING OFFENSIVE was about to begin. The enemy seemed to know this, as one afternoon a German reconnaissance plane flew over. It was flying very high, and was the first enemy plane we had seen for months. That evening, Willie Frame and I went to look at a vehicle that needed some attention, and Willie had drawn a bottle of whisky which NCOs of his rank and above were entitled to buy from the NAAFI duty free. Before we were able to get back to HQ, the German artillery began a bombardment, and we found ourselves at the receiving end. There was no cover, but we managed to find a depression in the ground where we lay flat while shells exploded around us. Presently, Willie uncorked his whisky and we both had one or two swigs, until we summoned enough Dutch courage to get up and make a dash for it when there was a slight lull, and succeeded in gaining the shelter of a substantially built farmhouse, where we found many of our comrades sitting on the floor with their backs to the thick stone walls.

Next day we were told that an estimated 1,000 shells had fallen around our position, but had caused no material damage. None of us were hurt, but unfortunately two infantrymen who were on their way back to a rest area were killed. The bombardment had been concentrated on a road junction and areas where our troops had been expected to assemble in readiness for our attack, but the Germans must have received misleading information, as they acted twenty-four hours too early.

That afternoon the battery assembled in a field, and Captain Knibbs explained to us the strategy of the coming offensive, which was to put paid to the German forces in Italy. The following day was to begin with a terrific artillery bombardment involving our field guns, medium guns, and long-range artillery. Waves of bombers would then drop their deadly loads on the German Army. After this, fighter planes would swoop down over the enemy front line, firing their guns to make the Germans take shelter in their foxholes, whilst our infantry and six-pounders would cross the river. Once the enemy began to retreat, they would be subject to a merciless non-stop bombardment by our artillery and from the air. As they retreated beyond the range of the gun firing from our rear, our forward guns which had been kept in reserve would begin to fire, whilst our rear-ward guns would leapfrog them to be ready to resume firing when the forward guns were no longer in range.

In the event this went exactly as planned, and the enemy were soon in headlong retreat, but fighting desperate rearguard actions with great bravery. They were suffering terrible losses, both in men and material, and they were desperately short of petrol. Many of their enormous guns had to be blown up or abandoned, as they had no means of moving them. So often did we have to advance, both by day and by night, that we were tired out, and actually found ourselves feeling sorry for the Germans, for whom the situation was so much worse. Once when we had to move in the early hours of the morning, I dozed in the cab of a truck Willie was driving just as dawn was breaking, and was awakened by a crash and my face coming into violent contact with the windscreen, which fortunately didn't break. It appeared that Willie had also dozed, with the result that we had collided with a stationary tank, from the interior of which came the muffled sound of obscene imprecations. Luckily the only damage seemed to have been caused to their tea-brewing tackle which was hanging on the side, and seeing this we beat a hasty retreat before the irate occupants had time to emerge and turn their gun on us for this desecration of their most essential equipment. Some nights there was so little time left for sleep that when we stopped, we just threw down a ground sheet wherever we happened to be, rolled in our blankets fully dressed, and went instantly to sleep, only to be roused again after an hour or two.

One evening we passed through the town of Argenta, part of which was still in German hands. Fierce fighting was going on, and some buildings were burning. The remains of the bodies of men who had been blown to pieces lay beside the road, a gruesome and sickening sight.

Wagon lines were usually situated some distance behind the guns, but that night they were in the next field. The wheels of our truck were straddling a gully, and I decided to sleep under the truck in this depression. Just as I was preparing to do so, the whine of a shell was heard, so I and one or two others dived into the gully. The shell landed close by, but did not explode. A moment later, another shell whined over, and that was also a dud. Then came a third shell, which landed with an almighty explosion, having scored a direct hit on one of our field guns. Then the cordite in the gun pit went up, burning fiercely. The gun was destroyed, but fortunately no one was hurt, as the two duds had given warning, and everyone was lying low. It was providential that no gunners were in the gun pit.

For months, the Germans had been leaving behind propaganda leaflets describing the horrors that awaited us if and when we reached their 'impregnable' defence line along the River Po. One bore an illustration of a skeleton standing in the river with a British steel helmet in one hand and an American steel helmet in the other, Allied soldiers pouring out of them into the river. However, when we reached the Po our momentum was so great and the Germans were under so much pressure that we encountered little effective resistance. The bridges had been destroyed, but we crossed on a quickly assembled pontoon bridge—a rather hair-raising experience as it swayed and undulated under the weight of the column of lorries and weapons that streamed over it. The motorcyclists found it particularly frightening, and we heard that one (not of our regiment) had been drowned. Within a short time this very wide river was spanned by a Bailey bridge.

Beyond the Po, our forces smashed ruthlessly on, and we were soon through Rovigo. Presently we came to the River Adige, where we found signs of frantic flight. Horses which had been pressed into service when petrol ran out had been slaughtered. Vehicles, guns, tanks and ammunition had been abandoned. The cooks had fled over the river so hastily that we found food still cooking in a pot.

We had reached a small village called Concadirame, and here we found billets. Happy, Reg and I found ourselves comfortably accommodated in a fairly large house with a young couple who had a little boy named Alberto, and the elderly parents of one of them. The young man seemed to be well educated, and he asked me questions about Shakespeare and Byron, and how to pronounce some English words. Another member of their family came on a bicycle from Rovigo to join the household, a young lady whose husband was a prisoner of war in England. One evening a visitor brought a piano accordion, and we all enjoyed a sing-song. They called me 'Signor Carlo'.

On May the 1st the German armies in Italy surrendered, and on the 8th came the welcome news that the Second World War was over, in Europe. On Sunday May the 6th there was a church parade of the whole regiment, and the padre conducted a service on the last battlefield. It was the only service I ever knew him to conduct, before or after. On the parade, we were as smart and well turned out as any troops in England, in spite of all we had been through. The Argyll and Sutherland Highlanders Pipe Band appeared, immaculate in full Highland dress, their kilts and pipes causing great astonishment among the local peasantry.

After the inspection, each battery marched through the battered village street, our boots clinking against the litter of spent cartridges, bits of enemy equipment, and fragments of metal. Twisted wrecks of lorries lay beside blackened and crumbling walls from which charred beams protruded. A horrible stench rose from the spot where the carcasses of the dead horses had been hurriedly buried. Past the village on a piece of open ground, the three batteries were drawn up to form three sides of a square. On the fourth side was our altar, a collapsible table covered with a Union Jack, a crucifix in the centre, and an orange-coloured altar cloth with an embroidered cross across the front. A few service books were distributed here and there, and the padre with a surplice and cassock over his battledress took charge. We sang 'Fight the Good Fight', 'When I Survey the Wond'rous Cross' and 'O God Our Help in Ages Past', and the service was conducted on simple C of E lines. The colonel read the lesson. In the course of his address, the padre mentioned those of our regiment who had fallen. I can hardly describe my emotions as the service proceeded, surrounded by the debris of war. Underlying all was a great thankfulness to God for having guided and preserved me through so many difficulties and dangers. The service ended, and we marched back, the colonel taking the salute.

A couple of days after the war ended, there was a terrible accident in the village. We were in our billet when we heard a loud explosion, followed by a piercing scream. Two small boys had picked up a German hand grenade which had exploded, killing one and maiming the other. The whole village was grief-stricken.

Chapter 32
'War is Over'

NOW THAT the war was over, we predictably reverted to all the aspects of Army life that I most detested: early morning PT, parade and drill. We fitters managed to invent jobs to do on the vehicles in order to dodge as much as possible. One welcome break was provided by a day trip to Venice, a city I had hoped to see. The ride there was very pleasant, passing through Padua with its domes. Everyone is so familiar with descriptions and pictures of Venice that there is little point in trying to describe what I saw there, but I was delighted to have this opportunity of seeing for myself the famous St Mark's Cathedral and Square, the Bridge of Sighs and the Grand Canal with its gondolas.

One day General Dudley Russell came to address us. Having duly praised us for the good job we had done, he went on to say that he had some very disappointing news for us. Everyone had expected us to return to England as a unit. Instead, the War Office had decreed that the regiments should be broken up, and the men sent piecemeal to units forming the Army of Occupation in Austria and Germany. Even Field Marshall Alexander was disgusted at the unfairness of this decision. Some of our men had been continuously abroad for as much as three years, and even before that had served in France, returning from Dunkirk. They claimed to have served in ten countries. Surely no more could be expected of them. Everyone was disappointed, dismayed and disgusted. However, there could be no appeal against a War Office order.

Leaving Concadirame, we travelled south, past the beautiful Lake Trasimeno, to a village called S. Enea, near Perugia. We had in our battery a lance sergeant whose name I forget, but who was generally known as 'Raggytash', by reason of his untidy moustache. He was an old regular, and went up and down in rank like a yo-yo. As fast as he reached the rank of sergeant, he would be 'busted' back to bombardier for drunkenness. His trouble was that a comparatively low intake of alcohol affected him, particularly when he was so foolish as to drink in the heat of the day. One afternoon I found him lying asleep on a dismantled tent, which was beginning to smoulder from a lighted cigarette he had dropped—a similar incident to the one at Huddersfield. Of course I pulled him off the tent and extinguished the fire. Later that afternoon a guard had to be mounted, and he was the guard commander. I was also one of the guard. Raggytash not having regained his sobriety, we marched to the guardpost with him in the middle so we could keep him upright. We then propped him against a wall, and proceeded to go through the ceremony of changing the guard without an order being given. If any officer noticed he must have turned a blind eye.

Afterwards, someone must have told Raggytash what had happened, and he suddenly became possessed of a great esteem for me, to the extent of regarding me as a bosom companion. He was hardly my type, but he was harmless and amiable, so I went along with him in a rather guarded sort of way. One evening we had gone into the village together, and he had entered into conversation with a farmer named Giovanni Minnelli, a genial character who wanted to know if we had anything to sell. It so happened that we had, for the German trucks which had been abandoned by the River Adige had contained lots of clothing and other necessities which the Germans had looted. As these items were now ownerless, we had helped ourselves to them, with the object of selling them to the needy and making a few lire for ourselves. Giovanni invited us to his farm the following evening, giving us detailed instructions how to get there, through a cornfield and over a footbridge.

The following evening, each carrying a bundle of garments, we set out for the farm. Having correctly interpreted our instructions we soon reached it, to be greeted by Giovanni, his elder brother Pasquale, their wives and children, spinster sister Elisa, and their aged parents. It was a large farm, with a spacious farmhouse which had the usual arrangement of animals on the ground floor and the living quarters for this numerous family above. They were all very cheerful and friendly, and of course eager to see what we had brought. When the bundles were opened up, their delight knew no bounds and they instantly bought all we had taken without any haggling. After this we were invited to share their evening meal, so we all sat down round a big table. In the centre was placed a bowl of *insalata*— salad drenched in olive oil—from which we all helped ourselves. Then came the inevitable spaghetti, and an unidentifiable but none the less appetising concoction resembling a thick savoury pancake. I suppose it would have been a pizza. To wash down this feast, a two-litre *fiasco* of *vino bianco* was provided. When all had eaten their fill and the table was cleared, there was some conversation, and then we all started to sing. By now I had picked up a number of the most popular Italian songs, so I was able to join in. All the members of this family obviously enjoyed singing, Pasquale in particular having a firm tenor voice.

During the time we were at S. Enea, we visited the farm almost every evening, never going empty-handed, for when we had sold everything we had for disposal, we acted as agents for our mates. We were always given supper, and then we settled down to a social evening which I'm sure our hosts enjoyed as much as we did. The weather was extremely hot, and our khaki drill uniforms needed frequent washing, which Elisa was glad to do for the sake of the soap which we always provided.

Whilst in this area, I availed myself of another opportunity to visit Assisi. I was still in love with the place, but sorry to see that since our entry into it almost exactly a year previously it had become more commercialised, and prices had risen steeply.

One evening, Giovanni showed me a small petrol engine he had bought from some Canadian soldiers, and asked whether I could adapt it to provide electric light. I promptly undertook to do this for him. Searching through the junk in our workshop truck, I unearthed a dynamo that had been taken from some unknown vehicle, a couple of pulleys and a fan belt. I mounted the engine on the end of a board, and the dynamo on the other end, fitted the pulleys and belt, and wired the dynamo through an old cut-out to a salvaged battery. When the engine started we had the satisfaction of seeing the arrangement charge the battery. Wires from this supplied current to headlamp bulbs, and the farm had electric light. The Minnelli family were delighted. Then came the anxious question: how much did I want for doing it? After first naming some astronomical number of lire which caused them to break out in a sweat, I astounded them even more by saying that I wanted nothing for doing it. It was a gesture of friendship. They were dumbfounded, and it took a while for them to grasp the fact that I seriously meant it. The parts I had used had all come from disabled enemy vehicles and would have been scrapped anyway. It so happened that the next day was our last in that area, and when we bade them farewell that evening we were presented with a newly baked cake, two roast pigeons and a bottle of wine each.

The break-up of the regiment had begun. Among those sent to Austria were all the vehicle mechanics except Will Frame (now promoted to full sergeant) and me. There now remained the officers and NCOs and the men in low class numbers who by reason of age and length of service would be the first eligible for demobilisation. Knowing that I was on the borderline, I had applied through Captain Knibbs to be posted to an entertainment section, in order to play for time. The men who were being posted to Austria were being exchanged for younger men of the same category, a gunner for a gunner, a driver for a driver, etc. Knowing that our regiment had one vehicle mechanic over its entitlement, I was aiming to be the odd one out, so I could return to England with the 'ballast'. Back in England the regiment was to be reconstituted and retrained for service in the Far East, but I knew that no man in any class below 27 would be sent there, and I was Class 25. Predictably, so far no reply had been received regarding my application, so while it was pending I remained with the regiment, as I had hoped.

Once more we were moving southward, and we stopped just outside Rome at a transit camp where we were to spend the night before proceeding to Naples. My pack was stuffed with notes to the value of thousands of lire as the result of my trading, and I wished to spend some of it on something worthwhile to take home. That evening we were allowed to go into Rome; in fact a truck was laid on to take us there. Once in the city, which was by now familiar to me, I made my way to what appeared to be a good-class shop in one of the main thoroughfares and bought a Roamer wristwatch, for which I paid 9,000 lire. At that time this represented £22.10s which was then a fair price for a chromium-plated watch. It proved to be a good buy, as nearly fifty years and many hard knocks later it is still a reliable and accurate timepiece.

The next morning we proceeded on our journey, passing Cassino with its grim memories. Already, a new town was being built beside the ruins of the old. We arrived at Naples, passed through it, and proceeded to a camp site in an orchard of peach trees at the foot of Vesuvius, where we pitched our little two-man bivouac tents. The previous year Vesuvius had erupted, and everywhere underfoot was fine black dust which rose in clouds as we walked about, penetrating all our clothing. Smoke continued to rise from the volcano all the time we were there, and we would have been in a very vulnerable position had it erupted again. There were ripe peaches on the trees, and they were very delicious.

On the first day we took all our vehicles to a disposal park. They were classified according to condition, A, B, C or D. After one glance our battered and battle-scarred old workshop truck was consigned to category D. There was a large piece of shrapnel embedded in the front bumper, a silent witness to the service it had given.

During the fortnight we spent at the camp, there was nothing to do, and we could go into Naples every day, or bathe at the Lido, a stretch of beach that had been commandeered for our use. The sand was volcanic, and therefore black, and under the blazing sun was so hot that duckboards had been laid on it so that men could walk down to the sea without burning their feet on it. A lot of prostitutes frequented this beach, and some of the men who were foolish enough to associate with them contracted venereal disease. This was doubly serious, as they would soon be going home to their wives.

On most days I went into Naples, usually with a young gun fitter named 'Tiffy' Benfell. The nickname 'tiffy' was an abbreviation of artificer. He had been an Army apprentice, and was an excellent gun fitter. At the Battle of El Alamein he had distinguished himself (and scared the living daylights out of the gunners) when a shell had jammed in one of the guns. The usual drill having failed to extricate it, he had calmly pushed a tent pole down the muzzle and knocked the shell out! At all times he was quite imperturbable, and his dry sense of humour greatly appealed to me. By reason of his training, skill and length of service he ought to have been an artificer sergeant major, but his contemptuous attitude to smartness, discipline, and what in the Army is known as 'bull' had impeded his chances of promotion until higher authority took note of his record and elevated him to bombardier. Together we saw the sights of Naples, and visited the cafés and places of entertainment, and partook of an occasional glass of wine. I cannot say that I was very impressed with the place. Apart from the main thoroughfares, it seemed to be a vast slum, with steep narrow cobbled streets where we didn't care to venture. The former palace of the King of Naples had been pressed into service as a NAAFI where we regaled ourselves with tea and buns. One evening I had gone into a café on my own, and two Brazilian soldiers came in and sat down at my table. We politely wished each other 'buona sera' (good evening), and as they spoke no English and I spoke no Portuguese we entered into conversation in the universal lingua franca, pidgin Italian. After a while one of them paid me a compliment by saying, 'You speak Italian very well for an Englishman. It is easier for us, as our language is similar, but yours is very different.'

Our camp being so near to Pompeii, I had hoped to be able to go there, but no one seemed to be able to tell me in which direction it lay, and I never found any means of getting there. Pompeii and Milan were the only two places in Italy I was disappointed not to have seen. I seemed to have seen almost every other notable place between Taranto in the south and Leghorn and Venice in the north. This narrative may give the impression that my period of service in the Italian campaign was one long round of sightseeing and enjoyment, but this was not so. Most of our time was spent working hard, often under appalling conditions, in constant danger, and undergoing much hardship. With the passage of time, our most vivid memories are of the better times, and we tend to forget the worst ones, which is all to the good.

Of course, the uppermost thought in my mind at that time was the prospect of getting home to see my wife and our baby daughter. There had been so many disappointments that I felt I would only believe that I was actually going when my feet were planted on the deck of the homeward-bound troopship. Two days before it was due to sail, one of the battery clerks called to me, 'We've received a letter concerning your application to be transferred to ENSA. You're to go for an audition.' I looked at him for a moment and then said, 'The feeling's gone off, Joe. I've lost my voice. You and I have known each other for a long time. Do you think you could lose that letter?' Joe grinned and replied, 'I think we might manage it.'

The next day our kitbags, packed with everything we should not need on the voyage, were loaded onto a lorry and taken to the docks, to which we marched the following morning. At last we climbed up the gangway and stood on the deck. Our old friends the Argyll and Sutherland Highlanders had sent their pipe band, and as the ship slowly began to move, the stirring strains of the pipes rose to us from the quay. The Argylls were coming home the following week.

The ship on which we were joyfully travelling homeward was the *Athlone Castle*, and our voyage was destined to be much more enjoyable and peaceable than the one I had experienced on the *Cameronia*. My last sight of Italy was the famous view of the Bay of Naples: blue sea, blue sky, the hilly city, and the backcloth of Vesuvius, all bathed in the brilliant sunlight. I don't know who first said 'see Naples and die' the famous German poet Goethe is credited with saying 'one who has seen Naples can never be sad'. Regarding it from the deck of the ship, I thought the most apt quotation must be 'distance lends enchantment'.

This time, no gun crew was required, but once again a ship's concert party was formed, and having survived the audition found myself participating in the twice-daily performances. It was calm summer weather, and the Mediterranean was as smooth as a millpond all the way. We passed through the Straits of Gibraltar at about four o'clock one afternoon, and had a fine view of the Rock, and also of the African coast. For a long time after that the coasts of Spain and Portugal were in sight, and we saw many porpoises in that area of the sea. The Bay of Biscay was characteristically rough, and I sang my songs on a heaving deck. We gave thirteen concerts in the seven days we were at sea.

On the 27th of June we reached Southampton. After a delay of several hours we disembarked and travelled by train to Leicester, where we found billets in the comfortable prefabricated huts of a former American Army camp. The next morning, all but twenty of us who had not been abroad as long as the rest were sent home on a month's disembarkation leave. We twenty had to maintain the camp, and would have our month's leave when the others returned. Our duties consisted of tidying the camp, manning the stores, driving the ration truck, ferrying German prisoners to and from their camp and their place of work, and guarding the gate. I managed to get a couple of weekend passes, one to Sheffield and one to Ashford, where for the first time I saw Christine, now about fifteen months old. She was standing in her cot, and immediately greeted me with a most friendly smile. I was as delighted to see my nearest and dearest once again as they were to see me back safe and sound. We were very glad when my month's leave came round, and we were able to spend it together.

Chapter 33
'Demob'

RETURNING from my month's leave, I found that the re-formed regiment had been training hard during that month for service in the Far East, but I doubt if they ever went there, as the dropping of the atomic bomb had ended the war in Japan. Some of the oldest men who had been abroad for years were almost immediately demobbed, but William Frame, Ray Smith, myself and some others found ourselves on a draft for Belgium, and were sent to Old Park Barracks, Dover. From there I made a flying visit to Ashford to see Lucy and Christine.

Very late at night, we were marched to the harbour through a howling gale, and boarded a cross-Channel boat, but the weather was so bad that it was decided not to sail, so we left the boat and returned to the barracks. Another day passed, and then at 2.00 am we again boarded the boat, and although the weather was still quite bad, we did sail. As soon as we were aboard I went below and claimed the nearest bunk and lay on it until we reached Ostend, and was not troubled by the prevalent seasickness.

In Ostend we had a meal in an old barracks which had the appearance of a fortress, and then travelled by train through Bruges and Ghent to a town to the north of Brussels with the French name of Termonde, and the Flemish name of Dendermonde. Here we were installed in another fortress-like barracks. We were informed that the daily programme would consist of spit and polish, parades, inspections, PT, weapon training, lectures and football matches. However, it transpired that their bark was worse than their bite, as nothing proved to be very irksome. It was really only a transit camp, and the officers were at their wits' end to know how to occupy us. On afternoon they marched us all to the cinema to see an Abbot and Costello film!

Day passes were sometimes available, and I went twice on the train to Brussels, which I found to be a fine city with broad streets and imposing buildings. I was amazed to see the quantities of goods in the shops so soon after the end of the war, though the prices were high. There were good facilities for the troops in the way of clubs and canteens, theatres and cinemas. On one of the evenings I saw the ballet 'Giselle'.

The Flemish language amused me, having a resemblance to our Yorkshire dialect. For 'cold', they say 'koud', just like our Yorkshire 'cowd'. As all the notices and signs were printed in both French and Flemish, it was usually possible to arrive at the meaning by one route or the other, though we found that nearly all the Belgians could speak English. I was also interested to see their little wooden milk wagons being pulled by large dogs.

One morning there was a barrack room inspection, after which the CO expressed his satisfaction, and said we could have the afternoon off. As there was little to do in Dendermonde, I went to the station to see if there was a train to Ghent, as I thought it might be worth a visit. There wasn't a train to Ghent, but there was one to Antwerp, so I decided to go there. The fare was only the equivalent of two shillings for a one-and-a-half-hour journey. My visit to this large and interesting city proved to be well worthwhile. From the south station, I walked along a wide boulevard a mile and a half in length, with a broad belt of trees down the centre. The city was rich in fine buildings, monuments and open spaces, and there were some well-kept decorative gardens. The services were well catered for with canteens, clubs and places of entertainment. At the NAAFI canteen I had a tongue sandwich for my tea, and later on, a supper that was really a dinner, with three courses at a very reasonable price, served in an attractive room with an orchestra playing.

When I arrived at Antwerp station I had noted the time, chalked on a board, of a train returning to Dendermonde, as I thought, at 8.30. Returning to the station a little before this time, I found to my consternation that I had misread the rather smudged writing on the board, which was not 8.30, but 18.30, so of course the train had gone at half past six. The next train would be about eleven o'clock, and I knew I should be therefore late getting back, and almost certainly in trouble, particularly as I had gone without a pass. Killing time, I noticed as I was exploring the vicinity of the station a pub bearing the sign 'Bass Hotel'. This was a curiosity in that it was under English management, and had inexplicably remained unmolested throughout the German occupation.

Eventually my train came in, and I settled down with some foreboding for the return journey. Arriving at the barracks, I reported to the guardroom, where I found to my relief that the guard commander was none other than Sergeant Willie Frame. His relief had arrived at midnight, and it was now 12.35, but knowing I had not reported in, he had remained in the guardroom worrying about me until I appeared. He thought I might have met with some mishap, as I had never before overstayed my time. He entered my name in the book as having been present, and after I had expressed my gratitude we both went to our beds with some relief. This was a good example of comradeship.

In Dendermonde there were several establishments bearing the sign 'Café Sport'. These had a bar at one side where very weak lager was served, and at the end was a mechanical organ, something like the ones on the old fairground roundabouts, equipped with piano accordions and other musical instruments which were operated by rolls similar to the ones that activate Pianolas. People danced up and down the room to the music of these instruments.

After a fortnight there, we embarked on a train for north-west Germany, I don't remember much about the journey, except that when we were approaching Rendsburg along a high ridge, the train came onto a remarkable bridge which curved and descended in a long spiral, crossing the Kiel canal to the level of Rendsburg station, where we had to change trains. Whilst we were waiting on the station, I was recounting some anecdote to another man, and happened to mention that the occurrence had been in a little village between Canterbury and Dover. A soldier who was unknown to me overheard and asked me, 'What was the name of the village?' 'Bishopsbourne', I replied. 'I come from there!' he said. Bishopsbourne was such a tiny place that the chance of meeting in Germany anyone from there must have been extremely remote.

We boarded another train, and eventually arrived at Bordesholm, a village beside a large picturesque lake, about three miles from Neumünster. Our billet was a very substantial building which had been the local government offices. We were now attached to the 146th Medium Artillery Regiment. The weather was now extremely cold, and soon after our arrival there was a heavy snowfall, followed by an intense frost. The lake froze over and the ice soon became very thick. Christmas card views encircled us.

Ray Smith, the little driver mechanic, and I were by now the only two remaining together from the old P Battery, 53rd Field Regiment, and we stayed at Bordesholm for six weeks. An officer interviewed the new arrivals separately, and when he found that I was an A2 vehicle mechanic he asked if I could give lectures on vehicle maintenance. I said I would be glad to do this, so he told me to remain in the billet and prepare my talks. In view of the prevailing climatic conditions, this suited me very well. I spread a lot of papers on the table, wrote a few notes, and spent most of the rest of my time writing letters and reading books. If anyone asked what I was doing, I simply answered 'MT lecturer, preparing a lecture', and no more questions were asked. The only parade I attended was pay parade, and my existence appeared to have been forgotten. Sometimes I went for a walk in the forest beside the frozen lake, and once I went to a regimental football match. I never gave a lecture.

One afternoon I joined a trip in a lorry to Schleswig, which although now part of Germany, was once in Denmark. The wintry landscape was interesting, and we passed several windmills. We went to a cinema in Schleswig, and returned rather late, very cold and ravenously hungry. I remember eating a vast quantity of bread and cheese.

A truck to take us into Neumünster was laid on each evening, and Ray and I went on it to see cinema and variety shows. The artists appearing on these were mostly displaced persons from such places as Latvia, Estonia, Lithuania and Poland, so in view of the language difficulty, all the acts were visual and silent, consisting of such things as conjuring, magic, trick cycling, acrobatics, juggling and balancing. Many of them were very good indeed.

My sixth Christmas in khaki was spent at Bordesholm, and followed much the same pattern as the previous ones. With the coming of the New Year, Ray and I were sent to a barracks at Harburg, a suburb of Hamburg. Here I was given a job in a workshop on vehicle maintenance along with some other fitters, and I also did some driving. Going to the petrol harbour, I saw the remains of the U-boat pens that had been bombed by the RAF. There were huge blocks of ice floating down the River Elbe. The cold was so intense that when I went from one temperature to another my nose began to bleed. This was a striking change from the heat I had experienced in Italy only a few months previously.

Hamburg, December 1945

Hamburg was terribly devastated, having been eighty per cent destroyed by bombing, but I was interested to see that the Atlantic Hotel, where my father had spent a night in 1939, was undamaged and was being used as an Allied officers' club. It stood beside the famous lake known as the Alster. On two Sunday afternoons I went to hear concerts being broadcast from the radio studios in Karl Muck Platz, and I have often wondered who Karl Muck might have been. I noticed that the sign bearing the indication 'Hermann Göring Platz' had been erased, and some other name substituted for that of the fallen idol.

All the time I had been in the Army I had contrived to avoid driving as I had quite enough to do with my other duties, but one day my name appeared on orders as duty driver. During the course of the day I drove a variety of vehicles, fetching various stores. In the evening I had to drive the 'passion wagon'—the truck in which the soldiers went into Hamburg for their evening's entertainments. It was a big, unfamiliar vehicle, and in the dark I had to grope around to find the various controls. On the way into the city, I had to pass a single-deck tram which was drawing two trailers. There was barely sufficient room between the tram and the tree-lined verge, and I drove very slowly and carefully. I passed the tram all right, but as I passed the first trailer, there was a sound of breaking glass. One of my wheels had dropped into a pothole, causing the truck to tilt slightly, and my driving mirror which was mounted on along arm had broken a window of the trailer. It must have been one of the few unbroken pieces of glass in Hamburg until I came along. I was relieved to see that none of the passengers had been cut. The driver and conductor jabbered in German, but we couldn't communicate, so I drove away.

Returning later that night, I took a different route along an autobahn which ran beside a canal. From time to time, the truck seemed to drift towards the canal, and I had to keep pulling it back. The next morning, some of the regular drivers returned, saying they couldn't drive on the autobahn, as it was a sheet of ice! A fool had rushed in where angels had feared to tread. It may have been fortunate that the previous night had been too dark for me to see the ice, as otherwise I might have lost my nerve, but we had been lucky not to have ended up in the canal.

The demobilisation of Group 25 began on January the 17th, and I was awaiting my turn with growing impatience. On the last day of January Ray Smith went, and the following day I left with another party for a transit camp, where we stayed until midnight, when we were taken to the station and boarded a train on which we were to remain for twenty-six hours. There was the usual scramble for the hard wooden seats, but I was lucky enough to find a dark narrow little luggage compartment empty, and promptly bagged it, Once in, I hauled out of my kitbag a quilt that had been issued by the Red Cross, and with that and a blanket proceeded to get comfortable on the floor. Another chap who couldn't find a seat came along and asked if there was room for him as well, so I let him squeeze in and contribute his blanket. We hadn't much room, but we were warm and fairly comfortable, much more so than those with seats.

We travelled right through the Ruhr, a scene of devastation after the many RAF bombing attacks, passing miles of destroyed rolling stock. When the train slowly crossed a long bridge over the Rhine, scores of men, women and children below called to us for food, and many of us threw our emergency rations down to them. I saw a lot of the places which had so often been mentioned on the radio during the latter years of the war, including Hannover and the marshalling yards at Hamm, the scene of so many bombings. We passed through a corner of Holland, and reached Tournai in Belgium, where we left the train and spent most of that day. Our money was changed into Belgian currency, and after we had been given an opportunity to go around the town, into English. Wandering around Tournai, I heard a clatter, and was astonished to see that it emanated from a steam tramcar. We slept in Tournai that night, and the next morning returned to the train which soon entered France, arriving at Calais about noon.

We should have gone aboard the boat almost immediately, but there was such a gale blowing that the sailing was cancelled, and we were issued with blankets and installed in huts. The next day the weather was still just as bad, and sailing was again cancelled, so we were really fed up, especially as it poured with rain. I thought Calais was one of the most depressing places I had ever seen. In the gift shop I bought two bottles of eau de Cologne, one for Lucy and one for Mother.

At last on the following day the wind abated a little, and we were able to cross to Folkestone. It was too rough for us to be allowed on deck, and almost everyone was being sick into paper bags. I had gone aboard suffering from indigestion as a result of the sausages we had been given for breakfast, and at last the sight and smell of everyone being sick affected me also.

On landing, we went straight through customs without any ceremony, and were taken to Shorncliffe Barracks, only twelve miles from Ashford. After dinner we handed in our webbing equipment and were told that we should not be moving again that day, so I just walked out of the barracks and jumped on an Ashford bus that was conveniently passing, taking with me all my personal possessions. I was with Lucy and Christine by half past three, returning after ten o'clock on the last bus back to Shorncliffe.

The next morning we started on the last lap to Guildford, which we reached just in time for dinner. After that we hung around for ages like cats on hot bricks, and it was nearly four o'clock before our turn for demobbing came. Once it started we moved along very quickly as there was a chain of about twenty clerks to process all our documents, and then we filed into the clothing department. Our luck was in this time as a new lot of stuff had just come in, and

I was able to get quite a nice suit, a darkish blue with a bit of grey in it that fitted me well. I selected a macintosh, a trilby hat, shoes, socks, tie, shirt, collars, studs and cufflinks. Many men changed into their civvies immediately, but I simply shoved mine into the carrier bags supplied, and raced out of the building towards the station. It was the 6th of February 1946, and I had been in the Army five years and seven months.

By three slow trains I made my way back to Ashford, getting there about half past nine. After all my travelling, I was very dirty, and was glad to have a bath, from which I emerged once more as Mr Hatfield, not 2346046.

Chapter 34
'Picking Up the Threads'

MY RELEASE from the Army filled me with unspeakable relief and deep thankfulness to my Maker for my preservation through so many perils and hardships. Many men had enjoyed life in the Services, with its freedom from responsibility, its opportunities for drinking, gambling and other vices, and also its sporting activities. None of this had appealed to me, and I regarded my Army service as a waste of what should have been some of the best years of my life. Nevertheless, I had made every effort to adapt myself to the conditions, and had carried out my duties to the best of my ability, and managed to retain my sense of humour in my relationship with my comrades. Now all this was behind me, and I had to begin anew to adapt myself to a very different way of life to the one I had known before the war.

I have always been very fond of children, and getting to know my little daughter, now about a year and nine months old, gave me great delight. She was a very happy and amusing child, and Lucy cared for her beautifully. We read to her so much that she soon learnt the stories in her picture books off by heart, and would repeat them to herself, turning the pages over at the right places so that she appeared to be actually reading.

We spent three or four weeks in Ashford, and then went to my parents' home in Sheffield and occupied my old bedroom. Soon I returned to my old job at Pawson & Brailsford's, where I picked up the threads very quickly and found myself binding and lettering books as though I had never been away.

At first we lived with my parents, but of course we were anxious to get a home of our own, which was not easy, as thousands of ex-service men and women had been demobilised; many houses had been bombed, and no more had been built during the war. Once again the hand of Providence intervened. Our minister's wife informed us that a property in the same road as our church was for sale at a ·price we could afford, with the help of a mortgage. We moved in on the 13th of June 1946. Thirteen is considered unlucky, but I do not believe in any superstitions—I had joined the Army on the 13th, and abroad I served in the 13th Corps. The house needed a good deal of renovation, but we were able to do a great deal of the work ourselves.

The year 1947 began with the worst winter in living memory. Snow began to fall in January, and there was still some around in May. On one of the very worst days of that worst of all winters, Sunday the 9th of February, our son Roger Charles was born. When Lucy returned home from the midwife's house, and Christine and I from my parents, we found all our pipes frozen, and we had nine bursts.

Chapter 35
'Middlewood'

IN 1948 I left Pawson & Brailsford's for an occupational therapy job at Wadsley Mental Hospital (later renamed Middlewood Hospital) where I thought I might be able to help some less fortunate members of the community. The hospital stood in a pleasant environment, the work was congenial, I was given a free hand, and could look forward to a retirement pension.

The bookbinding department was in the main building, and was equipped with the essentials for bookbinding and a Roneotype printing machine. There were plans to further develop the printing side, so I enrolled for a printing course at the College of Art. During the years I was there, a great many patients passed through my hands: sewing and binding the patients' books, making manilla case-sheet folders, and operating the Roneotype machine. Books needed for the offices I bound myself, including enormous books of wages sheets. None of these had been bound for several years, and in bringing them up to date I bound them much more substantially and lettered them in gold instead of sticking paper labels on. To say the wages office staff were impressed would be an understatement. Actually, this would have been considered quite a mundane job in my previous employment.

By the end of the first fortnight I had bound a good batch of the books that had been gathering dust on the shelves, and had delivered them to the deputy chief male nurse, who acted as librarian. He appeared both amazed and delighted, and said I had brought him more books than he had received in years. A few days later I saw the chief administrator who said he had been receiving glowing reports of my work, so I seized the opportunity to press for some additional equipment. This was immediately ordered.

Wadsley Mental Hospital was at that time much as it must have been since its opening in 1872. I had ample opportunity of observing the wards, as I had to collect my patients every morning at 8.30, take them back at 11.45, collect them again at 2.00 pm, and again return them to the wards at 4.45 pm. A bunch of large keys had been issued to me, with which I had to unlock and re-lock every door through which I had to pass. The nurses carried theirs on their belts, where they were also secured with a chain, but I had no wish to look like a jailer, so I simply carried mine in my hand.

The furniture in the wards was typical of the Victorian era, consisting of heavy bench-type seats, bentwood chairs, and deal dining tables. Every morning the floorboards were polished. First came a patient with a large tin of orange-coloured floor polish and a big spoon which he used to slap lumps of polish onto the floor. After him came another patient with a 'bumper': a heavy rectangular metal plate covered with a cloth, propelled backwards and forwards by a hinged handle. This device not only imparted a high shine to the floor, but also made it rather slippery. The floors were so impregnated with this polish that if workmen ever had to take up any floorboards they found polish hanging down between the joints like stalactites. It was a mystery to me that the place never caught fire, as this polish was so inflammable that it was stored in a special steel shed in the middle of the stores yard. Nearly all the patients smoked, and there were gas jets on the walls to enable them to light their pipes and cigarettes. They made spills from slips of paper, which they often threw behind radiators, where other rubbish could accumulate. I bound their library books without fly-leaves, so that they couldn't tear them out, thereby weakening the book. The wards were very cheerless, with hardly a picture on the walls to break the monotony.

After I had been there a while, a great improvement was made at the instigation of Dr Kino, a Polish Jew who had been in Dachau concentration camp during the Nazi regime. He was a small rotund man who wore blue glasses and suffered from a heart condition. To relieve the monotony of the wards, he introduced reproductions of pictures by famous artists, to the frames of which were appended cards on which our department had printed brief notes relating to the artist. He also introduced aquaria containing tropical fish, and aviaries in the airing courts where the patients took their daily exercise. Dr Kino came into my department more than any other doctor ever did, and sent me a good many patients for assessment. Some I found useful and able to benefit from instruction, others had not the mental capacity to assimilate anything, and had to be returned to the wards. Dr Kino always accepted my judgement on this without question. His premature death from a heart attack was a loss to the hospital, as he was an expert in the treatment of mental illness, and had enlightened views on patient care.

It may be wondered how I came to know anything at all about patient care, as I had never received any instruction. Amongst the books I had found in the workshop was a very old one entitled *Handbook for Attendants on the Insane*, which appeared to have been published early in the century. I re-bound this, and took it home to study it. Although it was outdated, it served to give me some basic knowledge which as time went on I supplemented by dipping into the medical and nursing publications which came in for binding, and by conversation with the male nurses. It is a well-known fact that Michael Faraday, the great British scientist, who invented amongst other things the first electric generator and transformer, started life as a bookbinder's apprentice and gained his early knowledge from the books he had to bind, so I was in good company. No doubt my friends thought I must have an affinity with crazy people, as I usually seemed to get along well with them. Fortunately I was blessed with two essential qualifications: patience and a sense of humour. I realised from the start that I must laugh with the patients, not at them.

In 1948, I believe there were 2,030 patients in the hospital, and they were segregated in different wards according to their mental categories. Ernest and Tom were in wards that catered for the more reasonable patients. These were given parole cards which enabled them to leave the wards; either grounds parole, or full parole, the latter giving them liberty to go outside the grounds.

One dark and dreary ward in a semi-basement was occupied by a pathetic collection of idiots and imbeciles, many of them incontinent, for whose defective brains there could be no effective treatment, but who must be cared for by the nurses to the best of their ability. Ward 7 was the refractory ward, presided over by the biggest and most powerfully built nurses. When I had a patient in this ward, I used to enter it, lock the door behind me, stand with my back to the wall, and bawl the name of the patient I wanted. Until he came I observed with interest the inmates flinging teacups at each other, taking running kicks at each other, and attempting to clout each other over the head with the sweeping brushes. The plumbers had a constant job replacing the windows in that ward.

Ward 8 was the semi-refractory ward, peopled by a slightly less belligerent crew. Just inside the door there nearly always sat a patient who had been a professional boxer. He had once fought for the world title, but had been beaten by a Frenchman. I always made a point of wishing him a courteous good morning. Actually, I was told that he caused little trouble, and would in fact assist the staff in quelling disturbances. Many years later he was discharged.

About four months after I commenced working at the hospital, the National Health Service came into being, and the control of the hospital passed from the West Riding Hospitals Board to the newly formed Sheffield Regional Hospitals Board. At the same time the name of the hospital was changed from Wadsley Mental Hospital to Middlewood Mental Hospital, but before long the word 'Mental' was dropped. This gave me an opportunity to restyle all the forms we printed, and I had persuaded the supplies officer to buy some fonts of more modern type which transformed the appearance of all our forms, and led to a big influx of work which had been going to printing firms. After a few months my department was moved to another building which had been a key lodge. This was supposed to be temporary, but we occupied it for nine years.

In 1950 I took part in an amateur pantomime—*Dick Whittington*—as the dame. My part was uproariously funny, and I tried to make it more so by constantly ad-libbing. I had many changes of costume, including one where I wore a purple veil, yellow baggy trousers, and two saucepan lids on my chest in a harem scene. I also joined the Middlewood Hospital concert party. This was organised by the foreman electrician (a former member of Leeds Thespians) and an assistant matron, who trained the chorus line of nurses. In this party I sang, recited monologues, and participated in comic sketches. After giving four performances in the hospital entertainment hall we took the show to three other mental hospitals: Storthes Hall, near Huddersfield; Menston, near Leeds; and Wakefield. We were allowed to rehearse in working hours, and transport was provided to take us, the band, scenery and props to the other hospitals, as entertainment of the patients was considered to be a valuable contribution towards their recovery. To us, it was all good fun.

As the hospital authorities were now considering the purchase of up-to-date printing equipment, I decided to join the College of Art printing class, and enrolled for the winter session. Thus I acquired a good deal of useful information which subsequently stood me in good stead.

Early in 1951, I received an SOS from members of the Sheffield Bach Choir who were performing Bach's cantata, 'Sleepers Wake', in a church at Rotherham. In that cantata there are two duets for soprano and baritone, and the baritone singer had become unavailable. Although I am not really a baritone, but a bass, the compass of the notes was just within my range, and I quickly learnt the duets and managed to sing my part satisfactorily. This led to my entry into the choir without the usual audition. I always regarded membership of this choir as an honour. The singing was of a very high standard, and although the repertoire of the choir came to extend far beyond the realm of Johann Sebastian Bach, only works of merit were performed. Occasionally I sang solo passages. I remained a member for twenty-two years, until I became so overwhelmed with other duties that I had to leave.

A much less pleasant feature of that year was the calling up for a fortnight's training of the Class Z Reserve, brought about by the Government's mistrust of the intentions of the Russians. In June, I had to undergo an Army medical examination. During the course of the preliminary form filling, I had replied in the negative to questions as to whether I had ever suffered from any of a depressing list of most of the ailments that afflict mankind when I was asked, 'Have you ever been in a mental hospital?' I must have brightened perceptibly when I answered, 'Yes, many a time. I've just had to get permission to come from one.' The suspicion thus implanted regarding my mental state was not lessened when we reached the family history section of the questionnaire, and in reply to a question about my mother's state of health, I exclaimed 'My mother? Surely you're not thinking of calling her up! The country must be in a right state!' The corporal gave me an aggrieved look. 'Now come on, let's have some sensible answers to these questions', he said. Unfortunately, this ploy got me nowhere, although I usually have much more difficulty in convincing my friends and acquaintances of my sanity, rather than the reverse.

Some time later, I received a travelling warrant and an order to report to P Battery, 539 Light Anti-Aircraft Regiment R.A. (T.A.) at

Morfa Camp, Towyn, Gwynedd, on August the 5th. It was evening when a crowd of us disgorged from the train at Towyn, where we were given a meal and shown to our tents. After having been out of the Army for five and a half years, I was far from happy to find myself once more lying on a straw palliasse in a tent. The next morning we were kitted out with new uniforms, which actually fitted, and new brown boots. Then we went on a parade, where I found myself going through the old drill just as if I had never left the Army.

There was immediate interest when it was learnt that I had been a vehicle mechanic. Whilst most of the men went off to the firing range, I was conducted to the wagon lines, where I was shown my first job. The nucleus of the unit was a Territorial Army regiment based in Lincoln, and one of their trucks which had just been in workshops there had caused trouble all the way on the journey to Wales. I soon traced the trouble to the ignition system, which I completely overhauled. My suggestion to the driver that we should then take the vehicle out on test was agreed to with alacrity, so we went for a pleasant ride around the Welsh countryside, calling at a tea shop.

After dinner, although the truck was now running perfectly, we thought we ought to make sure by taking it for a further test, which got the afternoon over nicely. My 'old soldier' tactics delighted the youngsters, and my row of Second World War medal ribbons earned me a certain amount of respect. I kept finding little jobs to do on the vehicles, and the fortnight passed fairly pleasantly, except for being marred by a good deal of rain. Most evenings I went for a fairly long walk, and once I took the bus to Aberdovey.

At that time, we always spent our annual holiday at Lucy's parents' home in Ashford. She and the children stayed for a month, whilst I of course could only stay for a fortnight. That year they went on holiday when I went to Wales. When I returned to Sheffield from soldiering, I went to work for the rest of the week, staying with my parents, drew my holiday pay, and went to join my family. As the Festival of Britain was on at the time, I broke my journey in London, where Lucy joined me, having left the children in her mother's care, and we visited the Festival, which we found very interesting.

Whilst we were on holiday in the summer of 1952, we received a letter from Mother, telling us that Dad had been taken ill, and had been to see a specialist. On our return, she told us the bad news that he had cancer of the prostrate gland. After a distressing illness, he died on the 19th of December 1953, at the age of 66. He had been a difficult patient, and Mother had had an exhausting six months caring for him. It was particularly unfortunate as my parents had just begun to enjoy the best period of their lives. Not long afterwards, my brother Douglas lost his job at the sweet factory, but luckily I was able to get him taken on as a porter at the hospital.

In 1955 I reached the highest point in my singing career, when I sang the part of Jesus in Bach's 'St John Passion' in the Victoria Hall. Realising that this was a great responsibility, I practised very assiduously. The implications of singing this part stirred me very deeply, and my former singing teacher, who was in the audience, said I had never sung as well, and had never made a single mistake. A couple of months later I again sang in the Victoria Hall, in a much lighter vein, in an International Concert in which the participants included Poles, Spaniards, Welshmen, West Indians, Scots, and an Italian tenor. I represented England, as I did again at a similar concert held in the City Memorial Hall.

Chapter 36
'The Fire Brigade'

OVER THE YEARS, the work of my department continued to expand. A new group secretary, Mr Carpenter, became chief administrator, and during his ten years in office more improvements were carried out than in the previous hundred years of the hospital's existence, and Middlewood changed from being a dingy backward Victorian institution into a pleasant home for the patients. Building was his special interest, and he installed a plan chest in his refurbished office. Over the years, the wards were redecorated and refurnished in a much more modern manner. Open fires disappeared, and the daily floor polishing discontinued as hygienic floor coverings were laid. The central kitchen was modernised, and the entertainment hall completely transformed with a new dance floor, panelled walls, a suspended ceiling, air conditioning, a new stage with lighting effects controlled from a console, and well-equipped new dressing rooms. Twin projectors were installed in a new projection room for cinema shows, and a mobile projector was obtained for the benefit of patients who were unable to leave the wards. Mr Carpenter took a keen interest in my department, which now boasted a hand-fed Multilith small offset printing machine. He realised that the premises were unsuitable, and moved me into a much more commodious building, which had been newly decorated and adapted to our needs. With a view to choosing modern professional printing equipment, I visited the International Printing Exhibition at Olympia, and returned with a sheaf of brochures. My recommendations were accepted, an automatically fed letterpress printing machine was purchased, along with type and composing equipment. We also acquired a perforator, paper drill, wire stitcher, etc. About this time I also took on an apprentice. As the years passed and the scope of the work widened, more and more equipment was obtained. Eventually a new Heidelberg platen printing machine was bought, and the first of what was in time to become a row of fast automatically fed Multilith litho machines.

Life in the hospital had its lighter moments, and it was a poor day that was not enlivened by some humorous occurrence. The incident I am about to relate may seem too absurd to be true, but it did actually happen as I shall describe.

Years ago, it was common for large works and institutions to have their own private fire brigade manned by members of the staff, and Middlewood Hospital was no exception. The amateur firemen, who were all employed in the Works Department, received some training and were familiar with the apparatus installed in the hospital and the position of the hydrants, so that they could have been of real use in an emergency. At least one of them was always on duty in the entertainment hall when it was in use during the evening. One day during the dinner hour, I happened to be in the works yard, talking to the blacksmith when we heard the rather muffled sound of a bell ringing. 'That's the fire bell!' said the blacksmith, pointing to a large electric bell fixed high up on a wall. The reason for the muffled quality of the tone became apparent when we noticed a bird's nest built behind the gong. Just then the foreman joiner passed us at a smart trot, carrying a red fire extinguisher in each hand. Some other members of the fire brigade who had been playing cards in the works canteen now emerged and congregated at the building which at a later date housed the porter's electric truck, but in those days was the fire station, proudly containing the fire engine. This was an old car, which in some remote era had been bought for £20, stripped of its body, painted red, and fitted with a ladder and some items of fire-fighting equipment.

There was some consternation when it was discovered that: (a) a cat had given birth to kittens in the centre of a coiled hose; (b) the driver's seat had been sent to be re-upholstered; and (c) the driver had gone on leave. Emergency procedure sprang into action. The cat and kittens were evicted without prior notice, the missing seat was replaced with an upturned bucket, and a swift messenger was dispatched to the transport department to find a driver. In due course, Abe, the transport manager arrived. He mounted the fire engine, sat on the bucket, started the engine, and drove off smoking his pipe and wearing his trilby hat, a model of calm competence. In record time the fire engine arrived at the seat of the fire, which was at least a hundred and fifty yards from the fire station. It was a little old outbuilding standing next to the incinerator about halfway down the farm drive, and was used to contain waste paper and rubbish which was to be burnt. By now it was well alight, and making a good enough blaze to gladden the heart of any amateur fireman. The nearest hydrant was a long way up the hill past the entertainment hall, and a notice has since been placed there enjoining motorists not to obstruct the hydrant by parking. A standpipe was affixed to the hydrant, and a fireman began to run down the hill in a very professional style, uncoiling the hose over his shoulder as he went. Unfortunately, the end had not been securely connected to the stand-pipe, with the result that he kept on running after all the hose was uncoiled, taking it with him down the hill. After a good deal of shouting, a sufficient length of hose was run out, one end con-nected to the standpipe, and a nozzle connected to the other. The foreman electrician aimed the nozzle at the fire, which was blazing merrily, and the water was turned on. The fire brigade was in action.

It immediately became apparent that the hose was of great age, and porous, as small jets of water began to squirt from it at all angles throughout its length, in the manner so often depicted by comic paper artists. There was an unfortunate contretemps when the clerk of works, who was also the chief fireman, came hurrying past the porter's lodge. Just at that precise time and place, the hose burst and he received the full force of the water, completely drench-ing him. The foreman electrician who was still holding the nozzle at an upward angle playing a jet on the flames, was somewhat non-plussed when the water suddenly lost its pressure and described a small arc towards his feet. The fireman called upon to replace the section of hose that had burst was appropriately enough the fore-man plumber. At that time a coil of hose was kept in a small glass-fronted cupboard affixed to the wall of the corridor near the entrance to the entertainment hall. The foreman plumber went to get this, but of course plumbers are notorious for coming without their tools, and this one had come without his keys. Fortunately, after a little delay, he was able to borrow a key, and after he had coupled a fresh length of hose, operations were resumed.

After a few minutes the hose burst again, near the path leading to the cricket field, deluging the baker, a somewhat morose man at the best of times, who was heard to moan, 'This would happen to me.' Again a fresh length of hose was inserted, and now that the roof of the stricken building had fallen in spectacularly, the door, window frame and contents of the building had been engulfed in the flames, the fire brigade was able to bring the conflagration under control with little or no difficulty.

Soon after this, the fire brigade was unaccountably disbanded, the fire brigade disposed of, and the City Fire Brigade contacted at the first sign of any fire.

The hospital concert party, which had been dormant for a number of years, was revived in 1961, with mostly new personnel. After we had given performances in our own entertainment hall, we no longer visited the West Riding mental hospitals, but entertained at local mental deficiency institutions and at senior citizens' clubs. Once, we hired a coach, and taking our respective partners went to an old-time music hall performance at the famous City Varieties Theatre in Leeds, with a meal at a Chinese restaurant.

First Christine and then Roger had been having piano lessons. Christine played quite well, but Roger, whilst having considerable ability, had never realised his true potential, as following in my Uncle George's footsteps, he disregarded the music and played by ear.

Since Dad's death, Mother had never been really well, and in December 1961 she was taken very ill. She died on the 19th, by a strange coincidence the eighth anniversary of my father's death. She had seen much sorrow and endured much suffering. Both her parents had been invalids for many years; three of her children had died, and another suffered from a disability; there had been years of poverty, and since her thirties she had suffered misery from the effects of mercurial poisoning resulting from the mistake made in the Royal Infirmary. Through all this adversity she had carried on bravely and cheerfully, making the most of her resources, being always gentle and kind, and setting a Christian example to us. Right until her death at the age of 72, she had been for twenty-two years the president of the church ladies' weekly meeting.

Our parents left identical wills, directing that everything should be equally divided between Douglas and I, except that he should have £100 more, because I had been given that amount for a wedding present. However, considering the fact that I had many advantages that he did not possess—physical fitness, my own home, a wife and family—I agreed that he should have the house and virtually all the contents, while I had a sum of money amounting to about a third of the value of the house alone.

Chapter 37
'Sunday School'

A S THE YEARS passed, life followed a steady pattern. Every Sunday we attended the church services, and on week nights there were the Bach Choir rehearsals, elders' meetings, church choir practices, and, once a month, Mess Night of the Fellowship of the Services, a sort of ex-servicemen's freemasonry which I had joined in 1959. Christine and Roger were involved in the usual activities of young people, and Lucy attended a dressmaking class. After leaving school Christine had taken a secretarial course at a business training college, leading to a job in the secretary's office of Samuel Osborne & Co. Ltd, steelmakers. Roger was serving an apprenticeship as a process engraver to the printing trade. Having abandoned piano lessons, he now took up the clarinet, on which instrument he became sufficiently proficient to join the Sheffield Youth Orchestra.

Our Morris Minor was eventually exchanged for a Morris Oxford Traveller, a larger car which served us well for six years, and which gave me a great deal of pleasure. Whilst we were still visiting Lucy's relations in Kent, now for a weekend at Easter and a week in the summer, we began to have holidays in other regions: the Lake District, Wales, and Cornwall. We were now accompanied by Christine's boyfriend, Michael.

In the spring of 1962 I reluctantly accepted another responsibility brought about by the long illness of one of my oldest friends, Reg Shaw. For some years he had been Sunday School superintendent, dedicated to this work, and with a great love of children. Most unfortunately, he was suffering from Hodgkin's Disease, and as his condition deteriorated he became unable to continue in Sunday School, where for lack of leadership, the situation became chaotic.

Although I was no longer a Sunday School teacher, I went annually to coach a class for the scripture examination, and to conduct the special singing at the anniversary services. On these occasions I was appalled by the unruly behaviour of the children, and the lack of preparation of some members of the staff. When, therefore, I was approached by a deputation of the teachers with a plea that I should take over the leadership, I felt unable to refuse.

Our minister at that time was an Irishman with a great propensity for circumlocution. He was an extremely kind man, and was concerned that my appointment should appear to Reg to be only temporary, pending his restoration to health, although we knew of course that his illness was terminal. Neither did he wish that one of my fellow elders who had been trying to hold the fort should appear to have been superseded, so we both received the unique and grandiose title of Joint Deputy Interim Sunday School Superintendent!

On the day I assumed leadership, all unruly behaviour ceased, the first indication having been nipped in the bud. My programme was always fully prepared, and we proceeded from each item to the next without any breaks in which the children could get out of hand. Copies of a new children's hymn book were obtained, and every Sunday I gave an address. At the end of each service, I convened a short teacher's meeting. I led Sunday School for fifteen and a half years, when to meet changed conditions, afternoon Sunday School was discontinued in favour of morning Family Service.

As far back as 1948, I had been ordained for life an elder of the Presbyterian Church of England, after having served as a deacon since before the war. An elder's duties consisted of assisting the minister at communion services and in the councils of the church, and visiting all the members in our allotted districts every three months. Because I had a car, I was given a very scattered 'district', extending from Loxley on the northern border of Sheffield, to Dronfield Woodhouse at its southern extremity.

Owing to the prevailing shortage of ministers in our denomination, I sometimes had to conduct church services in the absence of the minister. Although I always did this to the best of my ability, it was with a sense of great humility and unworthiness, and some reluctance, as I was acutely aware that my formal education had only been of elementary standard, and I had never received any training as a preacher. The preparation of a sermon usually occupied the whole of my spare time for a week, although once in a sudden emergency I had to prepare an evening service after finishing with afternoon Sunday School. The only reason why I ever preached was that otherwise there would have been no service. I tried to avoid a sanctimonious or 'holier than thou' approach especially as I was aware that my shortcomings were so well known to the congregation. Neither did I ever try to introduce any novelties into worship. I kept to the usual order of service, and in my address simply tried to explain what I found in the Bible, to the best of my ability.

A happy milestone was when Christine celebrated her twenty-first birthday with a party in the church hall. Her young man, Michael, had chosen to enter the legal profession, and had graduated at Birmingham University. After working for a firm of solicitors specialising in criminal defence, he eventually obtained a post in the Town Hall prosecution department. Christine also changed her job for the better, securing the post of secretary to the personnel manager of Sheffield Newspapers. They were married on the 'glorious 12th' of August 1967, and up to the time of writing are continuing to 'live happily ever after'. After living with us for a few months, they were fortunate in getting the key of a new high-rise flat in the Norfolk Park complex, where they lived very comfortably, until after five years of marriage Richard James was born and they moved to a larger house.

Baby Richard was a source of great delight to us, and we were no less pleased when three and a half years later his little brother John Charles was born.

In the '60s Harold MacMillan made his famous remark 'You've never had it so good', and I think for most of us this was very true. As far as I was concerned it was a time of quiet and unspectacular fulfilment. Although our income was very modest, our financial worries were behind us; we no longer had a mortgage, our house was comfortably furnished, we had a reasonably reliable second-hand car, and our son and daughter were making good progress and causing us no worry. My singing voice was at its best, and I frequently had the privilege of singing solos with the Bach Choir, including not only the part of Jesus in the 'St John Passion', but the part of Pilate in the 'St Matthew Passion', as well as the 'Messiah' and works by Purcell and other composers. On one occasion, we appeared on television as part of a huge massed Sheffield choir in the ITV programme *Stars on Sunday*.

Sheffield Bach Choir in the 1970s

Chapter 38
'The 1970s'

LUCY'S FATHER died in April 1968 at the age of 91, a fortnight after his sister Maud had died aged 95 at Devizes. After this my mother-in-law gave up her home in Ashford, and for alternate periods lived with us and with her other daughter in Kent. She was a remarkable old lady, and lived to be over 96, but unfortunately both her hearing and her sight were very much impaired towards the end of her life. I always got on very well with my in-laws.

Roger and Lesley were married on the 24th of July 1971, and in October they emigrated to South Africa. They both had excellent jobs in Johannesburg, but they could not come to terms with the political situation there, and after less than three years they returned to England. Roger found it very difficult to get employment, and was glad when I managed to get him temporary work, at first in the hospital supplies department, and later in my own department. Eventually he obtained a post in his own trade at Bradford with the *Telegraph and Argus* newspaper. He and Lesley bought a house at Keighley, but have since moved to Skipton. They now have two young girls, Jane Elizabeth and Rosemary Frances, so we are now blessed with a tidily arranged family of a daughter and a son, two grand-daughters and two grandsons.

A reorganisation of the National Health Service brought me some problems. I found myself no longer employed by Middlewood Hospital, but by the Sheffield Area Health Authority. The Royal Hospital printing department was closed down and transferred to Middlewood, and I now found myself responsible for printing for all the hospitals in the Sheffield area, all the school clinics, and all the community health centres. At first I had neither the space to accommodate all the equipment and stock that came from the Royal Hospital, nor the staff to cope with the work. No less than six people had been employed in the printing department at the Royal Hospital, and of these, the only ones who came to Middlewood were a full-time guillotine operator and two part-time women, one of whom was unfortunately off sick for seven months.

That year, 1972, was undoubtedly the worst year of my whole working life. There was hardly room to work, stock was piled in tea chests instead of being arranged on shelves, causing a great deal of time to be wasted in finding things, and because owing to a chronic shortage of staff I was having to do a great deal of the work myself, I had insufficient time to organise the work flow. The telephone hardly ever stopped ringing, and every official in every hospital and clinic demanded that his or her work should have priority. For all this extra work and responsibility I received not a penny more pay.

At last things came to a head when the area supplies officer and one of his henchmen came to complain that I wasn't doing my job properly. For once, I completely lost my temper, and gave full vent to my feelings. The result was that several people were employed on a temporary basis. The tailor, whose workshop was next door, was found other accommodation and I acquired his premises, losing no time in having steel shelving erected and reorganising the layout of the whole department. My overall was put away for good. I ceased to do any practical work, and installed myself in what had been the tailor's office. This was the turning point.

Although I had never done much office work, I soon adapted myself to it, and devised a filing system and costing system that met with approval. With the increased staff, I was able to organise the work flow, and the complaints of belated delivery ceased. After some coming and going in the first year, the staff settled down to some permanency, and we were all friends together. Very soon, our department recovered its reputation for being the happiest in the whole hospital.

I still had three patients for a time, although ours could hardly be regarded as an occupational therapy department any longer. I realised that the ladies were rather nervous of one unpredictable young man, who demonstrated his strength by carrying the enormously heavy base of a large bookbinding press the entire length of the shop. Although I didn't increase their nervousness by disclosing the fact that he had assaulted a policeman, I thought it prudent to dispense with his services, and he was transferred to a unit where concrete slabs were made. His replacement, a schizophrenic whose real name was Horace, but who preferred to be called Jim, was not very satisfactory, nor was another patient named Reuben who walked backwards and forwards along the same bit of floor until we expected him to wear a groove in it, so I got rid of the pair of them and was left with only Dennis, who had been with me for many years. He was one of our greatest successes, having improved out of all recognition during the time he had been with us. Long after I retired, he was still working there as a day patient, doing very useful work, and was very popular with the staff.

Chapter 39

'Retirement'

FOR A number of years we had considered moving from our house in Abbeyfield Road, which was old and really too big for the two of us, and situated in what had become a run-down area. As Lucy's mother had died and left us a little money, we decided to take the plunge, and began to look for a house in the Norton area near to where Christine and Michael were living. At length we discovered a house for sale at a price we thought we could afford. It was on a level road (a rarity in Sheffield) close to shops and a bus route—all advantages when one is getting older. After encountering some difficulty in selling the old house, we moved into our suburban semi on the 1st of December 1976, and have never regretted it. We had lived in Abbeyfield Road for thirty years.

At work, as my duties were now entirely clerical and supervisory, and as the person who had been in charge of the Royal Hospital printing department had been on higher clerical grade, with much less responsibility than I now had, I considered I had a good case for being regraded to the level of general administrative assistant, which would have meant a substantial increase in pay, and would have enhanced my retirement pension. Although all my superiors agreed that my pay bore no relationship to my responsibilities, and the area supplies officer, who was my ultimate boss, wrote twice to the Department of Health and Social Security in London supporting my application, it was turned down, and I only received a small rise. I believe ours was the only department under the jurisdiction of the Sheffield Area Health Authority that was more than self-supporting. A work study team that spent a fortnight investigating our department discovered that no job we did cost more than two-thirds, and in many cases only about half of contractors' prices, with the advantage of quick delivery, and with our newly bought modern equipment the quality of our work was beyond reproach. As the yearly output ran into millions of printed sheets, paper was bought by the ton, and the stock of material we carried was valued at over £20,000 at any time. The part of the building that had been the workshops of the shoemaker and the upholsterer now accommodated the area stationery store, with a separate staff with whom we worked in conjunction. My own staff consisted of four men and six women, all efficient, and of course the patient Dennis who was a great help.

When the job release scheme for early retirement was introduced, I decided to take advantage of it and to leave at the age of sixty-four. Under the provisions of the National Health Service superannuation scheme, service over twenty years counted double for a mental health officer, so my thirty years' service counted as forty, and as I was also able to count half my army service, I should be considerably better off retired than continuing to work for such low pay, especially as I would no longer have travelling expenses to and from work, nor stoppages for National Insurance or for superannuation, etc.

The date fixed for my retirement was March the 16th 1978. On the 7th my staff invited Lucy and me to a special dinner in the staff dining room. It was beautifully done, and at the end of the meal I was presented with a specially made volume entitled *This is Your Life*. This had been compiled after some surreptitious research by the young man who was to succeed me, and bound in red and lettered in gold by our compositor Reg, a versatile craftsman whose father had been a bookbinder with whom I had worked for a time during my apprenticeship. One of the ladies presented Lucy with a bouquet. It was a happy occasion, and I greatly appreciated the kindness of my colleagues.

The following Tuesday my official retirement party was held in the committee room, and was attended by my friends from many departments. A supply of refreshment, liquid and otherwise, had been provided. The chief administrative officer of Middlewood Hospital presented me with an Omega watch, the combined gift of the administration and my own colleagues, who had kindly subscribed. Lucy was given another bouquet, and we were also presented with a rose bowl by the area supplies staff. An illuminated address bearing the names of all the printing and stationery staff was given to me by one of the ladies, and another young lady presented me with a gift of money on behalf of the National Union of Public Employees in recognition of the fact that I had been a branch auditor for a number of years. Even the lady who supervised the staff dining room presented me with a bottle of home-made wine. Of course, I had to make a speech, recalling some of the funnier episodes of my thirty years' service. I was inundated with cards wishing me a long and happy retirement.

On my last day I turned everything over to my successor, and went around the various departments bidding my many friends and acquaintances goodbye. The area printing and stationery department now occupied the entire block—a far cry from the little room where I had started it all with three patients. Of the many patients who had been with me since those days, some had died, and I was glad to think that I had been able to help some towards rehabilitation.

From Roger came a brass paperweight in the form of my initial C which he had suitably engraved. Accompanying this was a little rhyme he had composed:

> A bit of type to keep in mind
> The fifty years of toil and grind;
> And will perhaps hold down your papers,
> When writing sermons and such capers.

Chapter 40
'South Sheffield Evangelical Church'

WHILST retirement was the end of an era, it was for me the exciting beginning of a new life, and the gateway to many possibilities. For the first time in my life, I was free from discipline, and at liberty to do what I liked in my own time. From the start, I resolved not to sit on my backside vegetating, but to employ myself in active pursuits. I began to go for long walks most days, usually in nearby Graves Park, which I believe covers about 220 acres, with playing fields, woodland, nurseries, three ponds, and a collection of unusual animals and birds. There is something to be seen there at all times of the year, and I have taken many photographs in the park. I also often walk in the opposite direction, to the library in Greenhill village.

As our garage now contained the contents of my former attic workshop, as well as those of my previous garage, there was no room for the car, which had to stand in the drive. Another disadvantage was that the redundant air raid shelter blocked most of our view from the kitchen and dining room windows. I therefore decided to have the whole lot demolished, and a new garage built of a sufficient size to accommodate the car and to enable me to pursue my various hobbies. A demolition firm made short work of the old building, an extended concrete base was laid, and a sectional pre-cast concrete garage measuring $24\frac{1}{2}$ feet by $10\frac{1}{2}$ feet was erected. Facing the windows in the far end my bookbinding bench and guillotine were placed. At the right-hand side I placed my woodworking bench, over which, fastened to the wall, was a cupboard containing a comprehensive assortment of joiner's tools. Facing this I placed my engineering bench, on which was bolted a large vice, a heavy-duty electric drill, and an electric grinder. Drawers under it and a cupboard bolted to the wall over it contained a very extensive array of engineering tools mostly inherited from my father. Shelves extending along the rest of this wall served to contain decorating materials, bookbinding material, nuts and bolts, and all manner of oddments. Here I spend a great many happy hours making and repairing all kinds of things. For friends and neighbours I have overhauled lawn mowers, vacuum cleaners, washing machines and cars, mended gates and clothes posts, and fixed locks. Occasionally I bind books. In short, I am a jack-of-all-trades, but I like to think I am master of at least one.

All these activities, together with home improvement and decorating, serve to keep me off the streets. Being so fond of music, I have stereo hi-fi, with about 400 records, and a growing collection of tapes. I am also keenly interested in photography, and over the years have taken over 4,000 colour slides, and occasionally give a slide show with a commentary and taped background music. The slides are permanent reminders of our travels in all the counties of England and Wales and some of Scotland, and a recent Continental holiday.

The author with his four grandchildren, circa 1983

For two and a half years after our removal we continued in our allegiance to the church that had played so great a part in my life, but I had come to realise that it was no longer practical to try to remain so involved from a distance of six miles, especially in bad weather, or at times when I might be without the car. The wisest course seemed to be to transfer to a local church before I became too old to be able to make some useful contribution to its life and work. After much consideration, we resigned our membership of St James's and joined the nearest church to our home, which was Greenhill Methodist, where Christine was already attending and Richard going to Sunday School. We were warmly welcomed, and began to worship there very happily.

After a few weeks, I was asked to return to a morning service in St James's, and to address the congregation on 'Life and work in St James's as I have known it'. Entering the building, I was gratified to see an unusually large attendance. During the course of the service, we were surprised and delighted to be presented with a beautiful silver-plated tray, together with a pair of cufflinks for me, and a potted plant and a bouquet for Lucy, in recognition of our many years of service in many capacities. Many people have said since how much they missed the monthly news-sheets I produced.

Although none of our family had been Methodists, along with Christine and Michael, we were happily attending Greenhill Methodist Church, and Richard and John were going to Sunday School there. In 1981 a difference of opinion regarding the preaching policy of the church arose, and as the minister was in any case nearing the time when he would have to move on, he decided to leave and start a new Evangelical church in a well-populated area where no church of any denomination existed. Along with many other families, we left Greenhill and joined the new venture, which became known as South Sheffield Evangelical Church.

The first service was held in a small hall at Bradway, and was very well attended. Duplicated hymn sheets were used that first day, but by the next Sunday we had a supply of new hymn books. Everyone was bursting with enthusiasm, and new items of equipment appeared each week. Someone donated a lectern, and someone else a communion set. My own contribution was a hymn board I had made, and a set of numbers for it. Only a few services were held in the small Bradway Hall, before we settled down to a regular routine of holding the evening service in a much larger and pleasanter room in the United Reformed church at Low Edges, where only a morning service was previously held. A building fund was started, all money being raised by direct giving, with none of the jumble sales and money-raising efforts, although we have enjoyable social events. I can only regard my membership of the South Sheffield Evangelical Church as one of the best things that ever happened to me, as in it I have found all I have been seeking. It has given me a new purpose in life. The minister and lay worker are completely dedicated, efficient, and an inspiration to all of us. The sincerity, devotion and enthusiasm of the members passes belief. All seem happy, friendly, helpful and generous, and their numbers steadily increase. The sneering parrot cry we so often hear that the church is middle class and middle-aged has no meaning here. Every age group is cared for, from babies in the creche to octogenarians, and a good deal of the work is (as usual) done by the much-maligned middle class and middle-aged. I can say this without rancour, because I am well past middle age, and if I am considered to be middle class, it can only be because I have managed to lift myself to that dizzy elevation by my bootlaces.

Our church has no off-beat beliefs. We simply believe in the teaching of the Bible, and in salvation through Jesus Christ, and our brand of religion is very uncomplicated. Nevertheless, there is no place for the boring uneducated type of preacher once so prevalent in chapels. It is also a caring church. The sick and elderly are cared for in a practical way, and those with cars use them unstintingly in the service of those who have not. Not only do the members care for each other in a very real way, but a great interest is taken in caring for deprived people in other parts of the world. Even when our members were making sacrifices to give to the building fund, the entire Harvest Festival offerings were given to TEAR fund, and we also support the Slavic Gospel Association, and missions in Japan, India, and Malawi. The £200,000 cost of building and furnishing the church was entirely raised by direct giving.

Although we were happily worshipping in rented premises, our ambition was to build a church of our own as soon as possible. Adjoining the fire station at Bradway was a level field which seemed to be the ideal location, exactly on the boundaries of three residential areas: Bradway, Low Edges, and Greenhill, with no other place of worship close by. It was owned by the City Council's Recreation Department, with whom negotiations for a lease were initiated. Eventually our application succeeded, as also did our application for planning permission to build a church on the site.

The plan of the proposed building, which was initially drawn by our minister, and then modified in some particulars by an architect, was admirable. There were to be no steps, and the layout of church, hall, classrooms, lounge, vestry, kitchen, boiler room and store—all with access to a central corridor—was most sensible. In order to save expense, we decided to do as much as was possible of the work ourselves—the main fabric of course being erected by a construction firm. Enthusiastic volunteers of both sexes and all ages soon formed themselves into a band willing to have a go at almost anything, under the capable leadership of the minister who was to be seen almost every day working on the site in old clothes, a woollen cap and wellingtons.

I rejoiced that here was something to which I could make a real contribution. Woodwork has always been one of my skills, and I am fortunate in having the facilities of my well-equipped garage-cum-workshop. My first task was to make doors and frames for the brick-built enclosures for the gas and electricity meters. Then I made all the frames for the internal doors—eleven for single doors, and two for double doors—all with provision for a glazed opening at the top. Later, often with the assistance of one or other of two friends, I was involved in making notice boards for the foyer and the class-rooms, and some built-in cupboards. We fitted all the skirting boards and window ledges, and helped to construct a suspended ceiling in the foyer. Fitting up the kitchen was probably our greatest triumph. Other volunteers dug for foundations and drains, laid quarry tiles on the kitchen and toilet floors, laid a marvellous hardwood block floor in the hall, and perhaps the most impressive feat of all, those with a head for heights put a wooden ceiling in the church. All the electric wiring, plumbing and painting was done by our members.

Although he was supervising the work on the site at every stage and doing a great deal of manual work, the minister still kept his pastoral work in the forefront, and continued to preach excellent sermons week by week. During every working session on the site, we had a coffee break, when one of our number would lead us in prayer. Nor did our prayers go unanswered, for people who had never done manual work were given unsuspected skills, and every difficulty was somehow overcome. Many of our members gave interest-free loans, which supplemented loans from two evangelical bodies. The congregation's standard of giving remained surprisingly high, and it was evident that many were giving beyond the point of sacrifice.

At last the great day came when the building was completed, decorated, carpeted and furnished, and we held our opening service with every one of the 250 chairs occupied, and others brought in from the hall. It was a beautiful building, sensible and functional, and has been greatly admired. I feel greatly privileged to have been able to make an active contribution to it at this late stage in my life. I still enjoy singing in the choir, although now in my late seventies my voice is well past its best. Occasionally I read the lesson, and I continue to write every quarter for the magazine *Contact*. We have many sincere friends in the church whose company we enjoy.

With the church building completed, I have turned increasingly to my hobby, Meccano construction. To those who would say that this is a sign that I have entered my second childhood, I can only answer that the ingenious and elaborate working models that are constructed by enthusiasts of all ages—many of them university graduates—are anything but child's play. In addition to being a member of the Sheffield Meccano Guild, I am a member of the North Midlands Meccano Club, and as well as exhibiting my models at all their meetings I am a regular contributor to the quarterly magazines of both clubs, and also to the very fine international magazine *Constructor Quarterly*.

Chapter 41
'Epilogue'

I BELIEVE my lifetime has seen more changes than any similar period in history. When I was born, Britain was the greatest power the world had ever known: the head of a mighty Empire, of which I think we were justly proud. Britain was also called 'the workshop of the world', with an unrivalled export market. The Industrial Revolution had originated here, and nearly all important inventions were born in Britain. Football and cricket were English inventions. But we taught the world how to beat us. We survived the two greatest wars the world has ever known unbeaten. I won't say we won them—nobody ever wins a war—all are losers. I have seen advances in technology that a previous generation could never envisage. When I was born, no home had radio, television or video. Fridges, freezers, washing machines and dishwashers were unknown; calculators and computers had not been invented. Few people had a car. No one had flown the Atlantic. Now we are even blasé about the fact that men have walked on the moon.

Looking back on my life, I believe that every age has its compensations, but I think the present time is the happiest I have personally known. Our two children grew up to be good and useful citizens, and we now take a great delight in our four grandchildren. Whilst wealth has never come our way, we find ourselves better off in retirement than we have ever been in our our lives, and are content with our lot. Above all, we are thankful that we both enjoy good health, so that we are not a burden to anybody, and can continue to make some contribution, however small, to the welfare of the community.

How does one conclude an autobiography? I am uncomfortably aware that throughout this narrative I seem to have blown my own trumpet, although in my case a more fitting metaphor might be to have 'sung my own praises'. The less creditable episodes of my career have received scant mention, but they are a matter for my own personal regret.

Since I started laboriously to tap out this long rigmarole on my old typewriter, I have long since passed my allotted span of three score years and ten. During all these years, whether in gloom or gleam, I have known that God's hand was guiding me, and that He had a purpose for me. I sometimes wonder if I shall live to see the year 2000. If so, I shall be 86. But as the hymn says:

> If life be long I shall be glad
> That I may long obey;
> But if short, why should I be sad
> To welcome endless day?

My brother Douglas continued to live alone in what had been our family home for twenty-nine years. In July 1990 he went into hospital with ulcerated legs, and remained there until the end of October. He had never kept the house clean, nor had necessary repairs done. The roof leaked, and the wiring was unsafe, so Michael and I obtained power of attorney to manage his affairs. We managed to get him a council flat closer to where we lived, and had it decorated and fitted with a new carpet, fridge and cooker, together with the necessary furniture from the old house. He was never happy there, and had only lived there for six weeks when Lucy and I found him lying dead on the floor. There were signs that he had died the previous night. Of course there was a post-mortem and an inquest, which showed he had died from heart failure. Remarkably, my father, mother, and brother all died on the same date—the 19th of December.

Over the years, Douglas had filled the house with an incredible collection of second-hand articles—particularly tools—most of which had to be disposed of. The house and many of the contents were sold by auction. As a result of this period of stress, I had a series of blackouts, which ceased after a pacemaker had been inserted.

In conclusion, I feel I must pay tribute to my dear wife who has been my helpmate for fifty years. She has been hard-working, and a loving, wife, mother, and grandmother, and a very caring person towards others. God bless her.

40th Wedding Anniversary, 26th of July, 1983